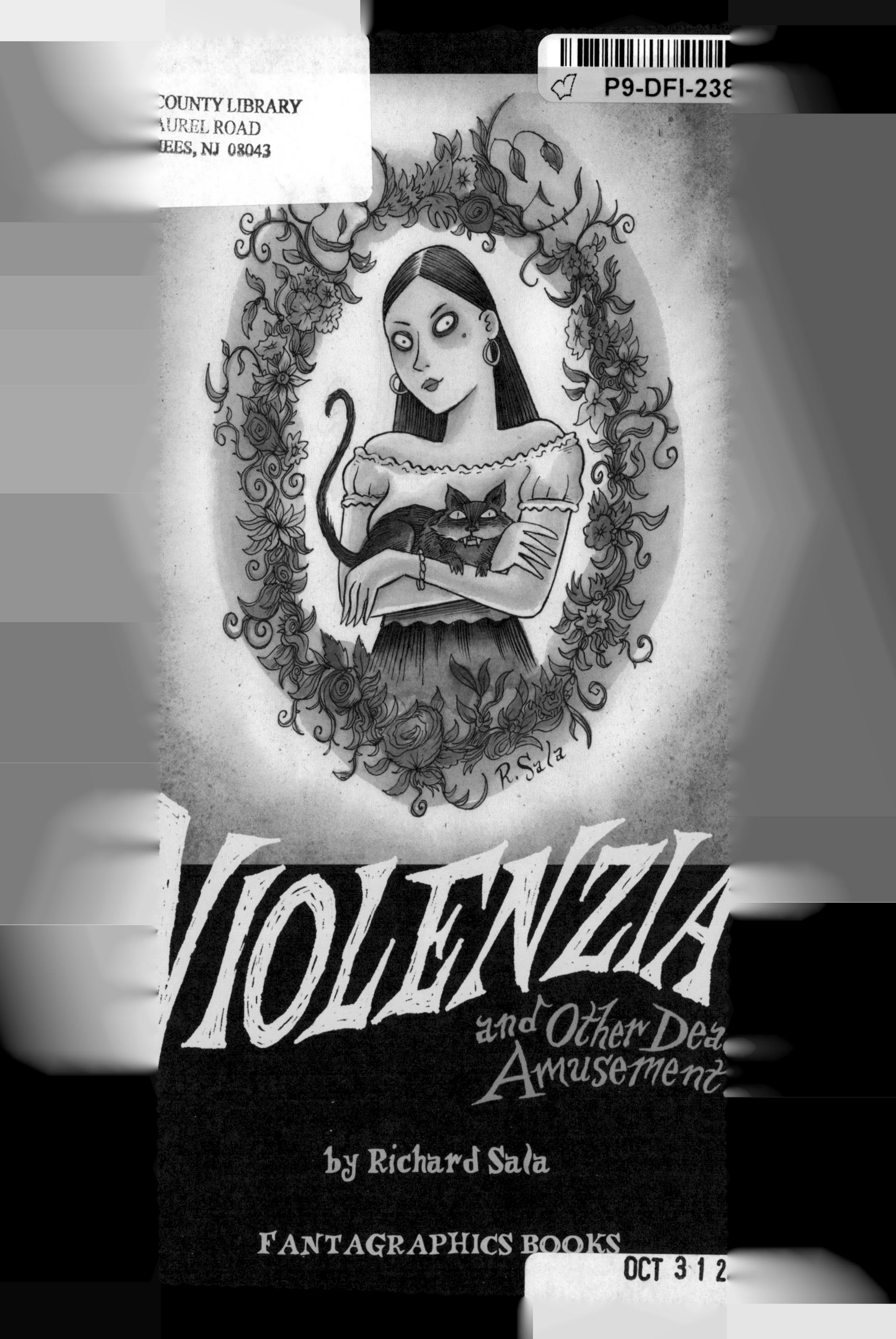
R. Sala

VIOLENZIA

and Other Dea
Amusement

by Richard Sala

FANTAGRAPHICS BOOKS

Editor and associate publisher: Eric Reynolds
Book Design: Richard Sala with Michael Heck
Production: Paul Baresh
Publisher: Gary Groth

FANTAGRAPHICS BOOKS INC.
7563 Lake City Way NE
Seattle, Washington, 98115

ISBN 978-1-60699-885-4
Library of Congress Control Number: 2015945052

First printing: October 2015
Printed in China

CONTENTS

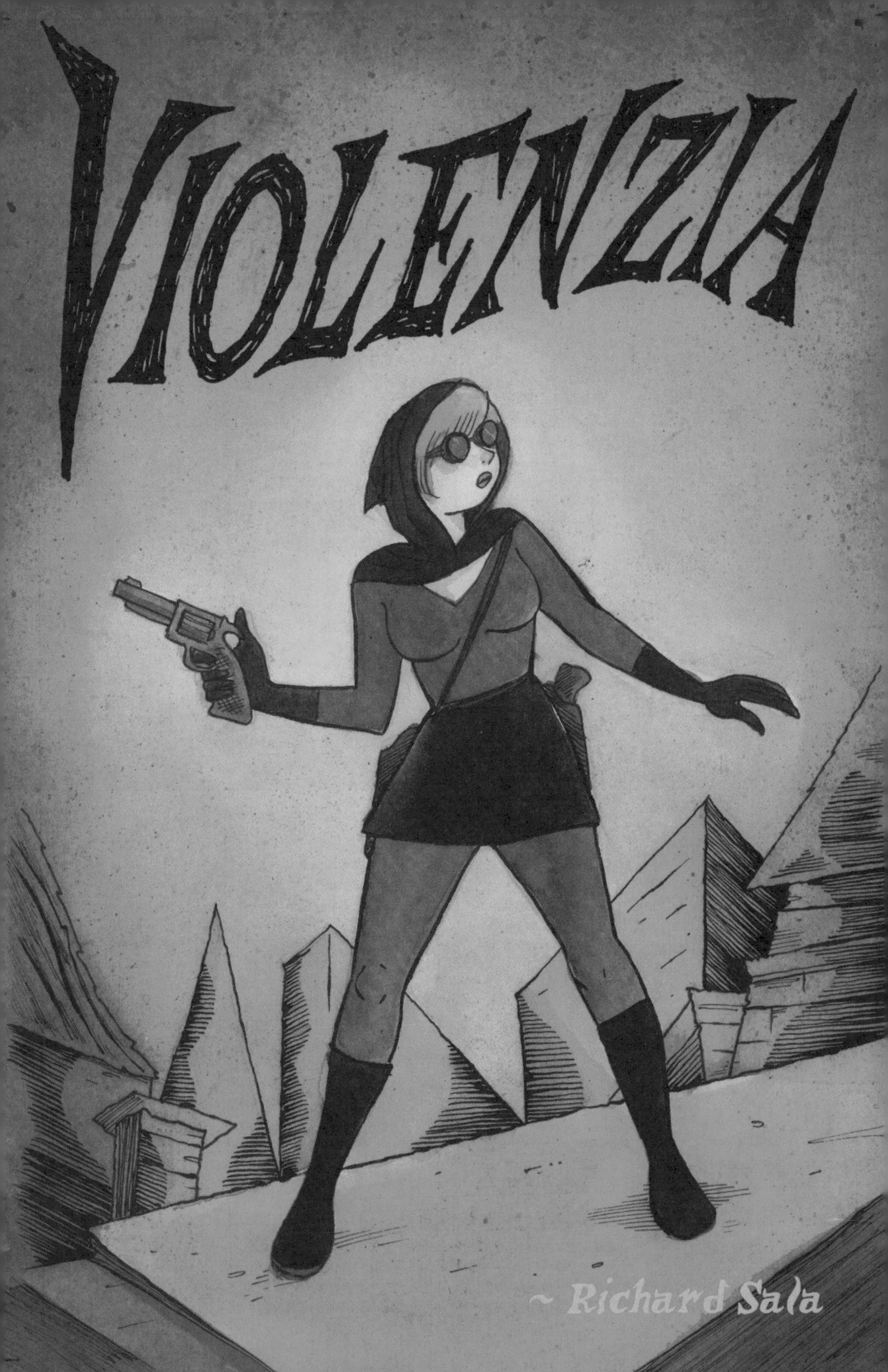
VIOLENZIA
~ Richard Sala

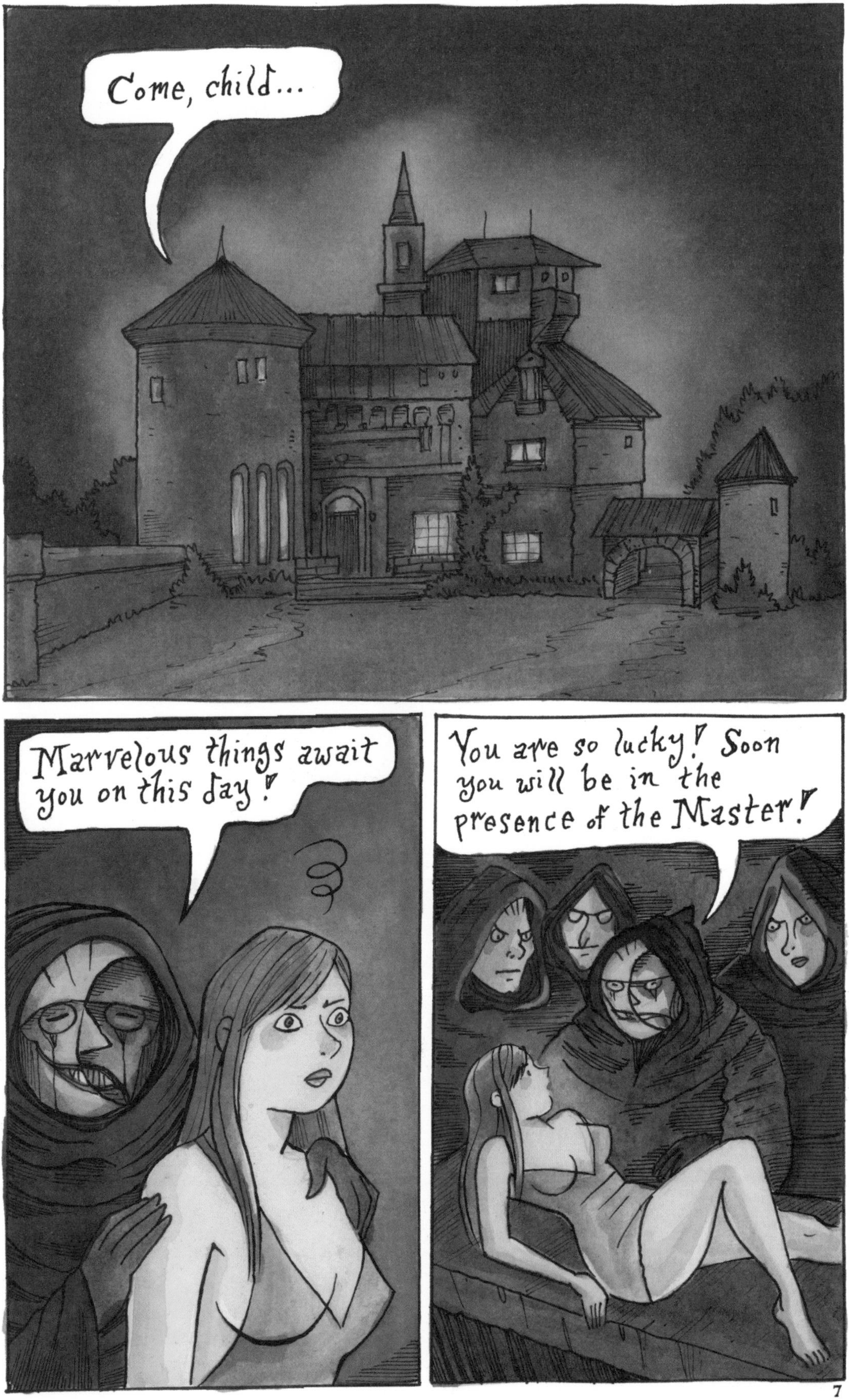
Come, child...
Marvelous things await you on this day!
You are so lucky! Soon you will be in the presence of the Master!

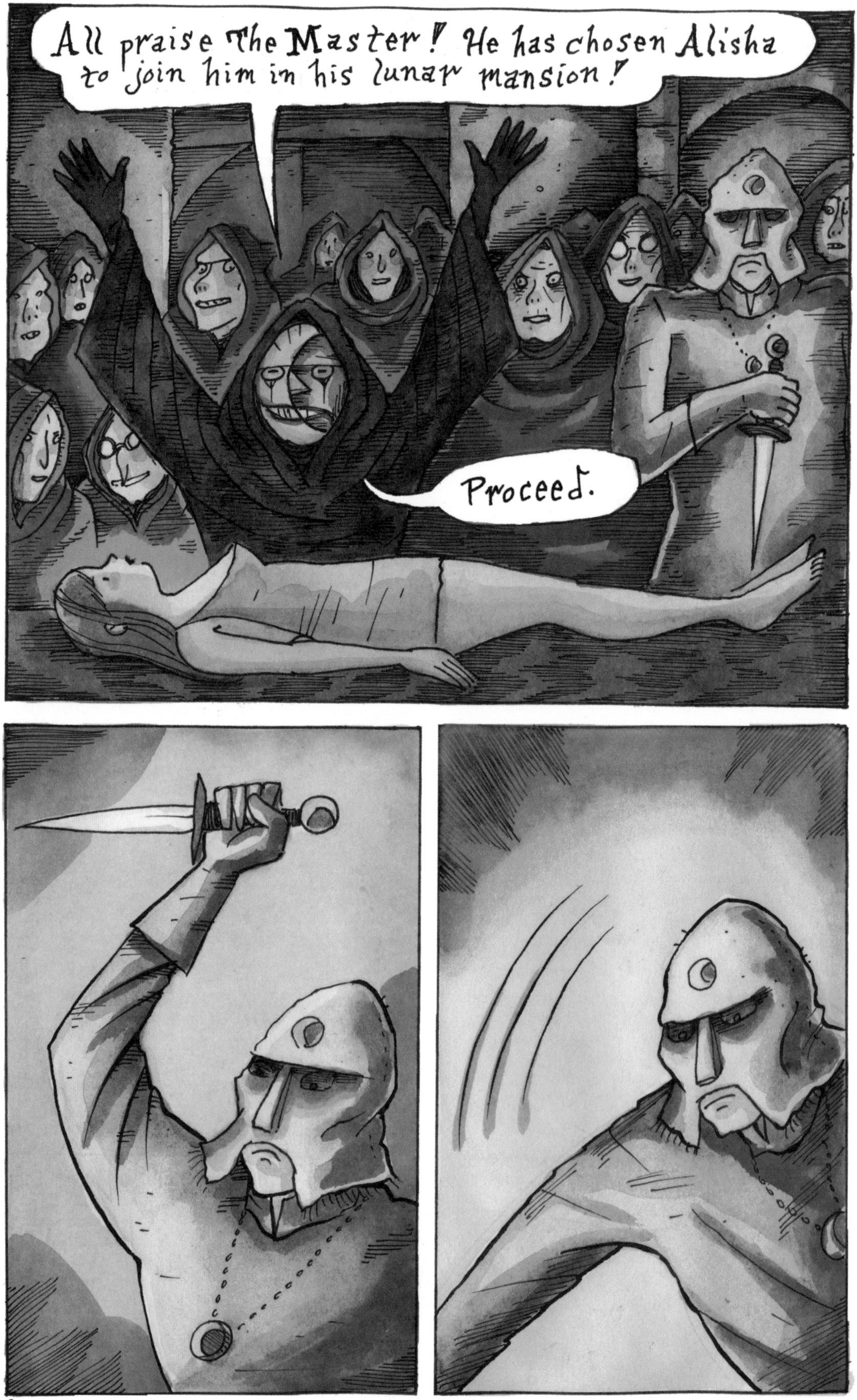
All praise The Master! He has chosen Alisha to join him in his lunar mansion!
Proceed.

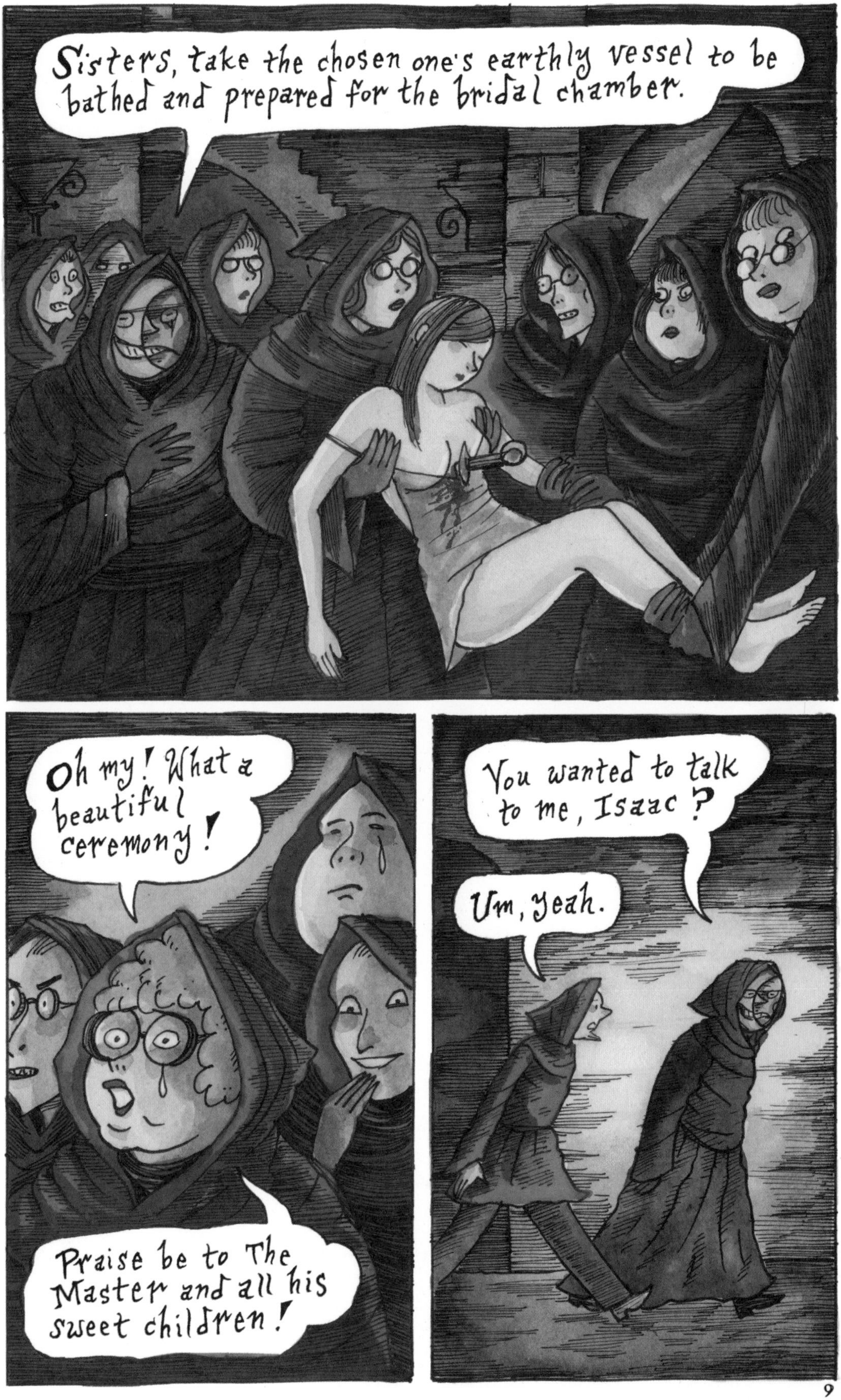
Sisters, take the chosen one's earthly vessel to be bathed and prepared for the bridal chamber.
Oh my! What a beautiful ceremony!
Praise be to The Master and all his sweet children!
You wanted to talk to me, Isaac?
Um, yeah.

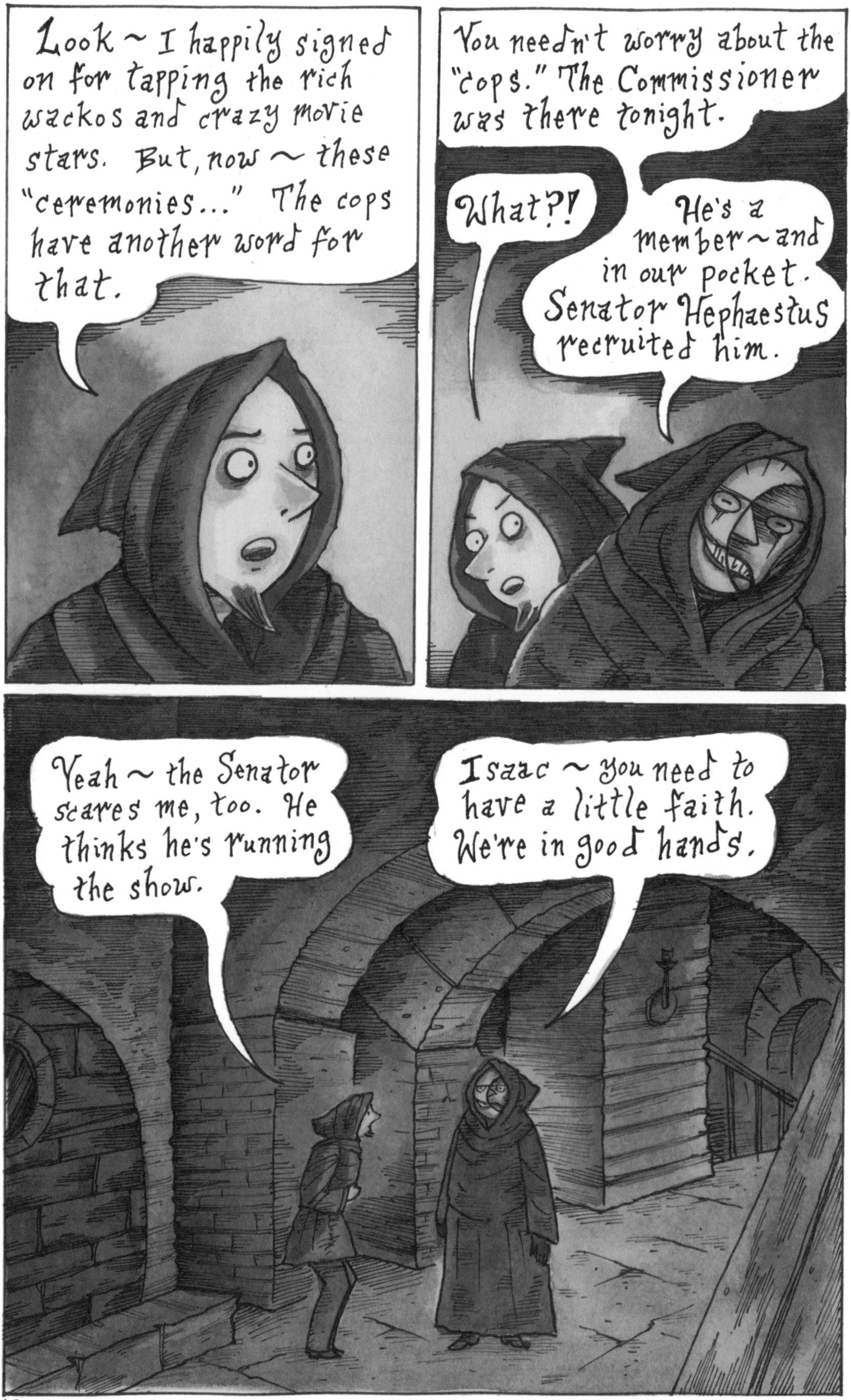
Look ~ I happily signed on for tapping the rich wackos and crazy movie stars. But, now ~ these "ceremonies..." The cops have another word for that.
You needn't worry about the "cops." The Commissioner was there tonight.
What?!
He's a member ~ and in our pocket. Senator Hephaestus recruited him.
Yeah ~ the Senator scares me, too. He thinks he's running the show.
Isaac ~ you need to have a little faith. We're in good hands.

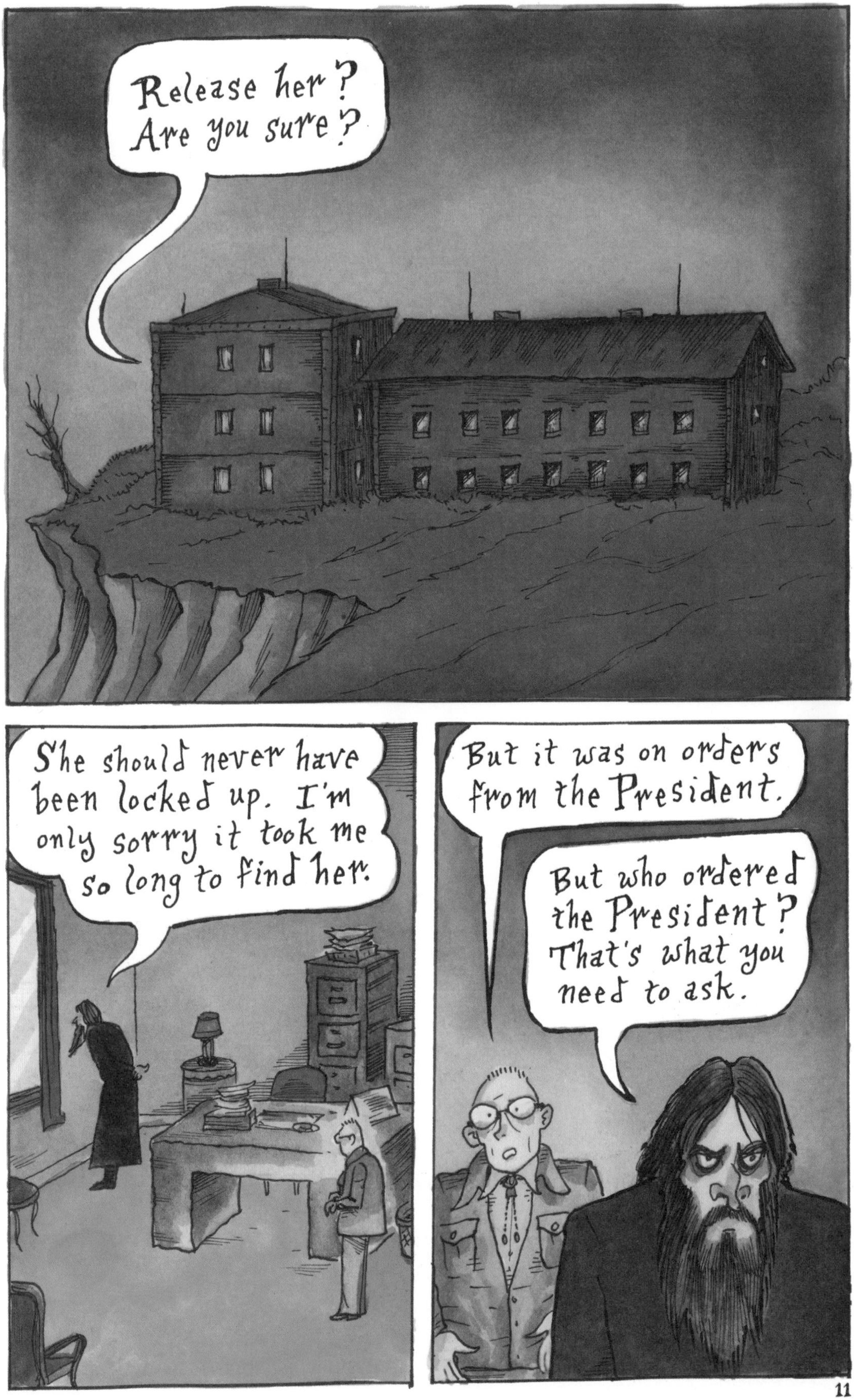
Release her? Are you sure?
She should never have been locked up. I'm only sorry it took me so long to find her.
But it was on orders from the President.
But who ordered the President? That's what you need to ask.

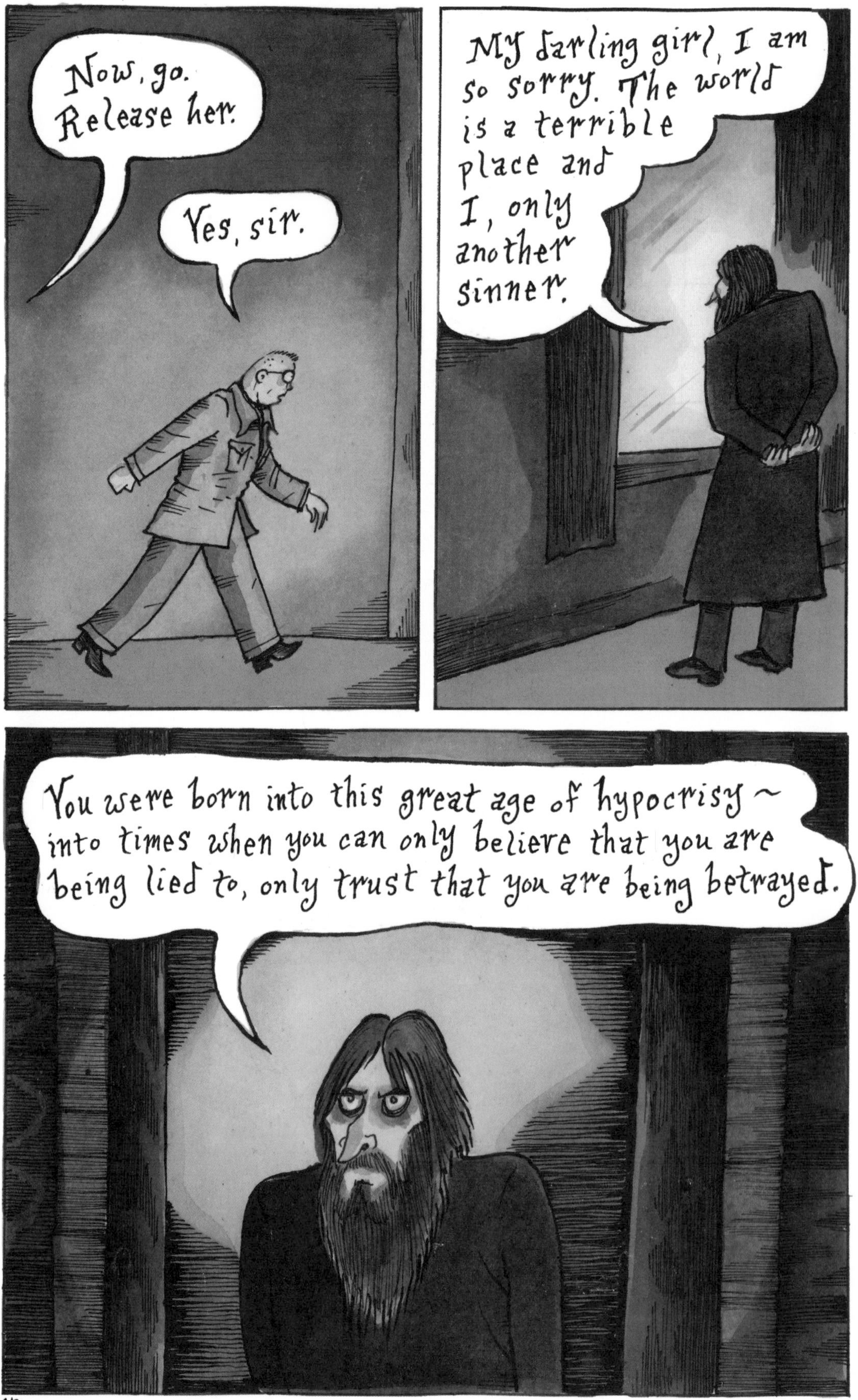
Now, go. Release her.
Yes, sir.
My darling girl, I am so sorry. The world is a terrible place and I, only another sinner.
You were born into this great age of hypocrisy ~ into times when you can only believe that you are being lied to, only trust that you are being betrayed.

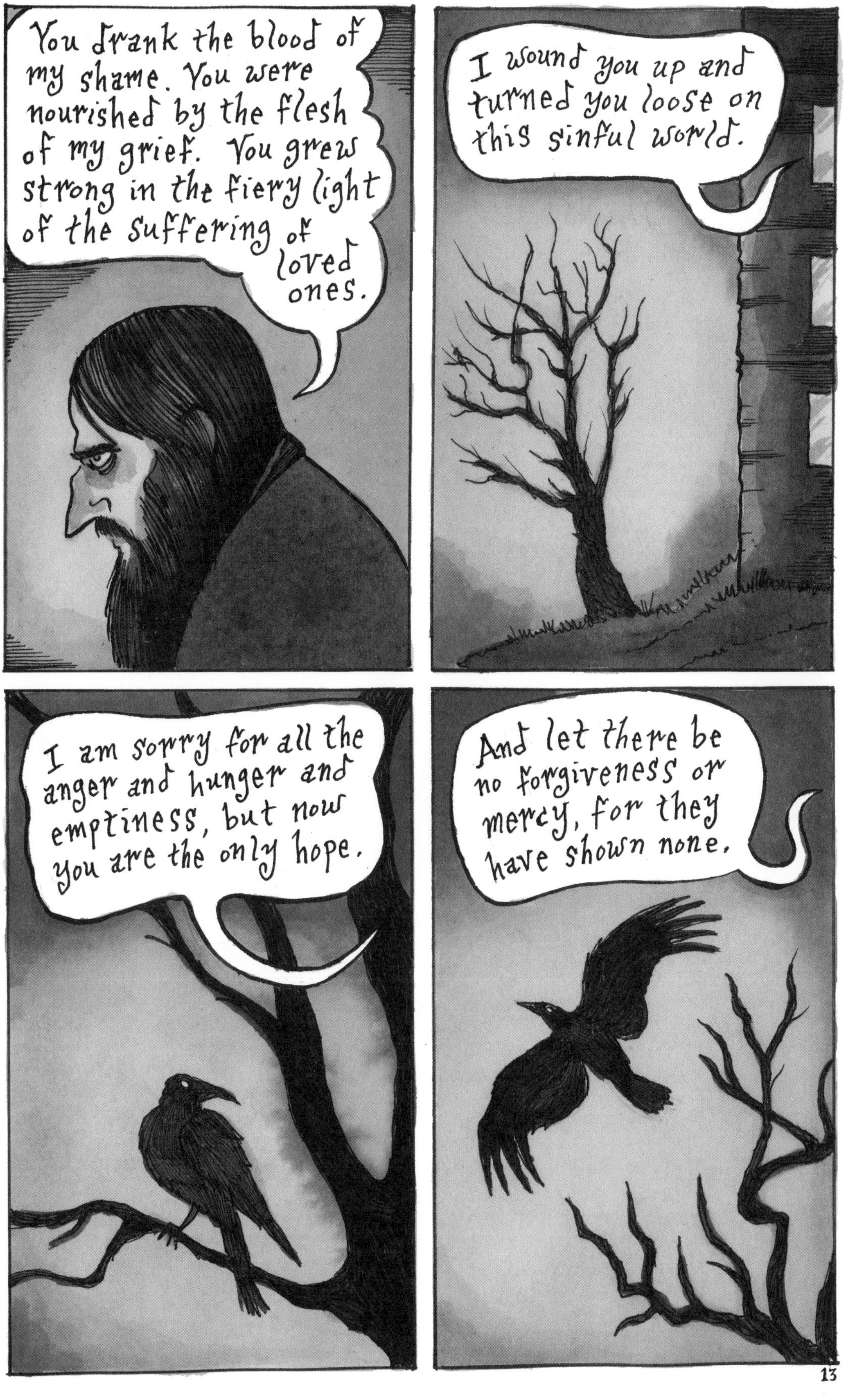
You drank the blood of my shame. You were nourished by the flesh of my grief. You grew strong in the fiery light of the suffering of loved ones.
I wound you up and turned you loose on this sinful world.
I am sorry for all the anger and hunger and emptiness, but now you are the only hope.
And let there be no forgiveness or mercy, for they have shown none.

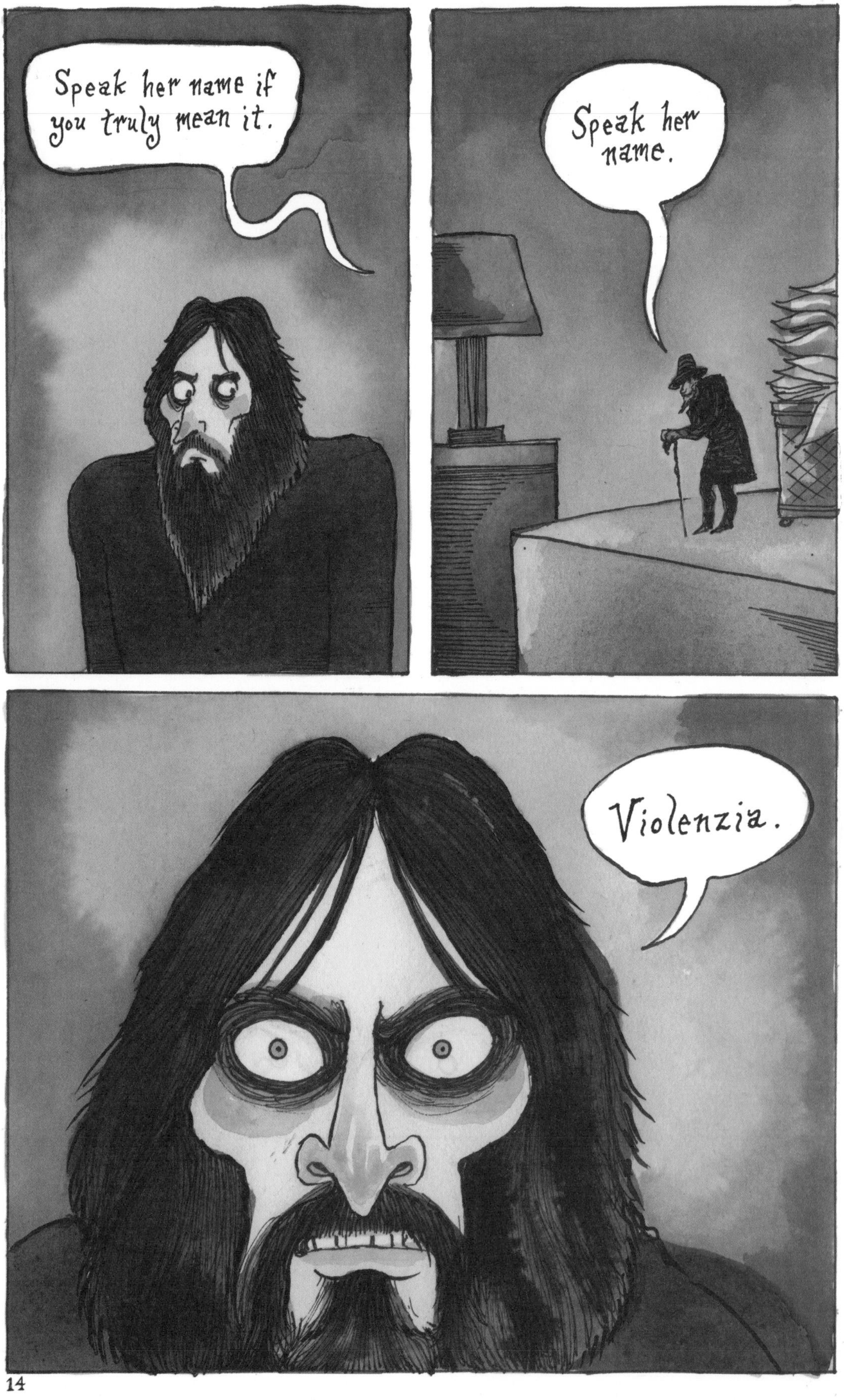
Speak her name if you truly mean it.
Speak her name.
Violenzia.

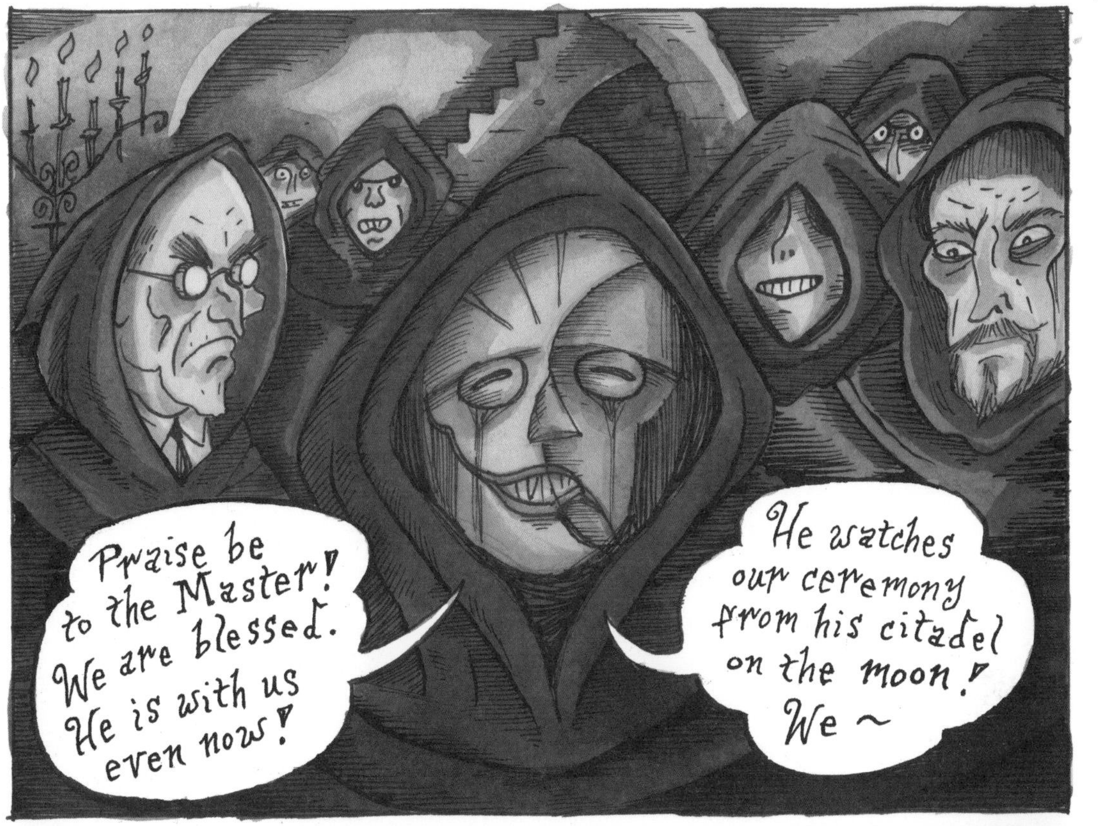
Praise be to the Master! We are blessed. He is with us even now!
He watches our ceremony from his citadel on the moon! We ~

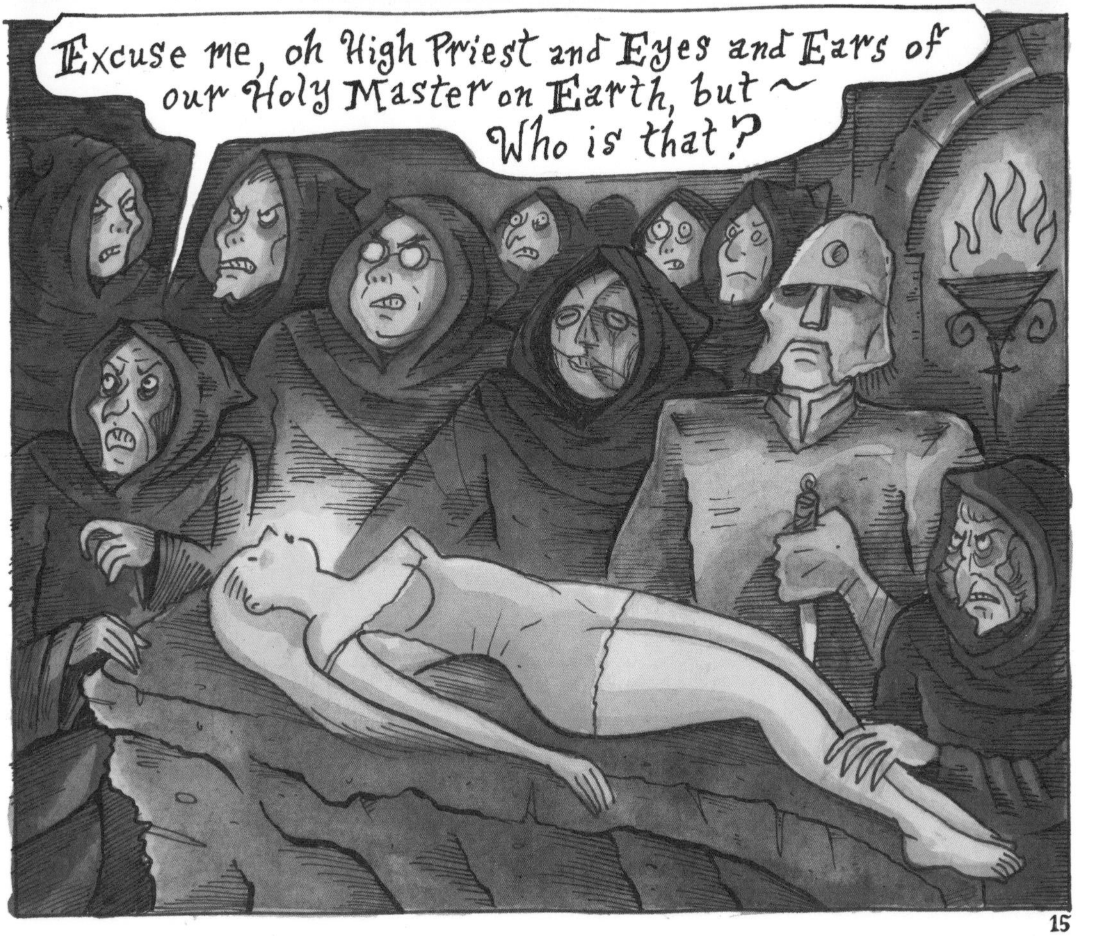
Excuse me, oh High Priest and Eyes and Ears of our Holy Master on Earth, but ~ Who is that?

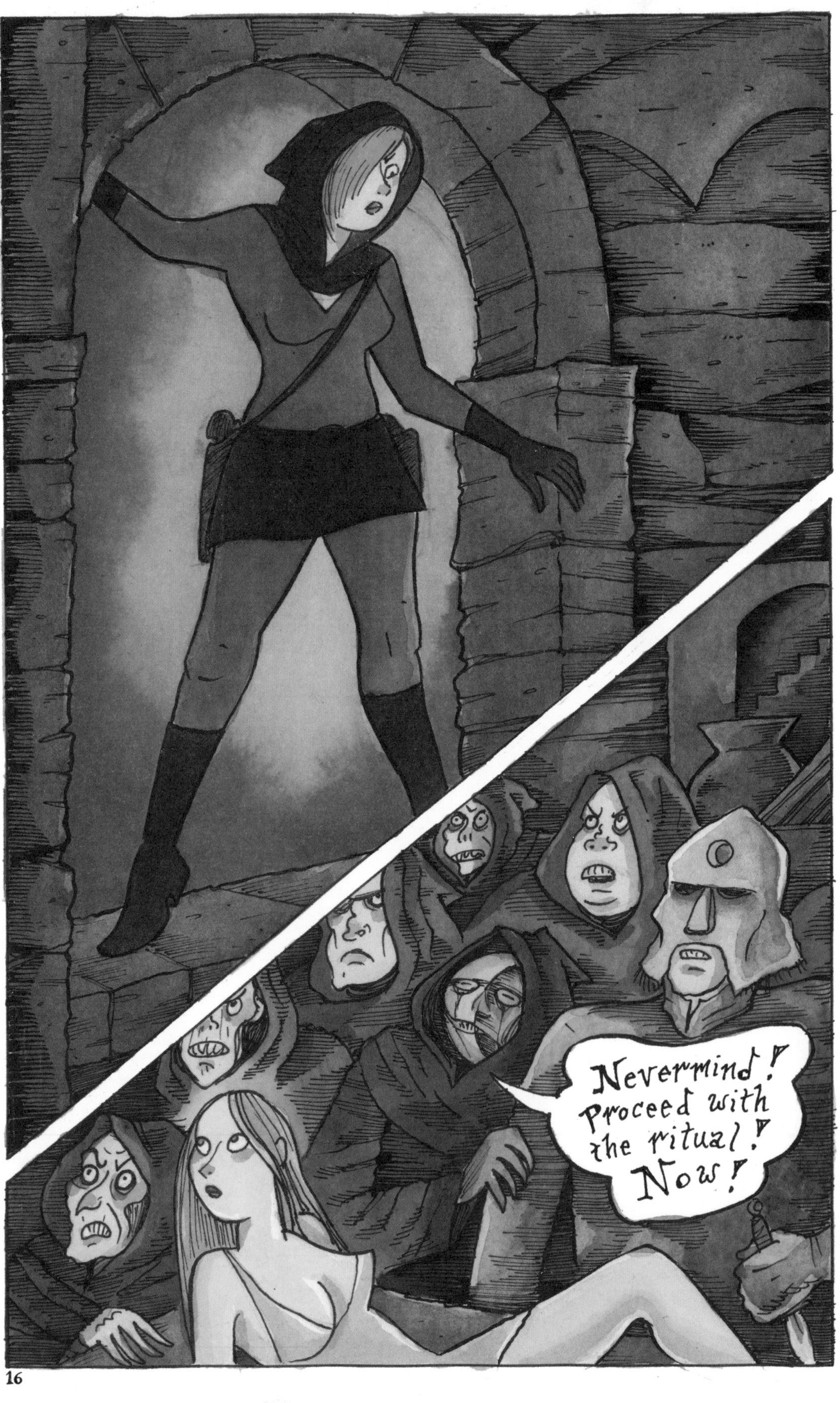
Nevermind! Proceed with the ritual! Now!

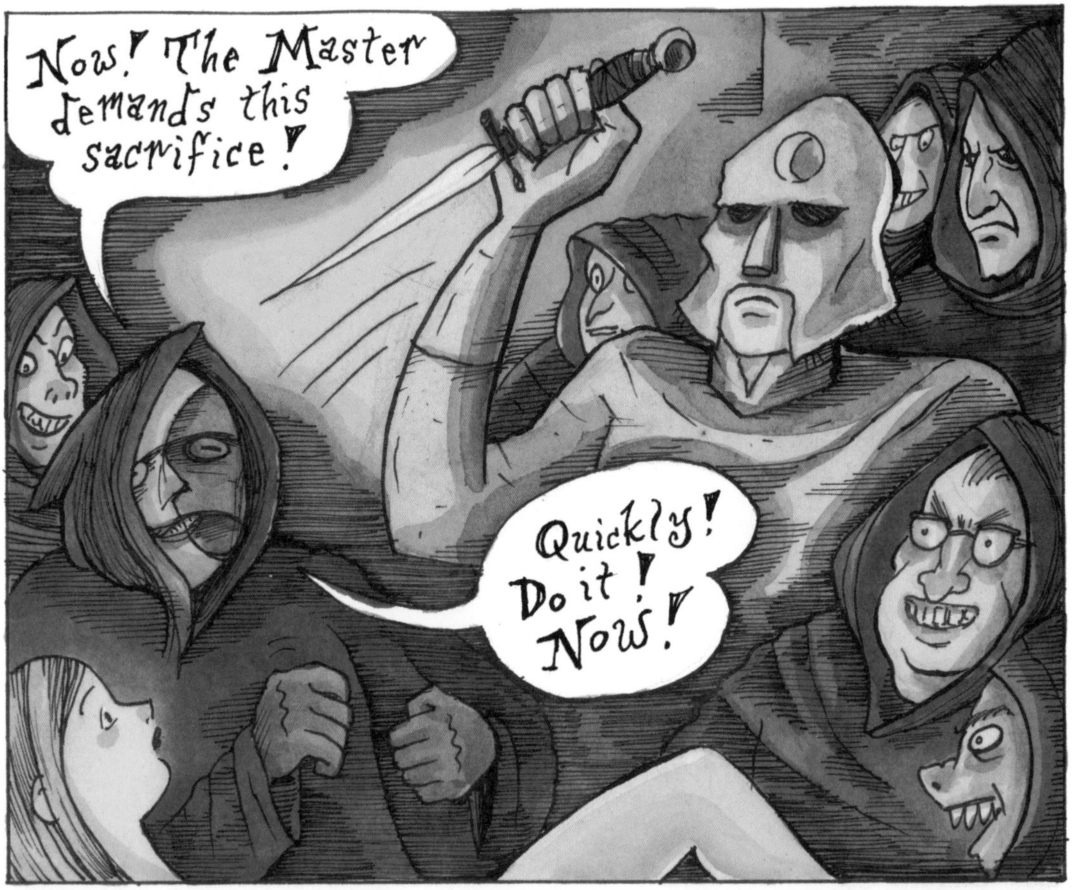
Now! The Master demands this sacrifice!
Quickly! Do it! Now!

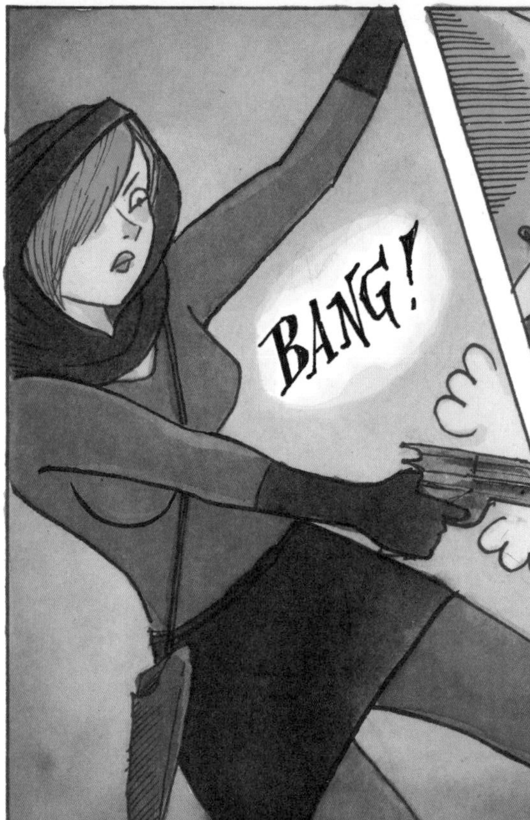
BANG!

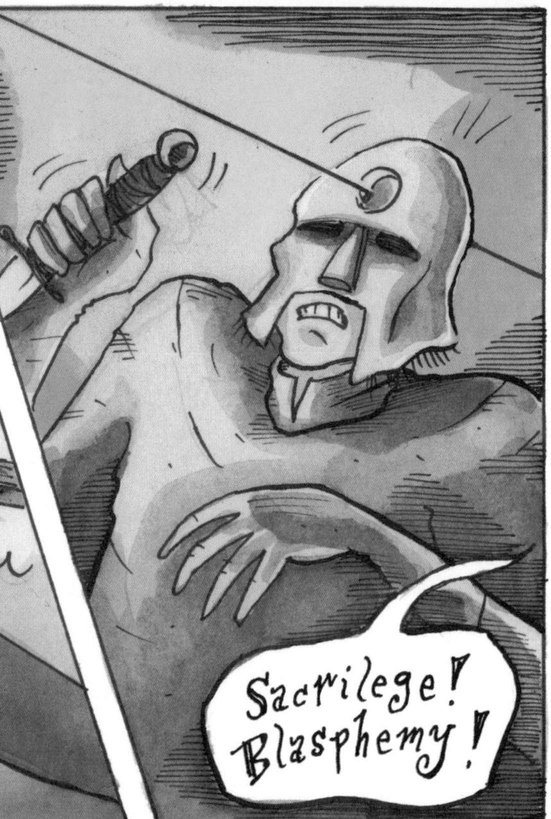
Sacrilege! Blasphemy!

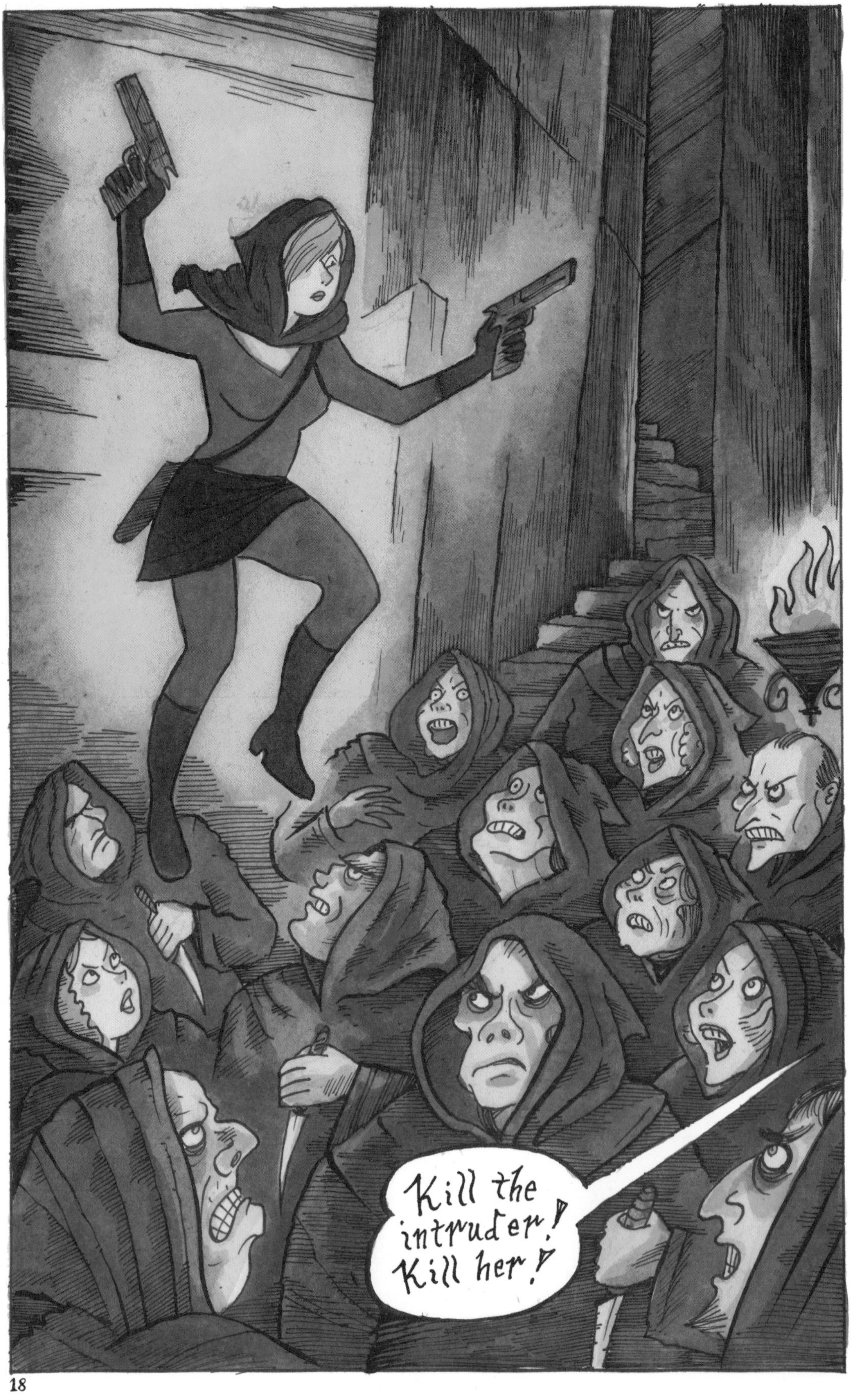
Kill the intruder! Kill her!

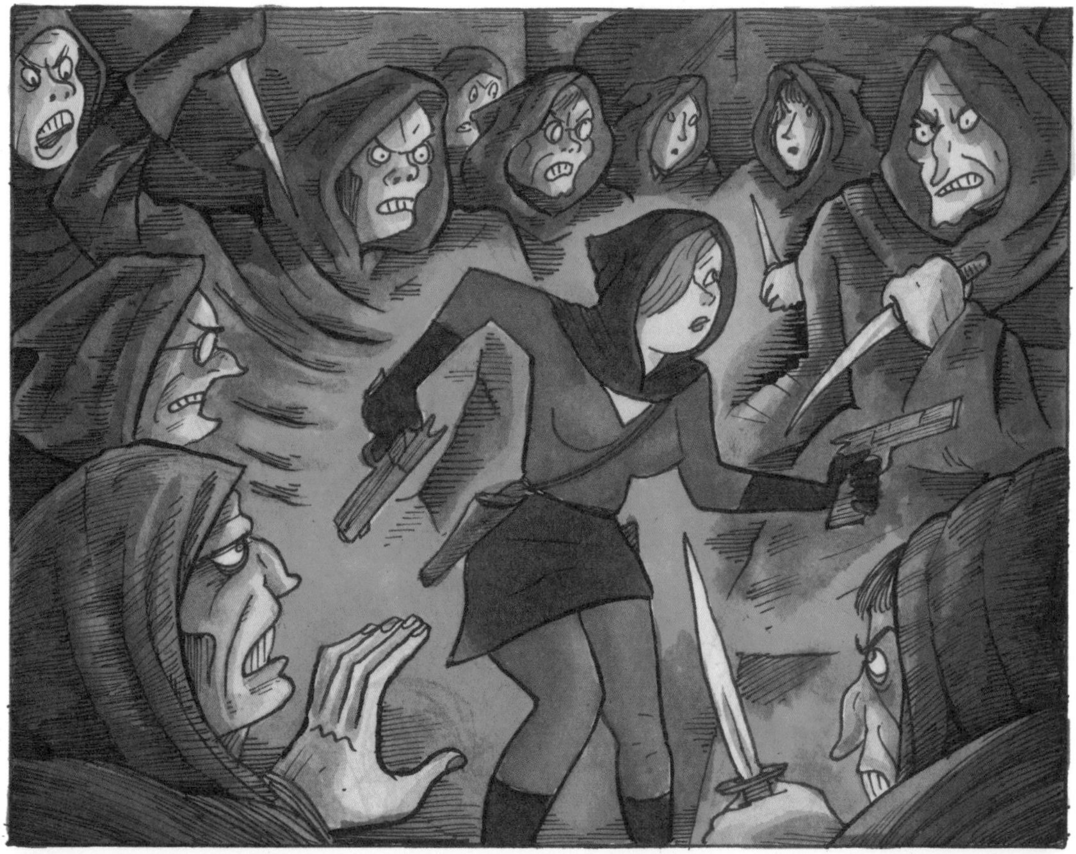

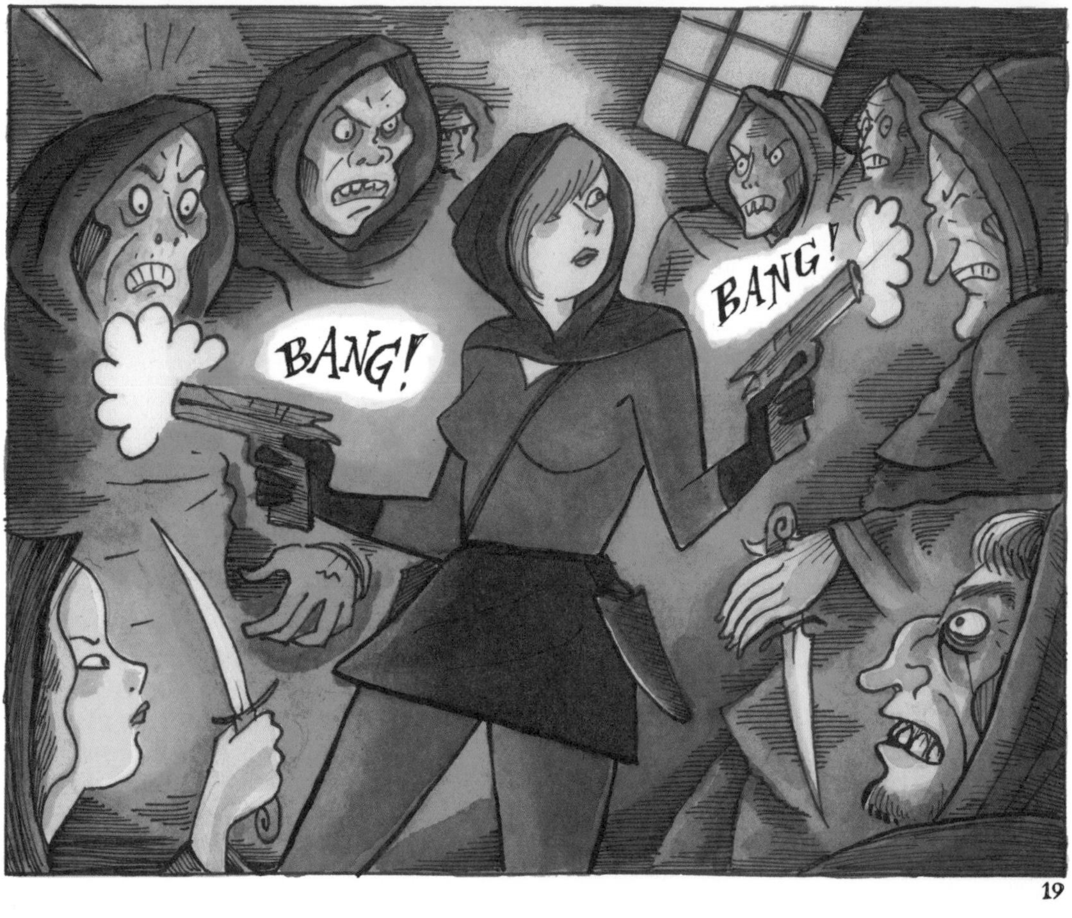
BANG!
BANG!

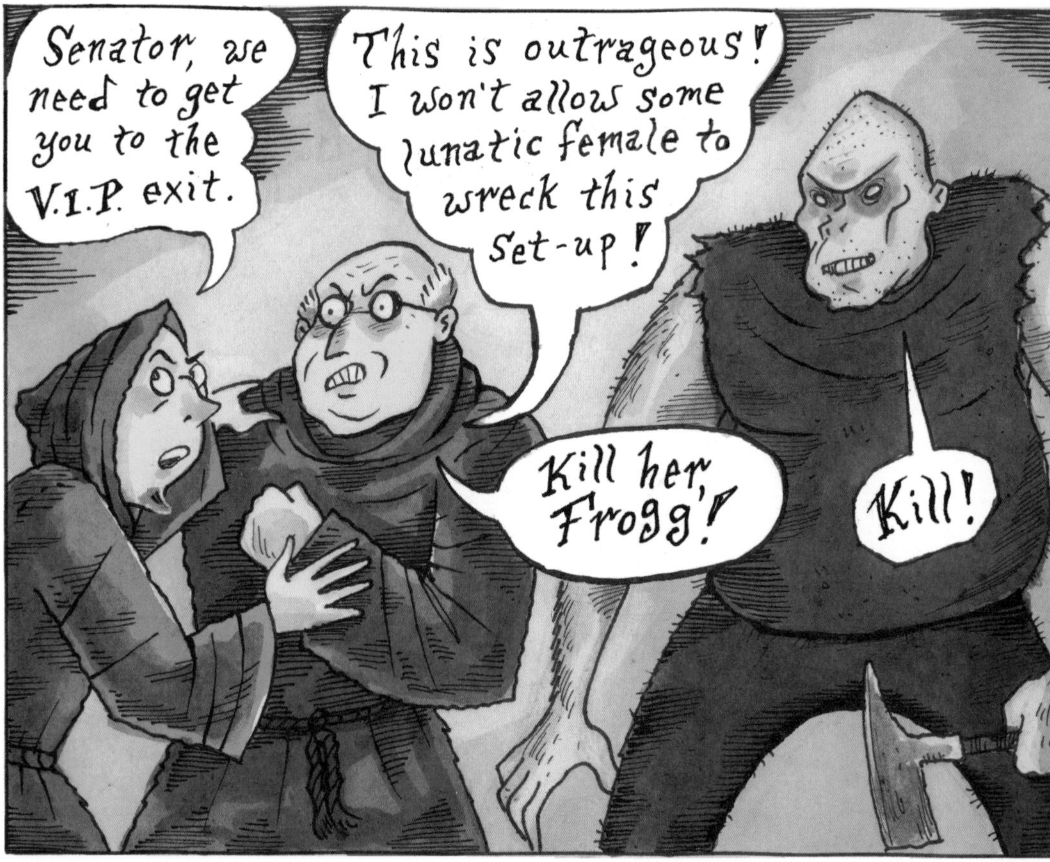
Senator, we need to get you to the V.I.P. exit.
This is outrageous! I won't allow some lunatic female to wreck this set-up!
Kill her, Frogg!
Kill!

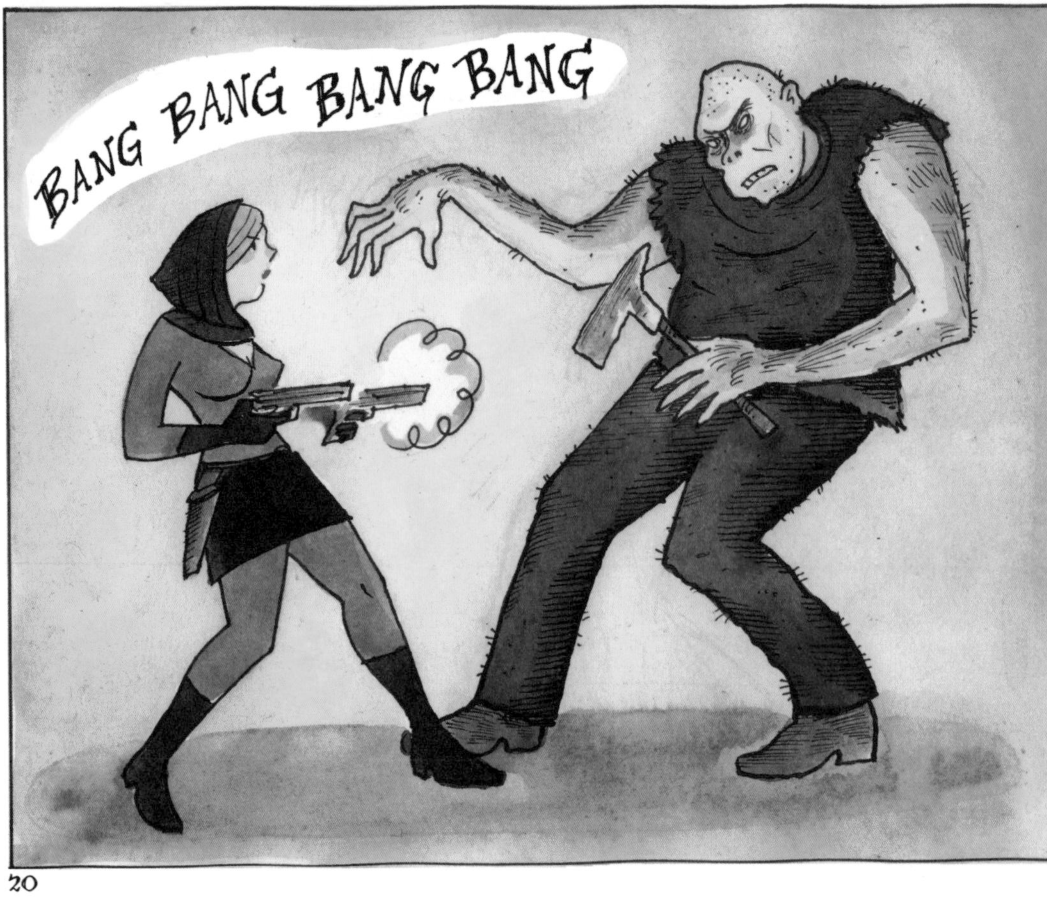
BANG BANG BANG BANG

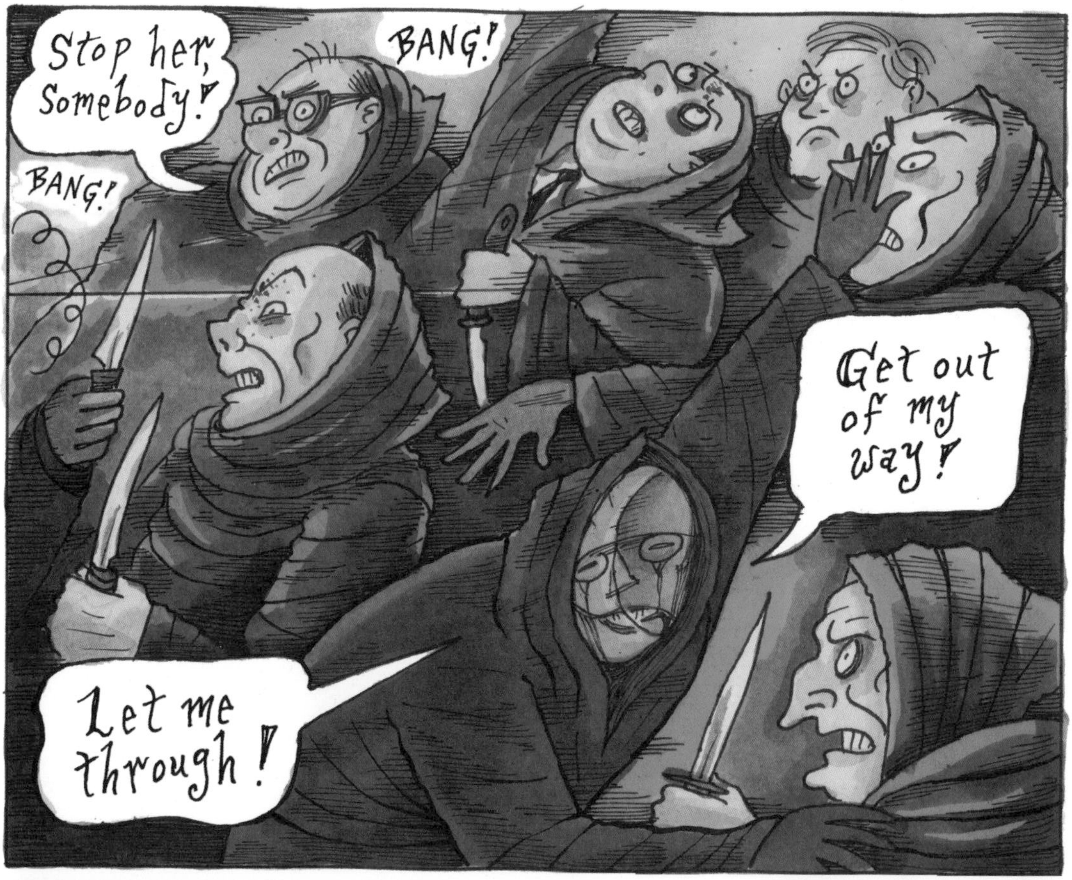
Stop her, Somebody!
BANG!
BANG!
Get out of my way!
Let me through!

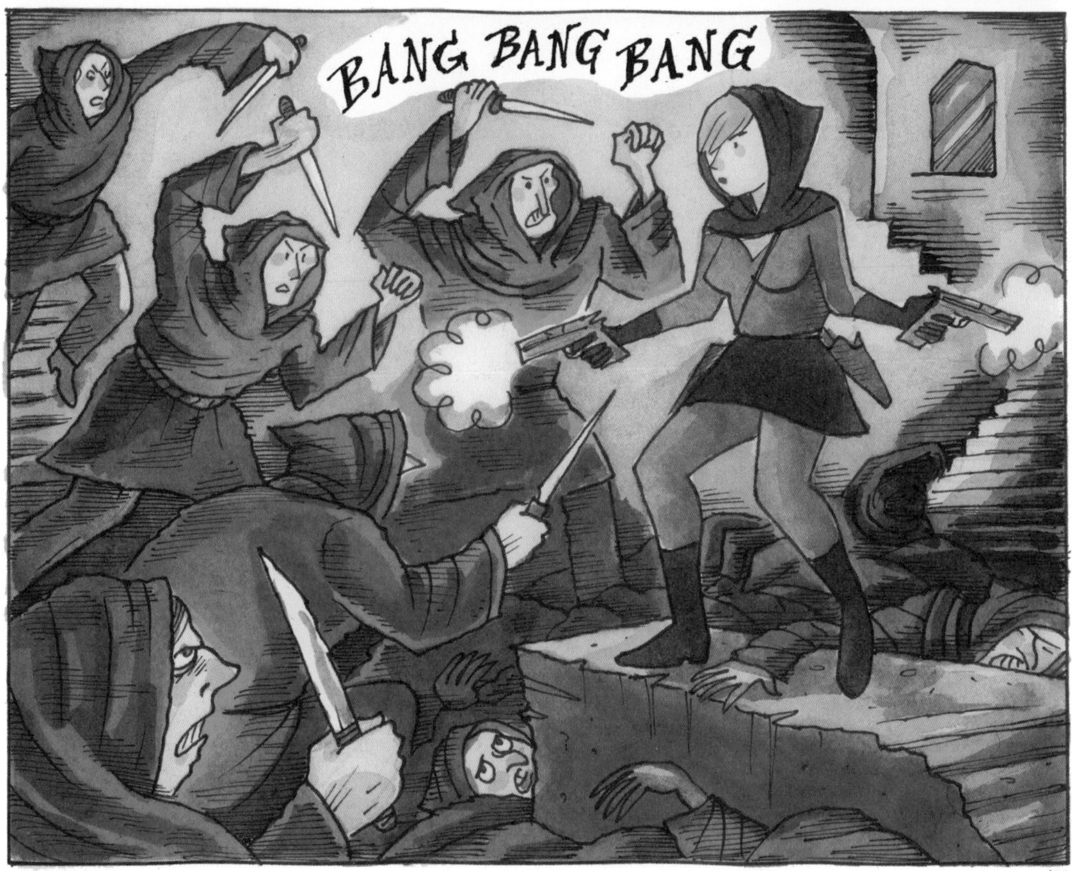
BANG BANG BANG

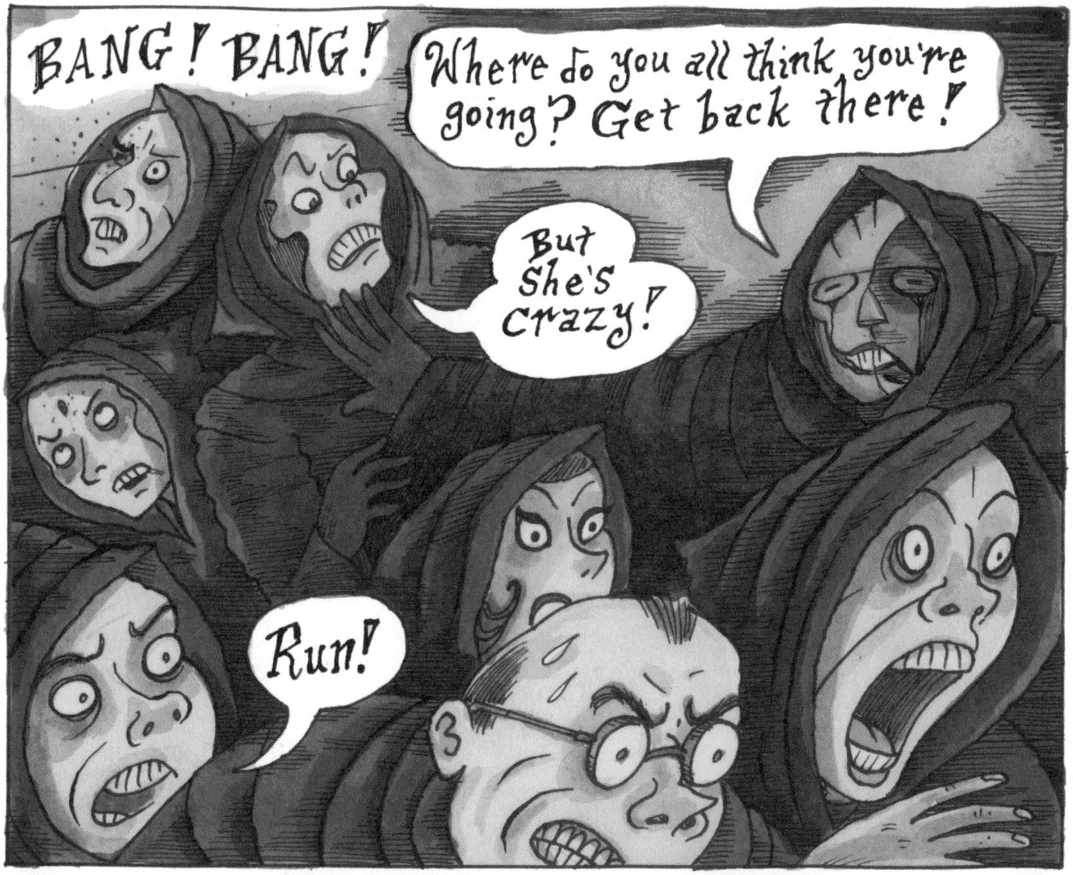
BANG! BANG!
Where do you all think you're going? Get back there!
But she's crazy!
Run!

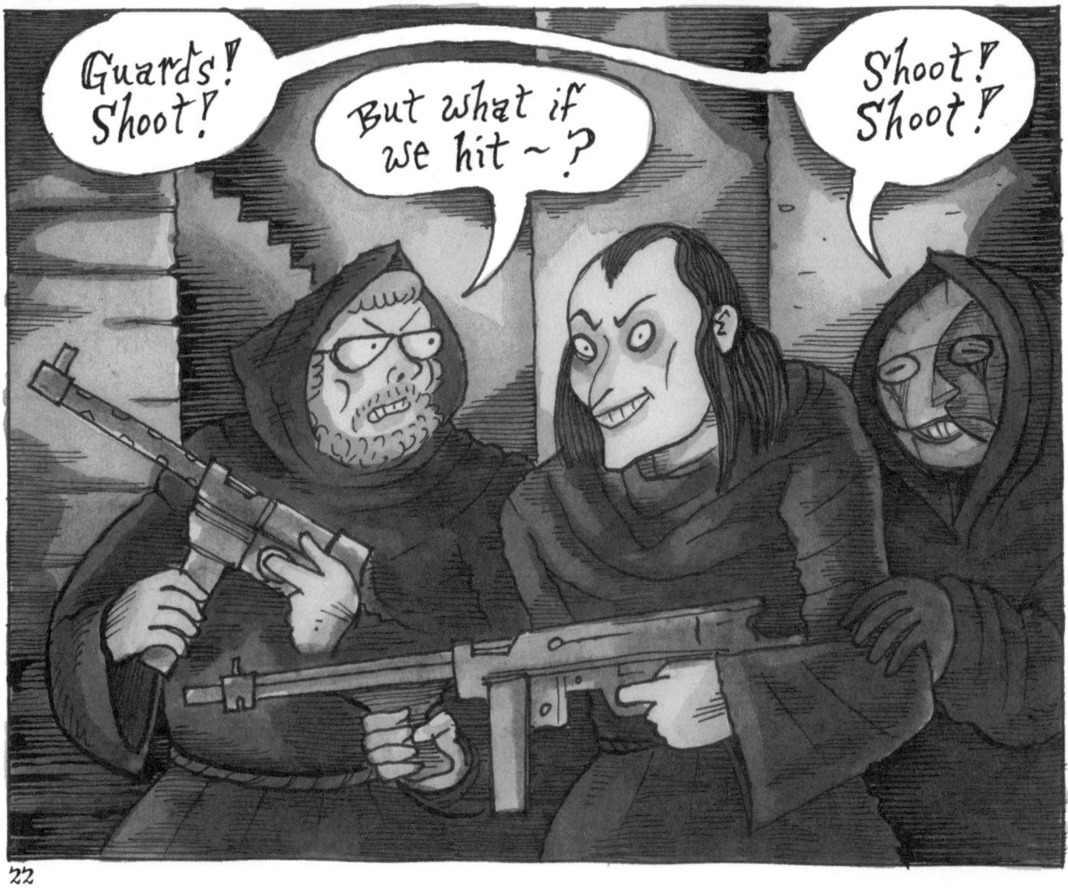
Guards! Shoot!
But what if we hit ~?
Shoot! Shoot!

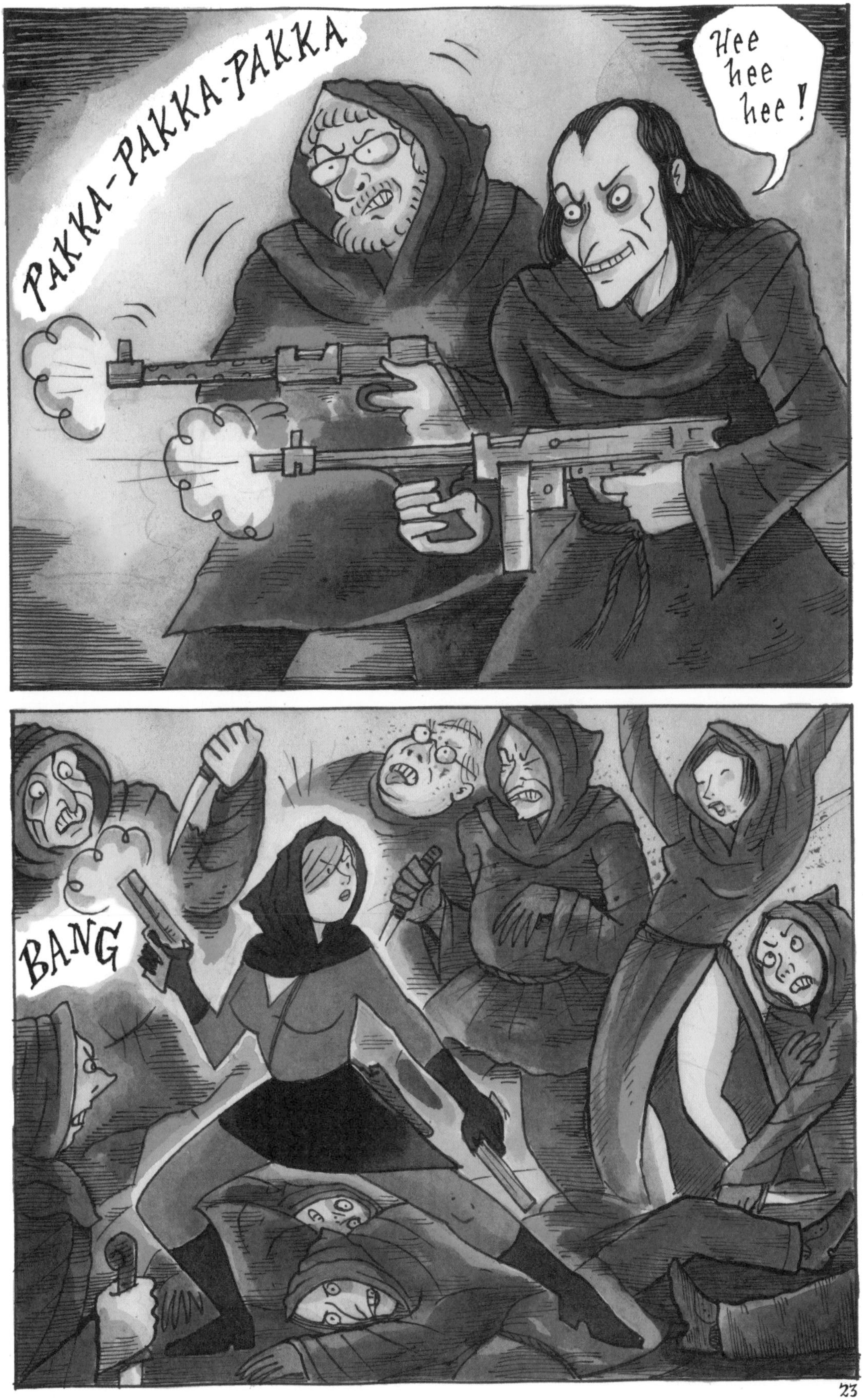
PAKKA-PAKKA-PAKKA
Hee hee hee!
BANG

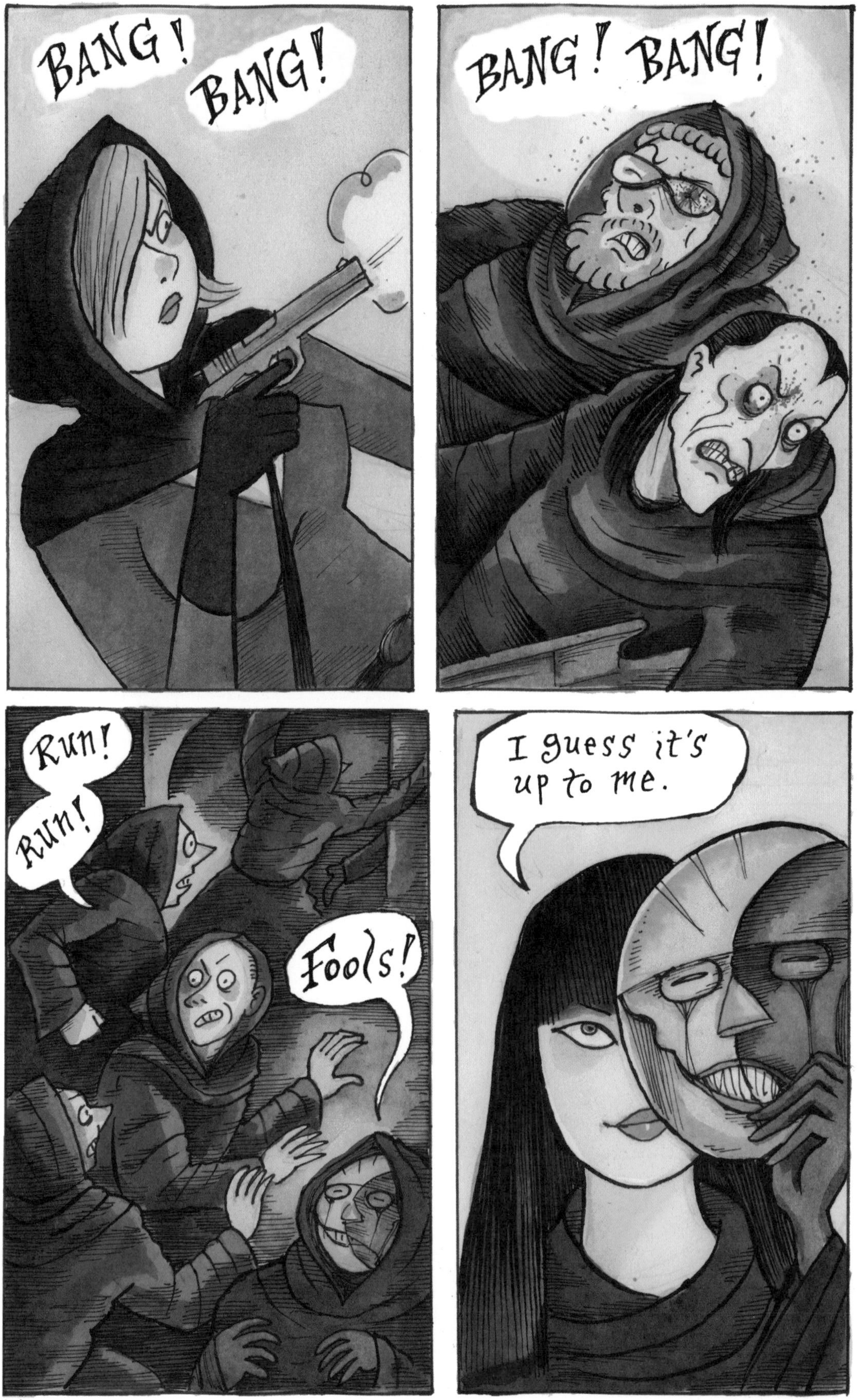
BANG!
BANG!
BANG! BANG!
Run!
Run!
Fools!
I guess it's up to me.

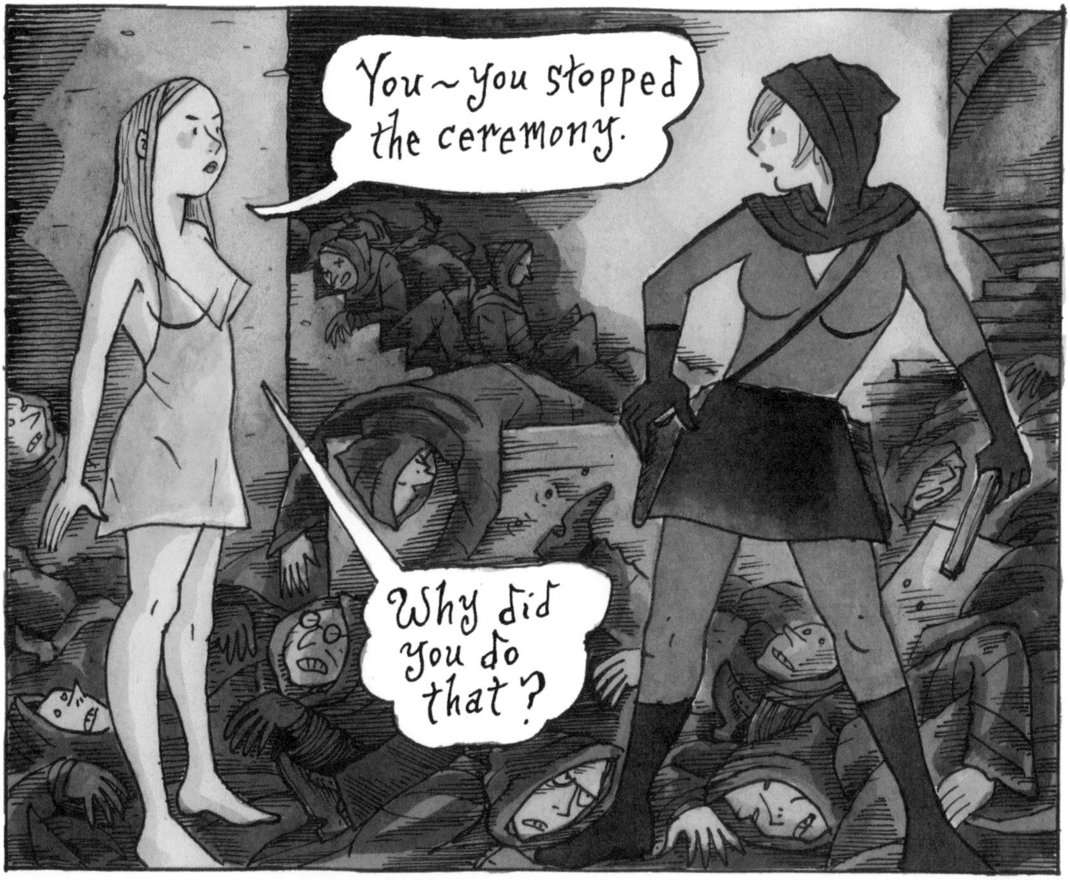
You ~ you stopped the ceremony.
Why did you do that?
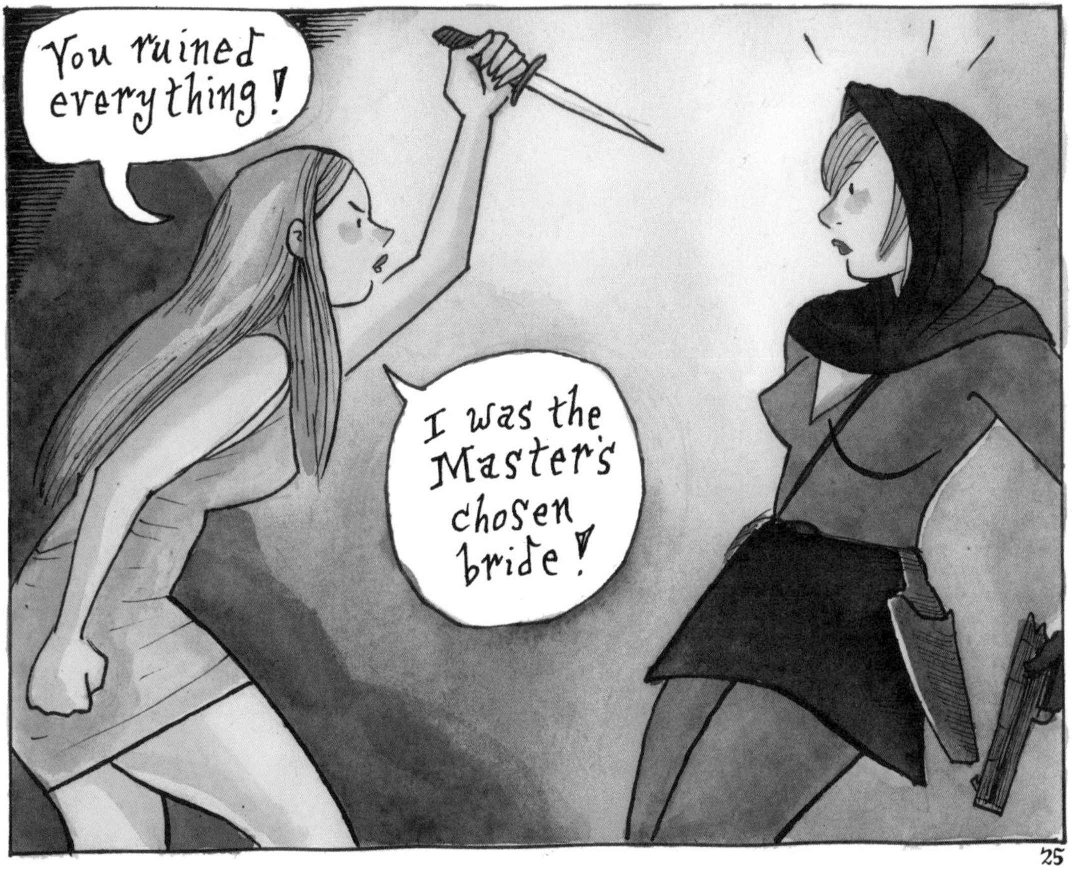
You ruined everything!
I was the Master's chosen bride!

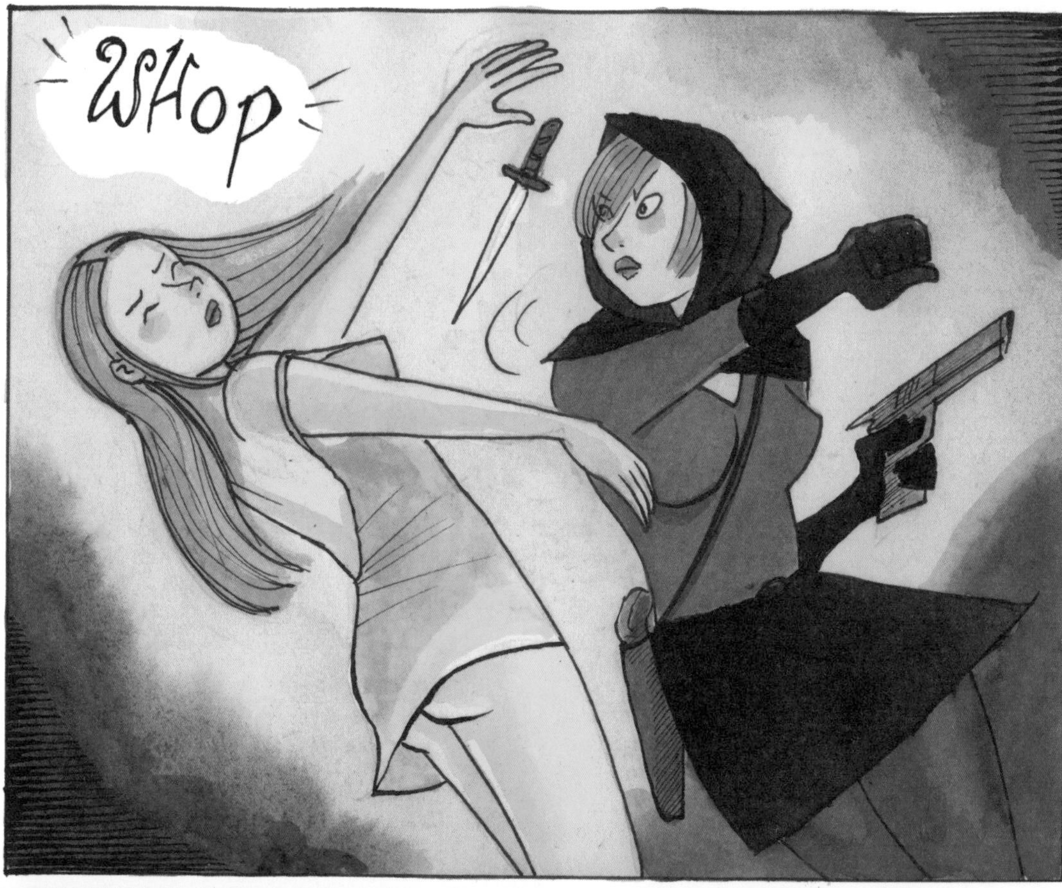
WHOP

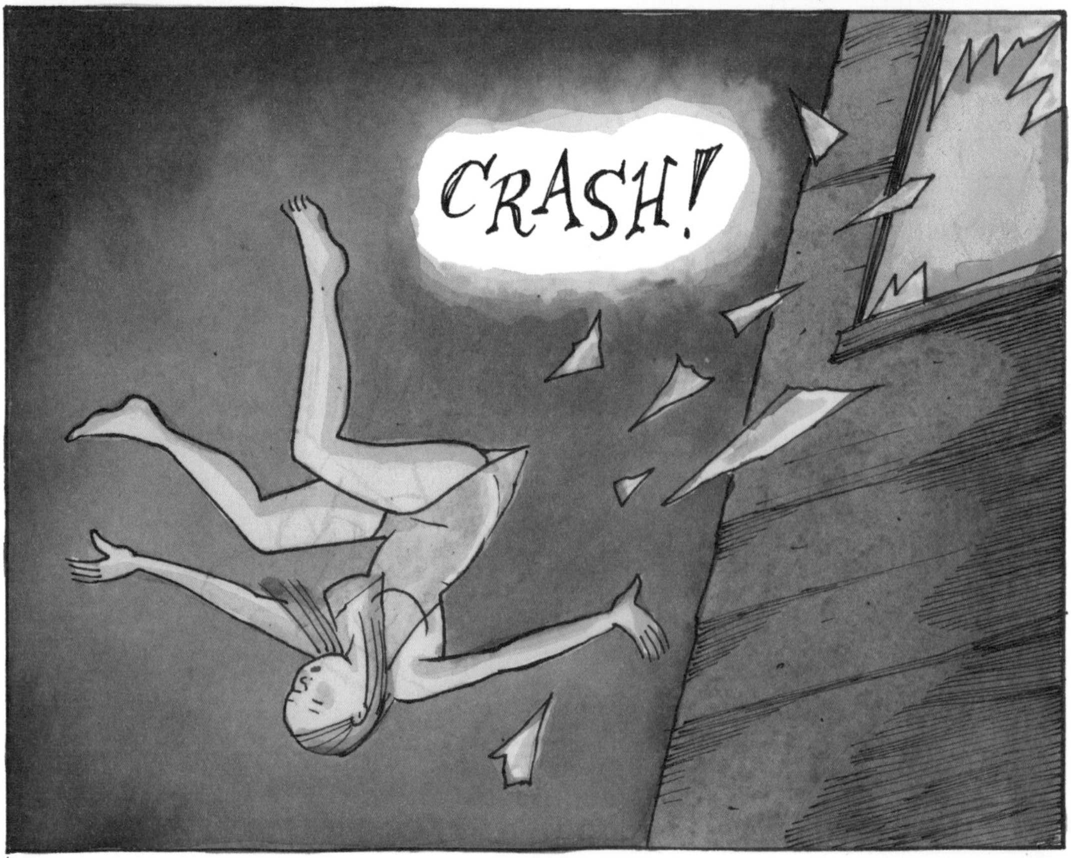
CRASH!

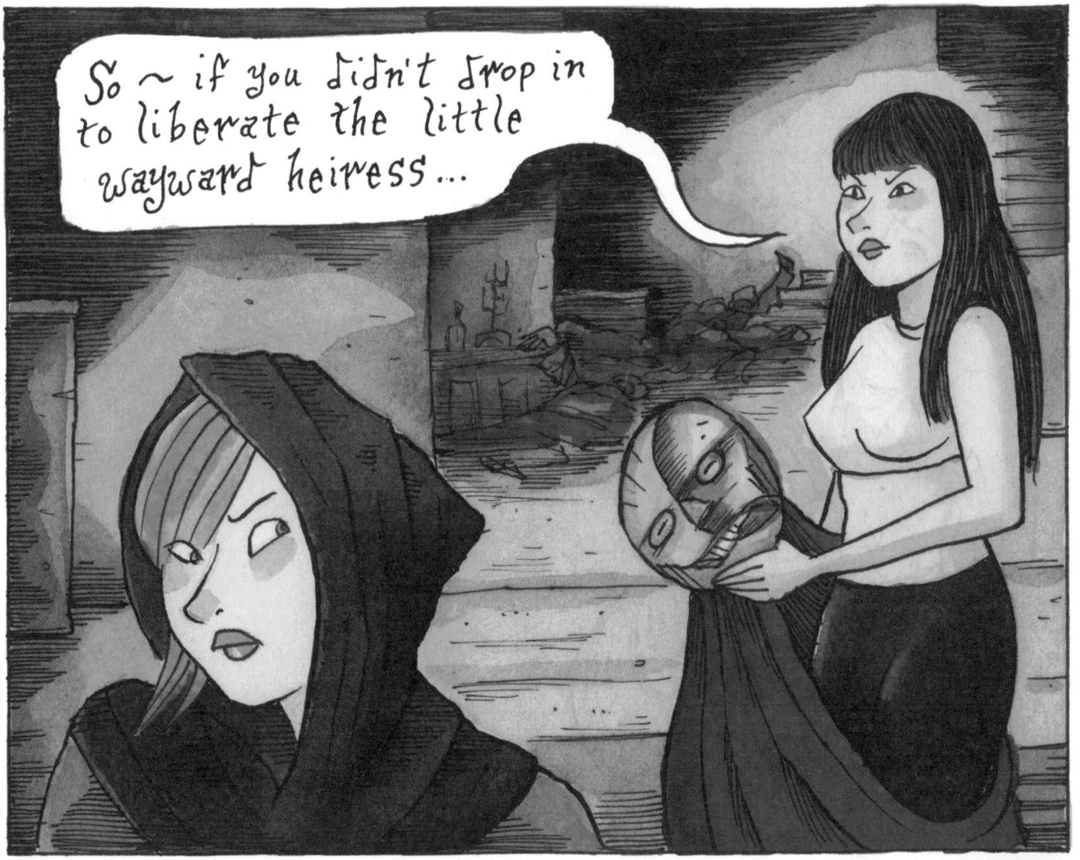
So ~ if you didn't drop in to liberate the little wayward heiress...

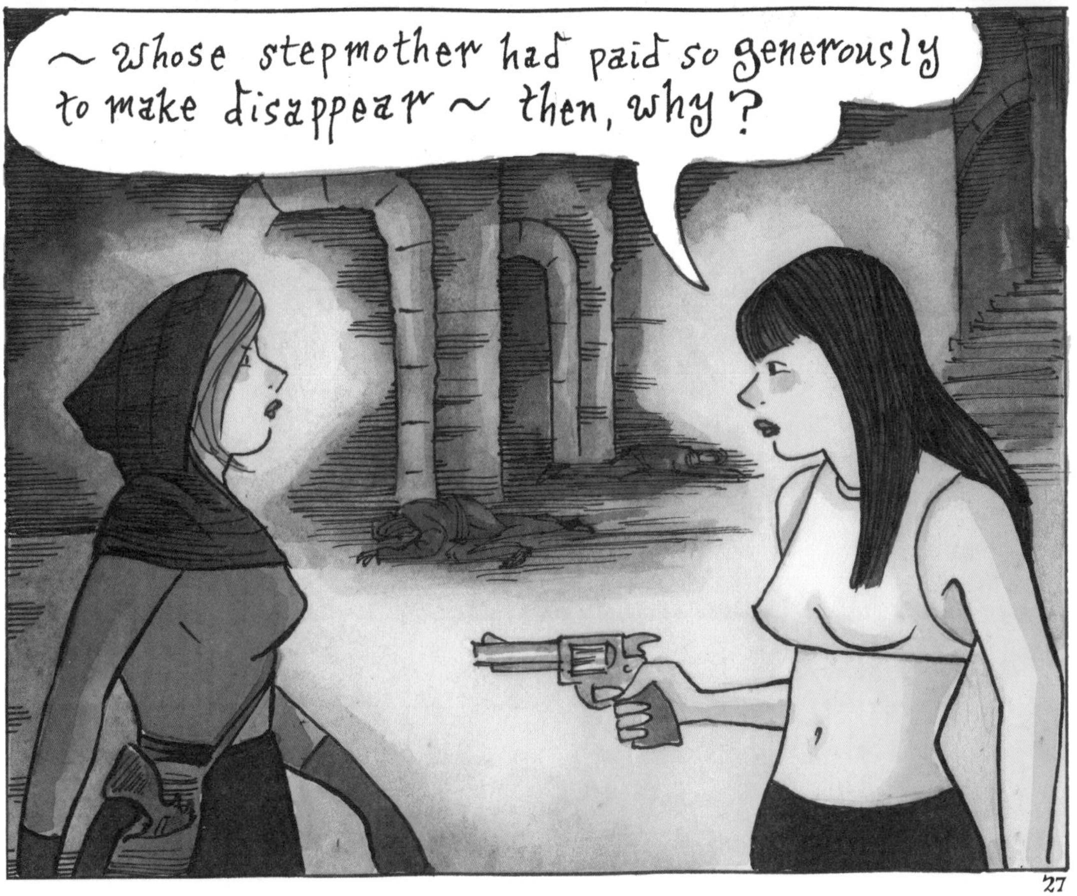
~ whose stepmother had paid so generously to make disappear ~ then, why?

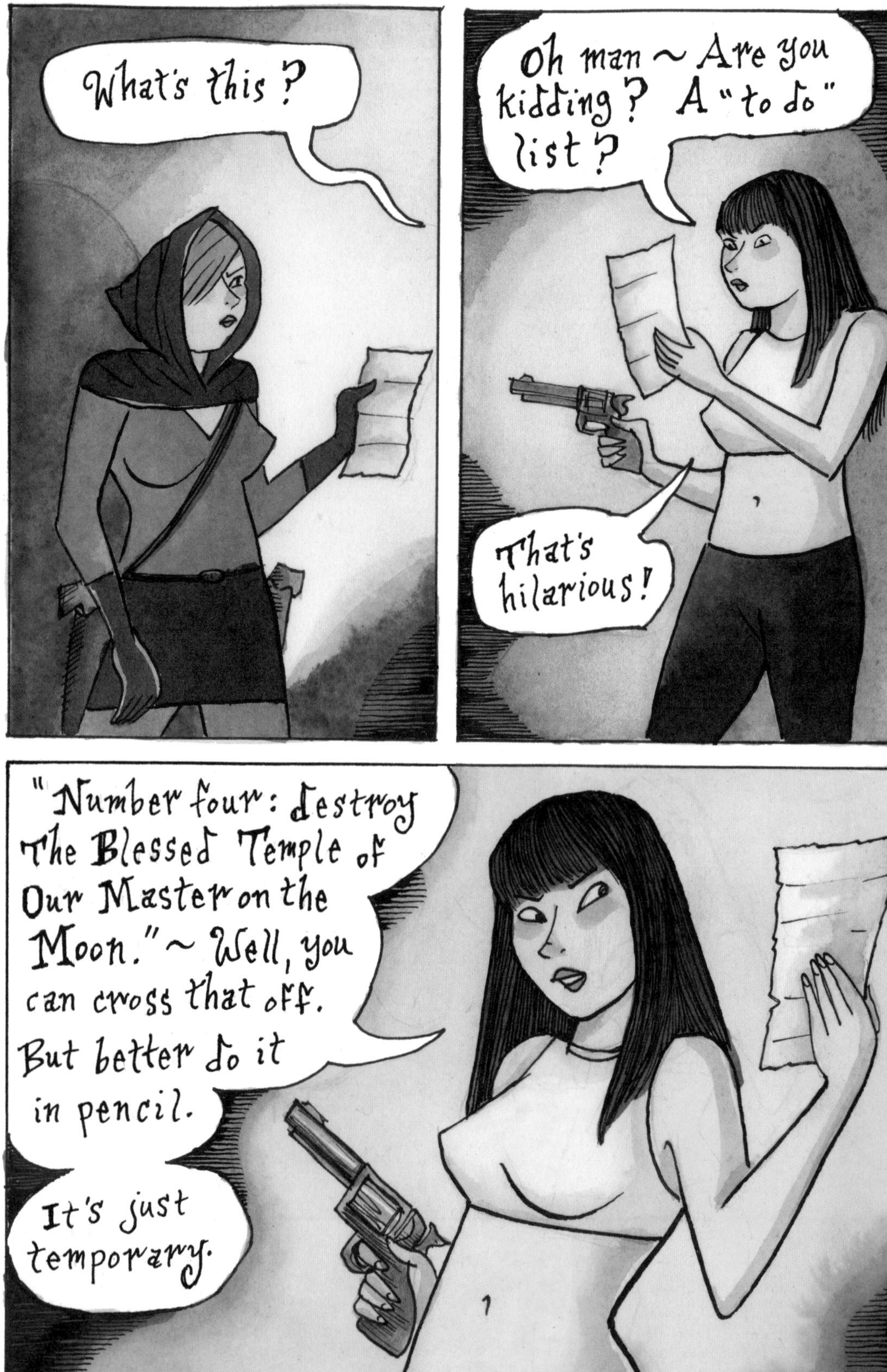
What's this?
Oh man ~ Are you kidding? A "to do" list?
That's hilarious!
"Number four: destroy The Blessed Temple of Our Master on the Moon." ~ Well, you can cross that off. But better do it in pencil.
It's just temporary.

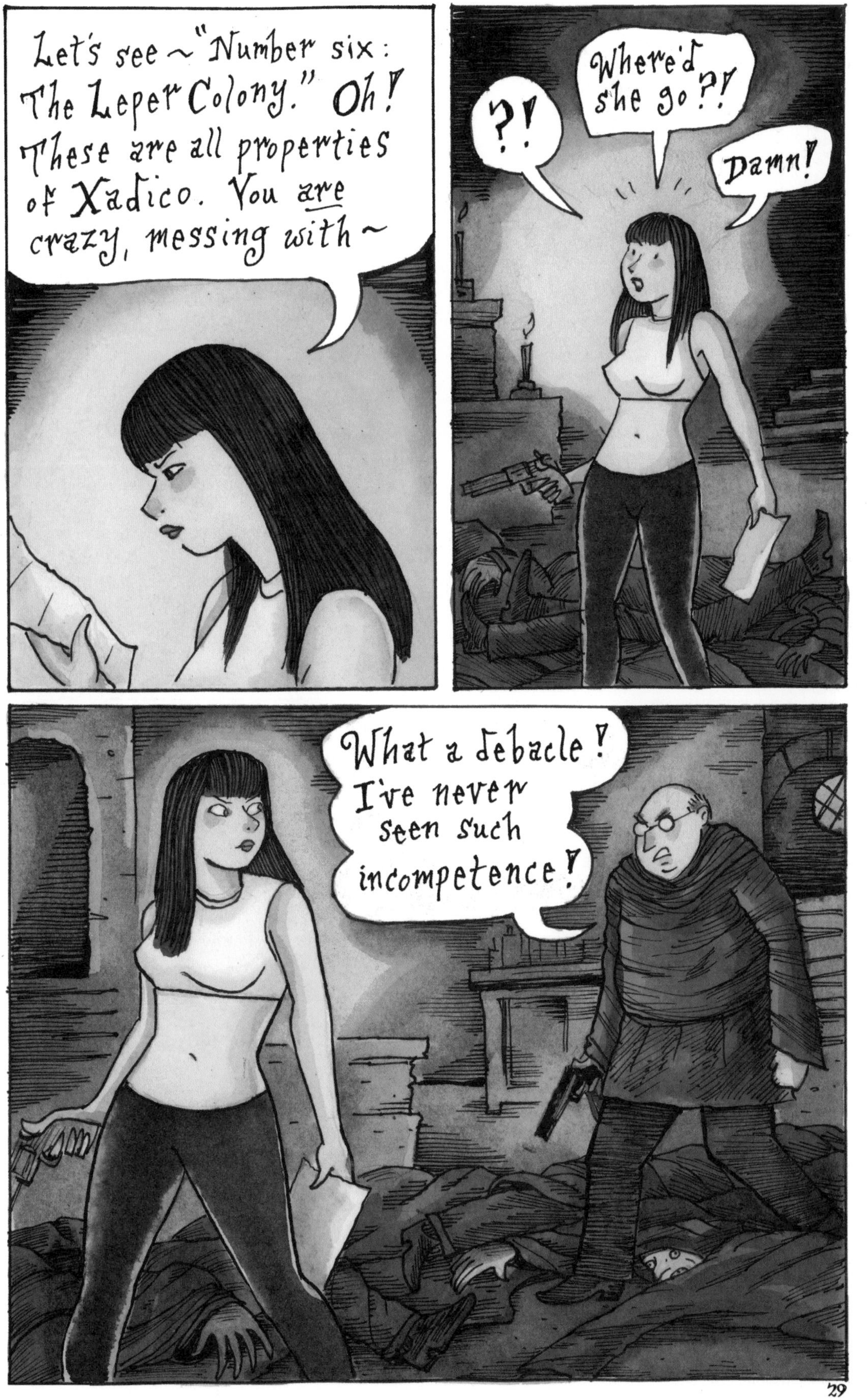
Let's see ~ "Number six: The Leper Colony." Oh! These are all properties of Xadico. You are crazy, messing with ~
?!
Where'd she go?!
Damn!
What a debacle! I've never seen such incompetence!

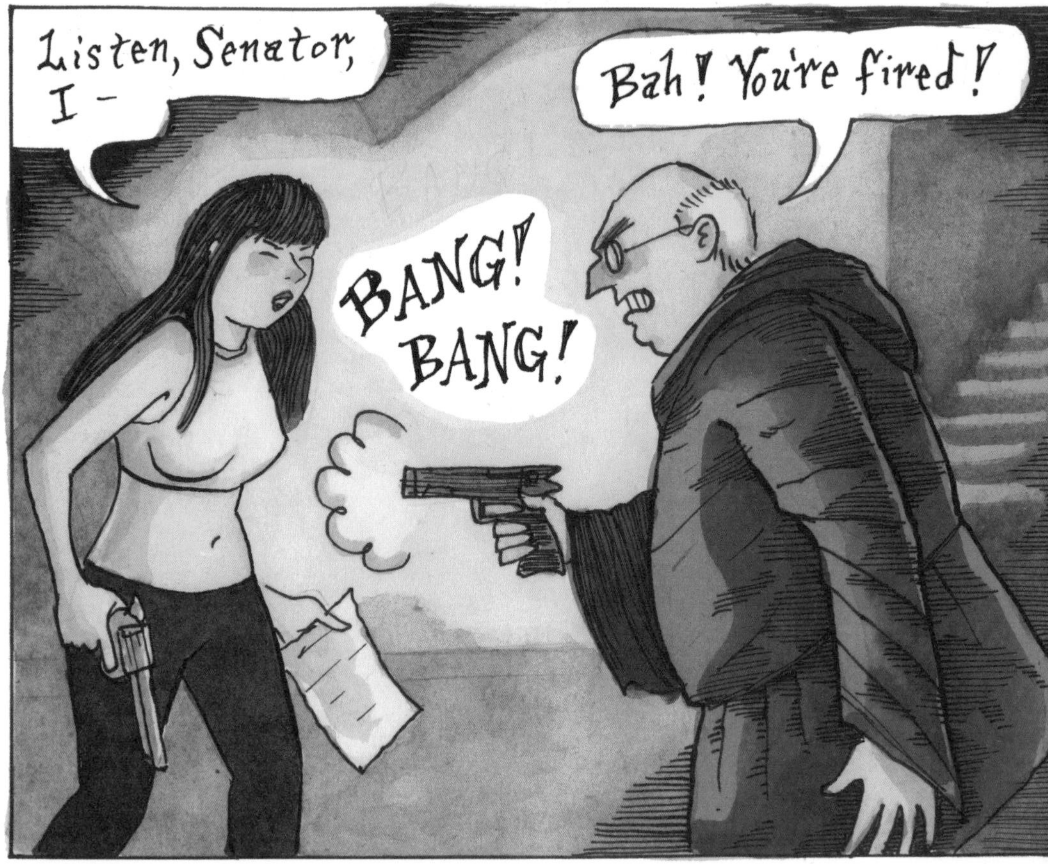
Listen, Senator, I -
Bah! You're fired!
BANG! BANG!
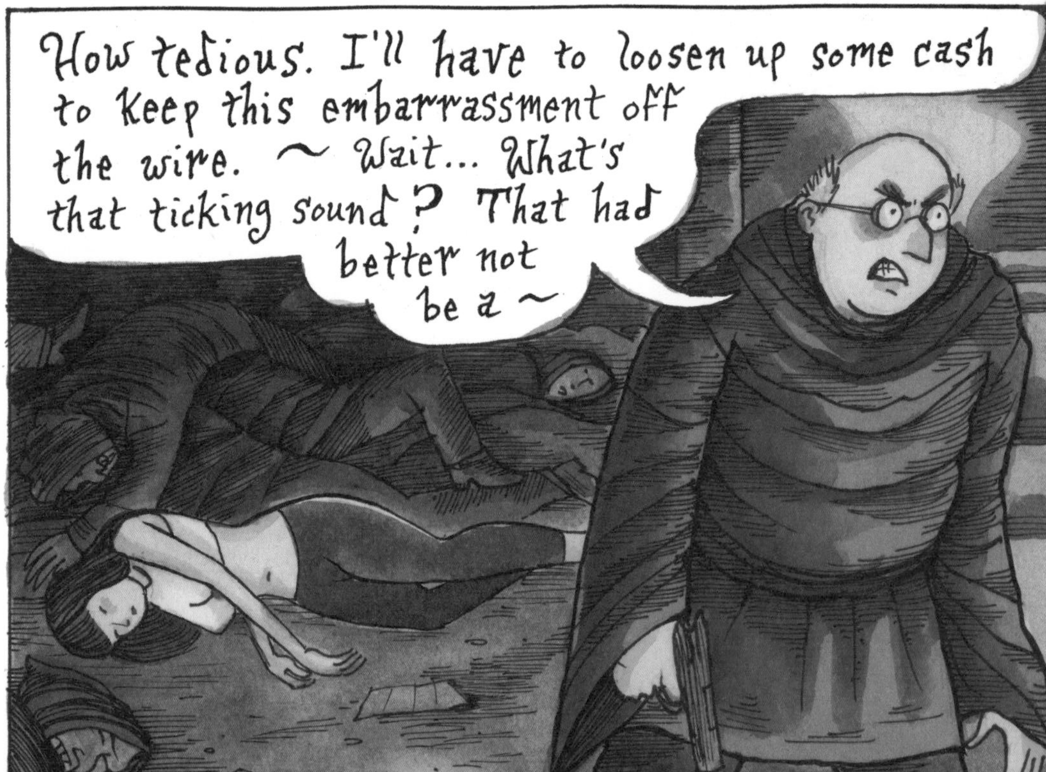
How tedious. I'll have to loosen up some cash to keep this embarrassment off the wire. ~ Wait... What's that ticking sound? That had better not be a ~

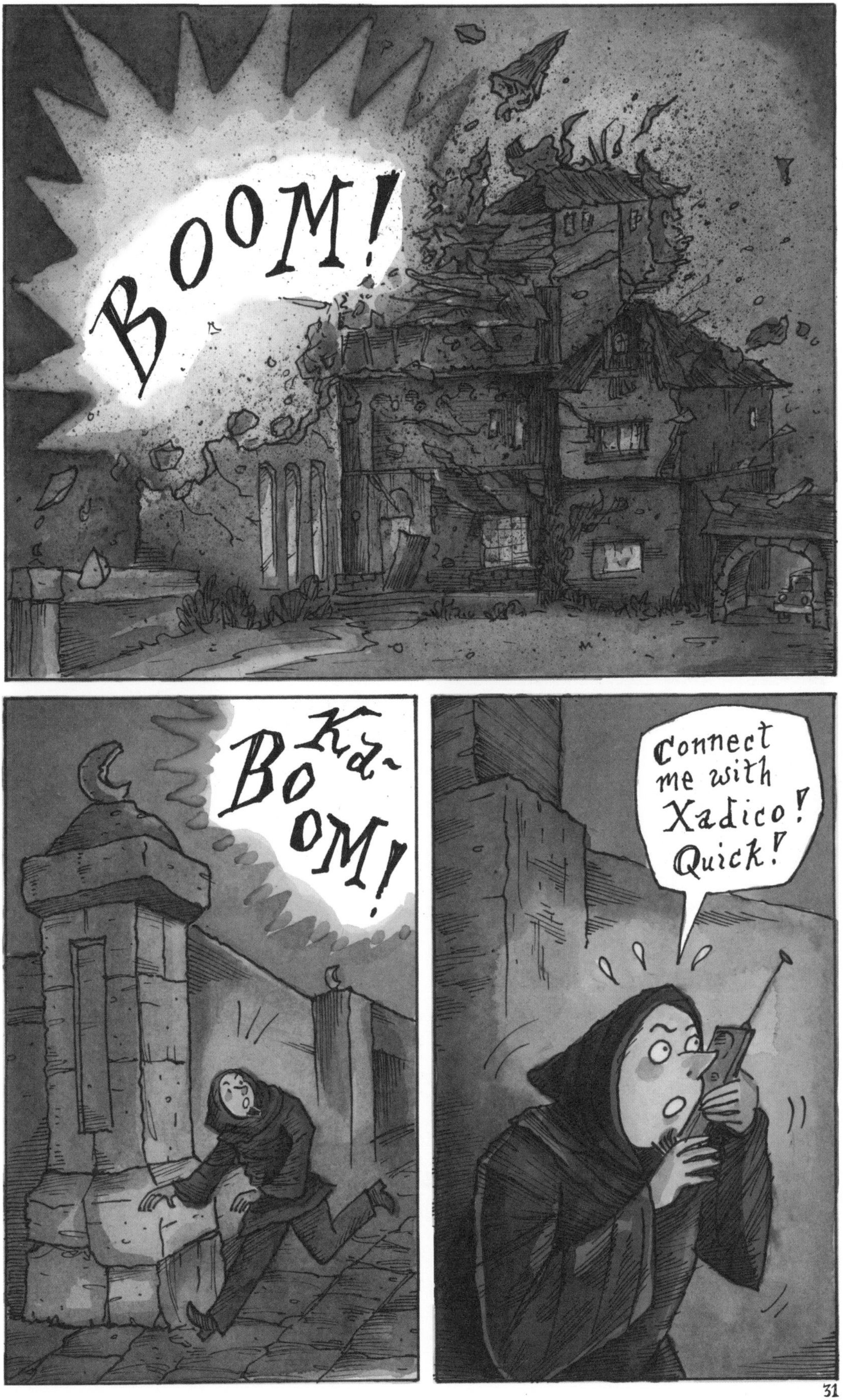
BOOM!
Ka-BOOM!
Connect me with Xadico! Quick!

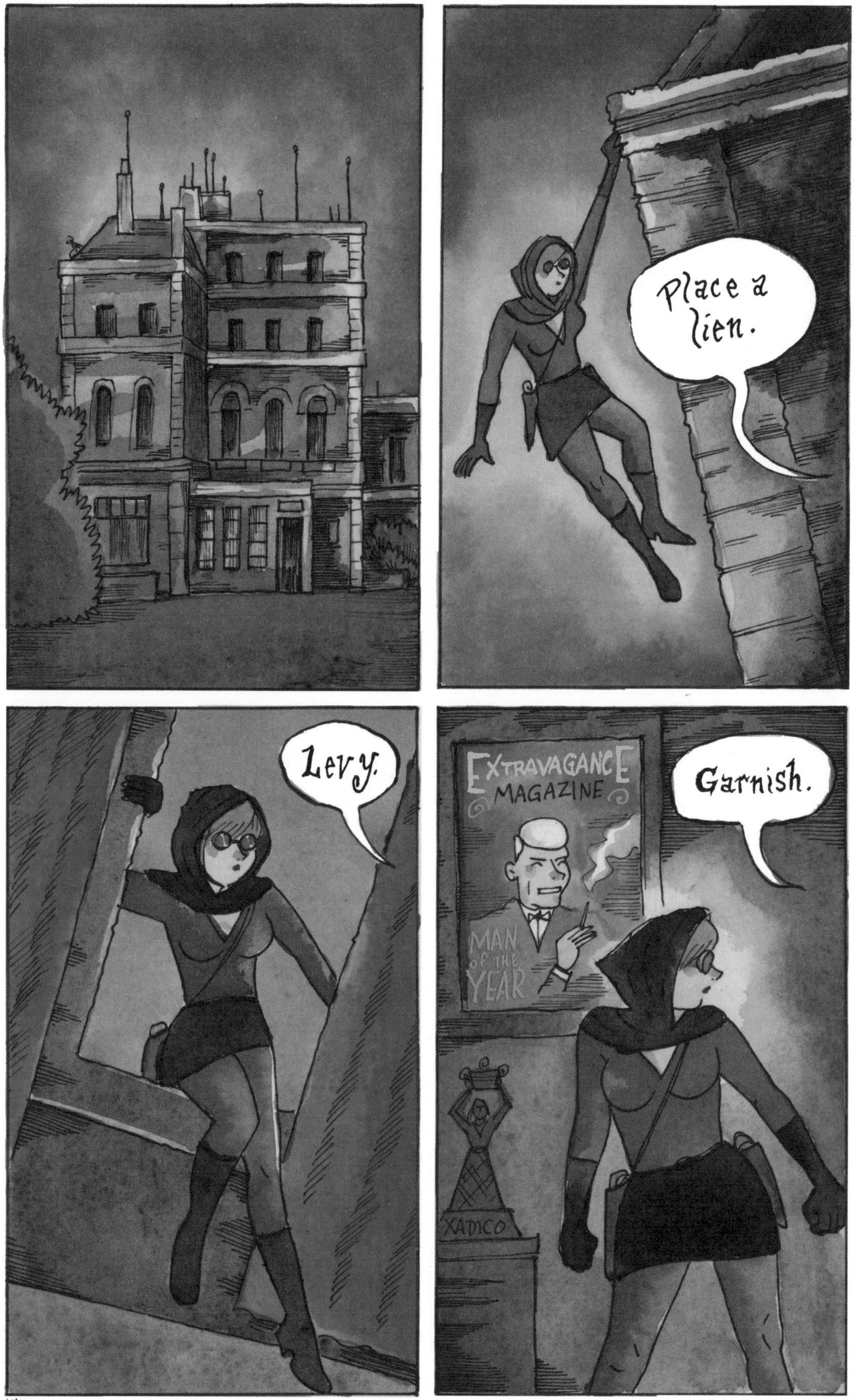
Place a lien.
Levy.
EXTRAVAGANCE MAGAZINE
MAN OF THE YEAR
XADICO
Garnish.

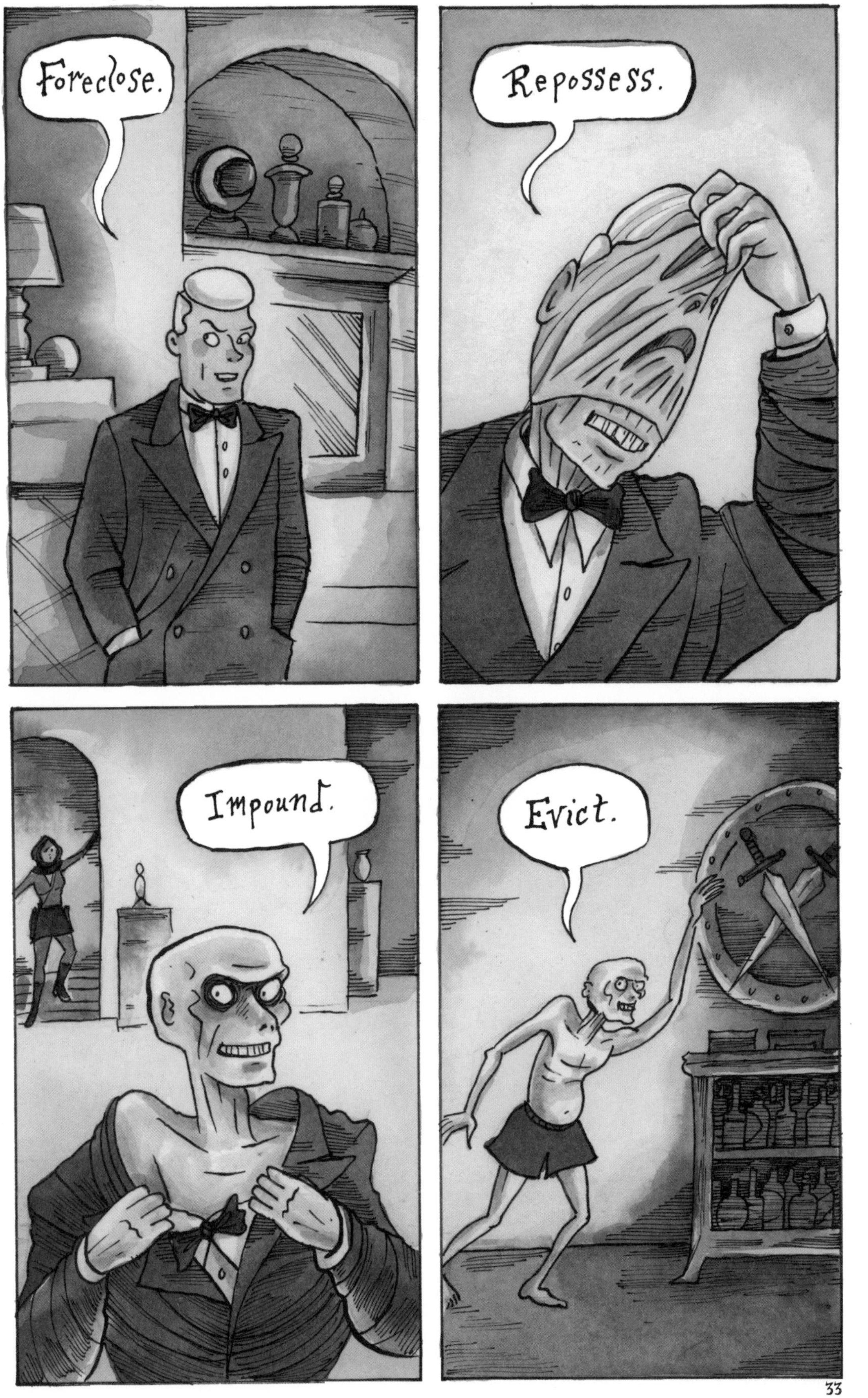
Foreclose.
Repossess.
Impound.
Evict.

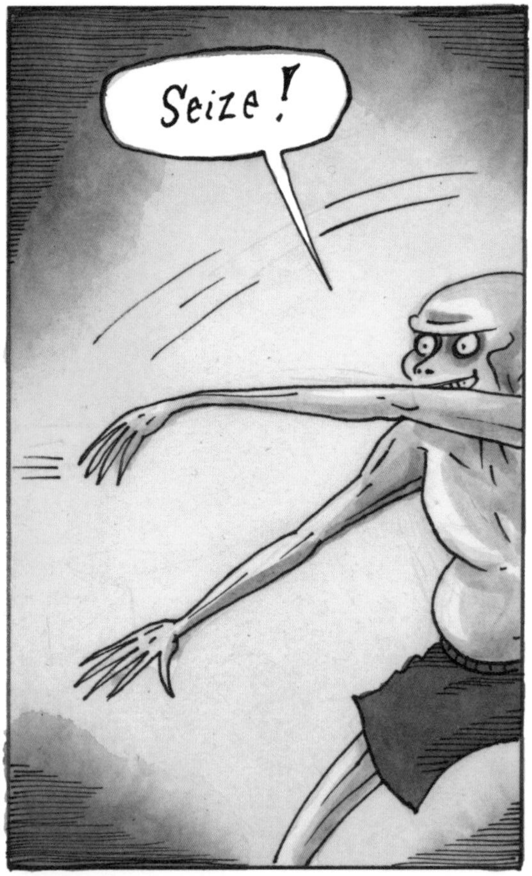
Seize!

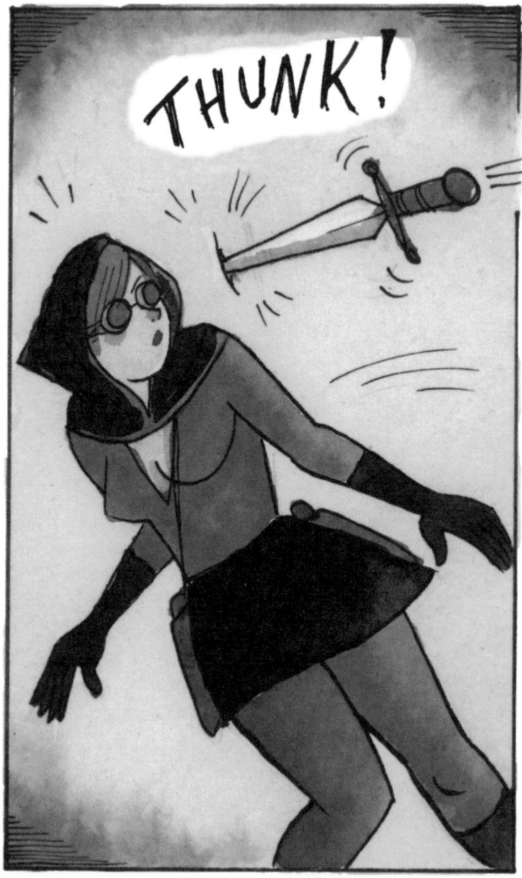
THUNK!

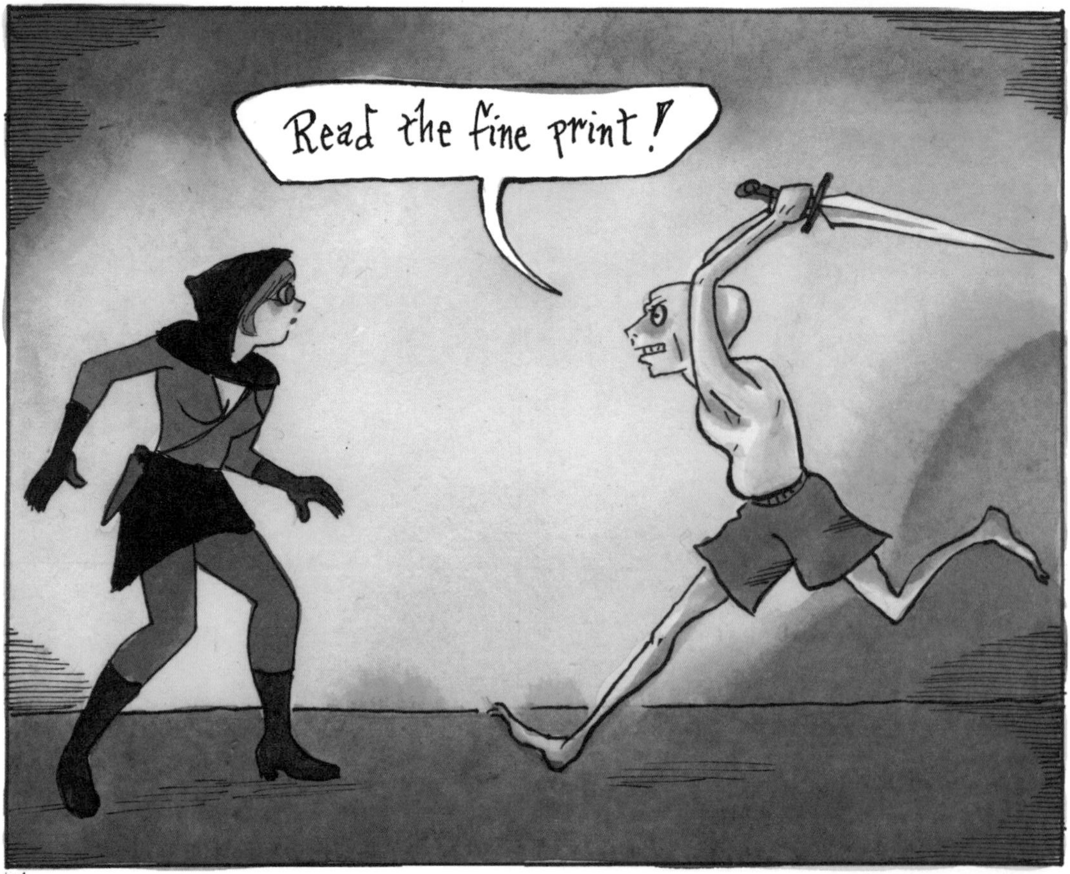
Read the fine print!

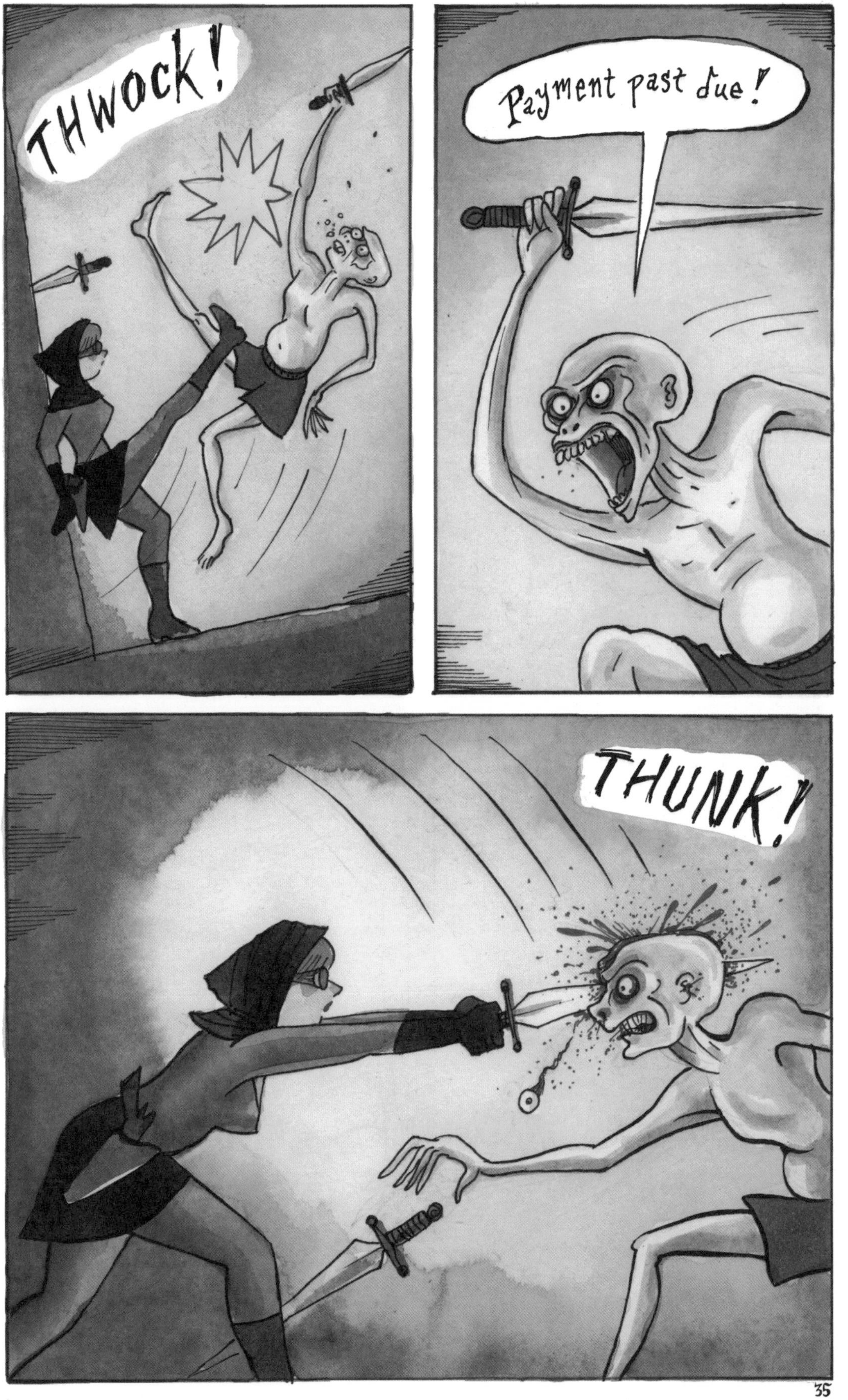
THWOCK!
Payment past due!
THUNK!

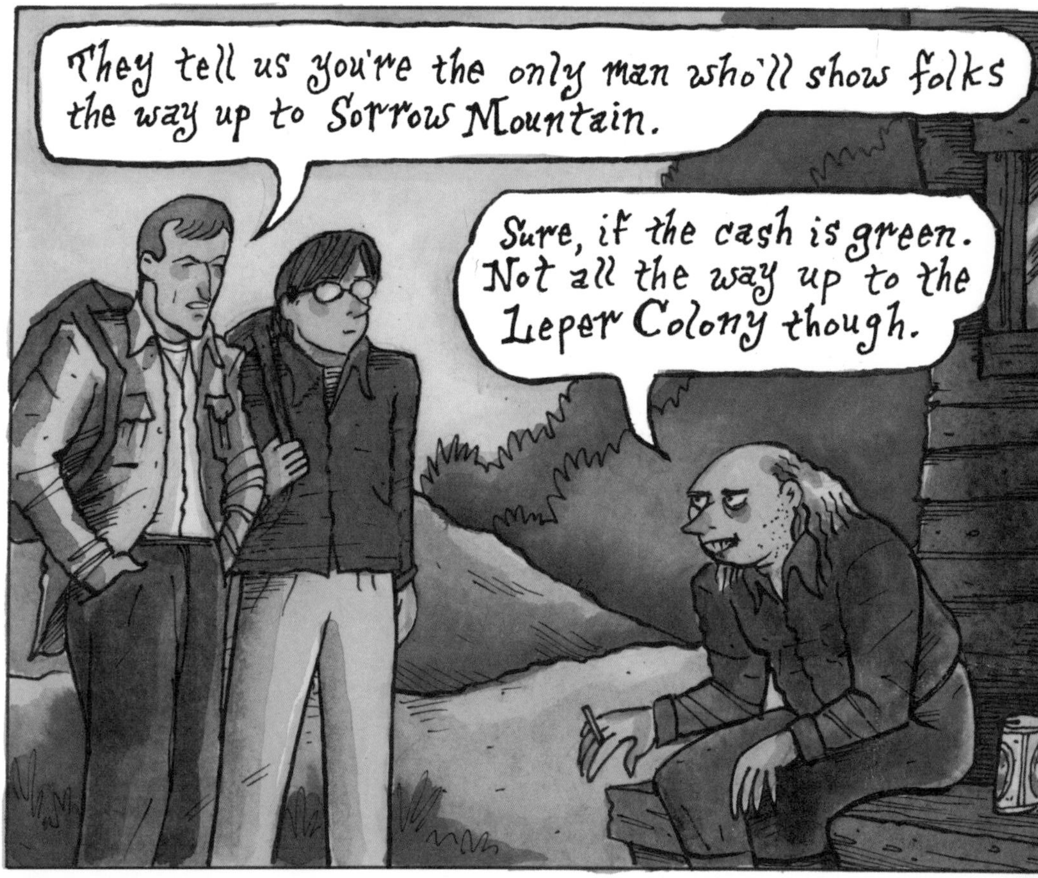
They tell us you're the only man who'll show folks the way up to Sorrow Mountain.
Sure, if the cash is green. Not all the way up to the Leper Colony though.

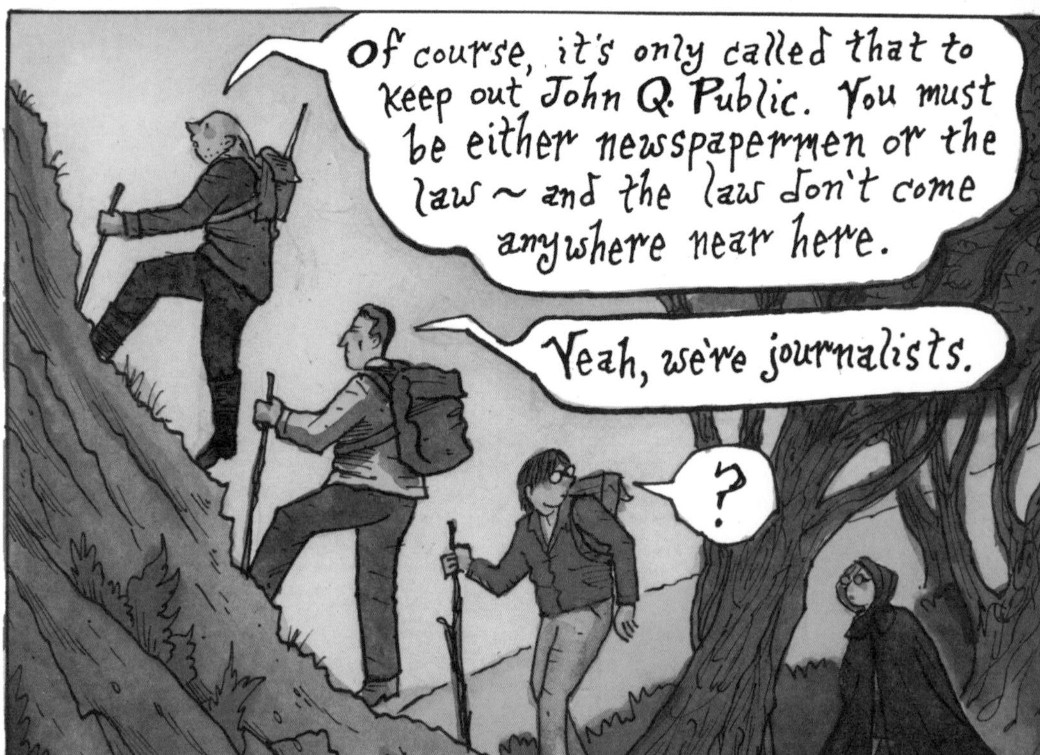
Of course, it's only called that to keep out John Q. Public. You must be either newspapermen or the law ~ and the law don't come anywhere near here.
Yeah, we're journalists.
?

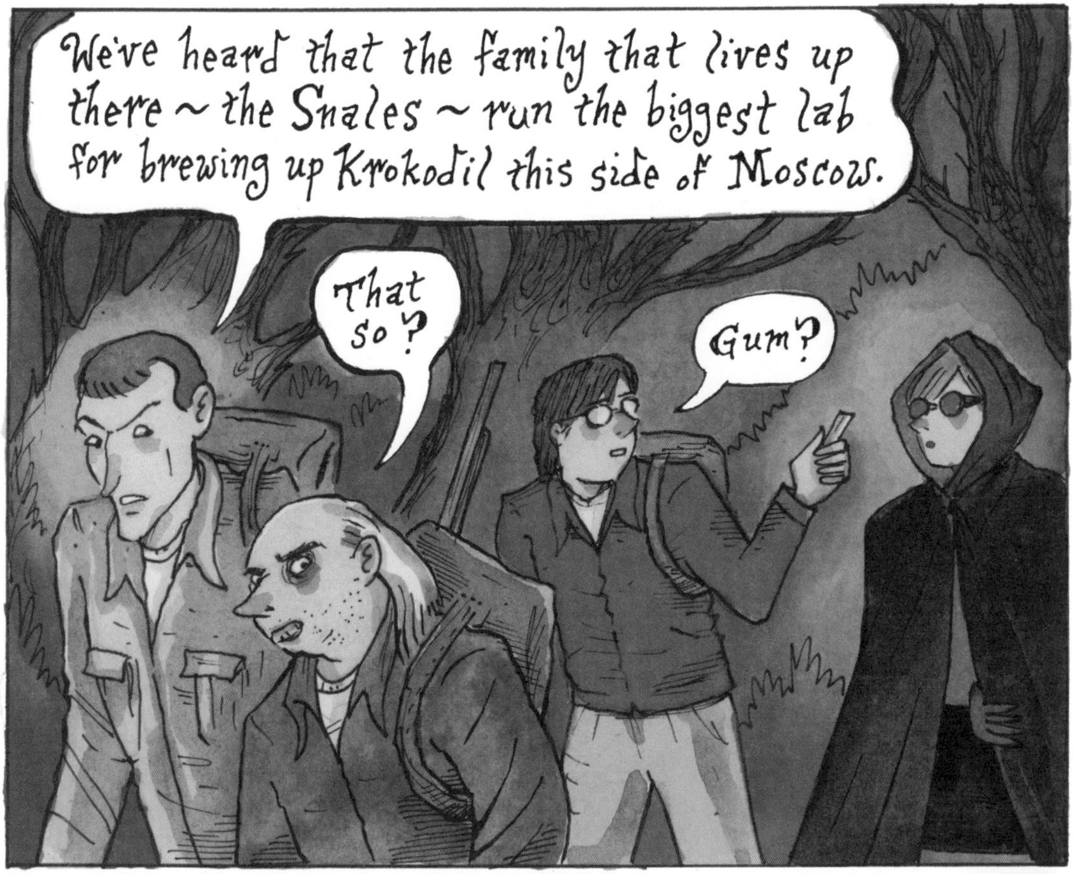
We've heard that the family that lives up there ~ the Snales ~ run the biggest lab for brewing up Krokodil this side of Moscow.
That so?
Gum?

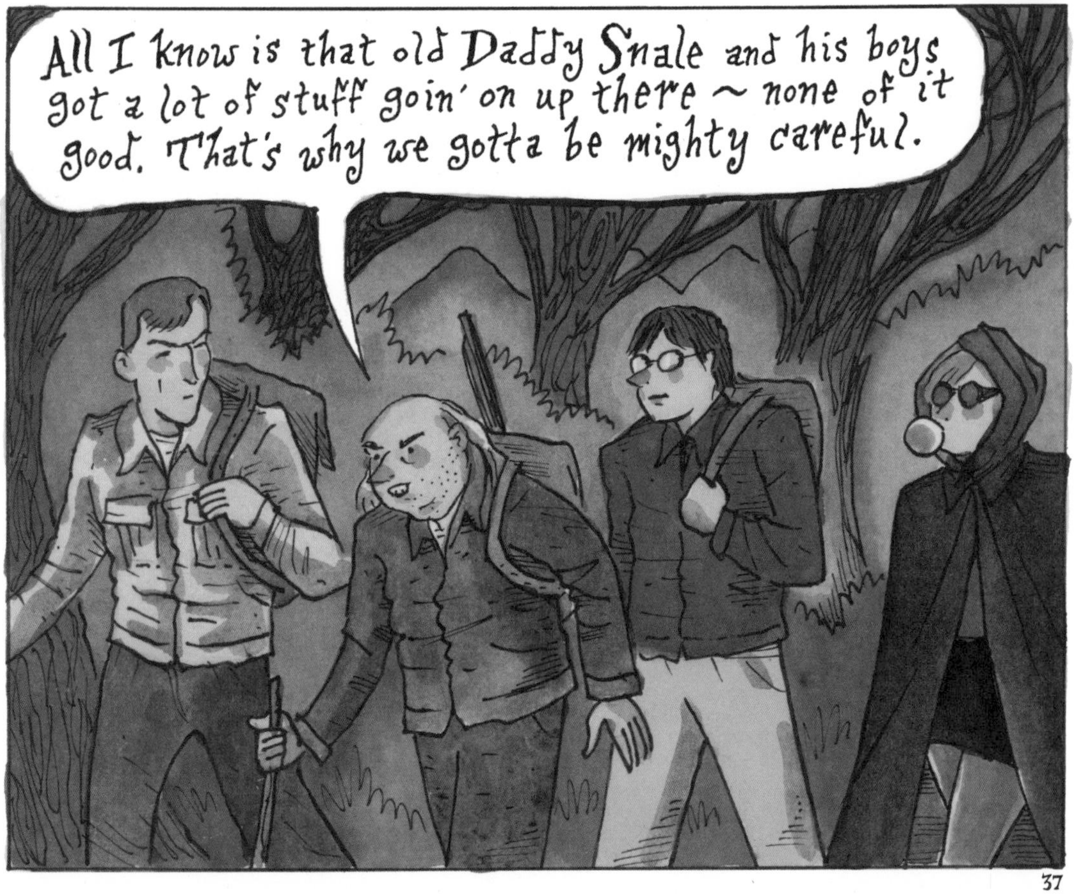
All I know is that old Daddy Snale and his boys got a lot of stuff goin' on up there ~ none of it good. That's why we gotta be mighty careful.

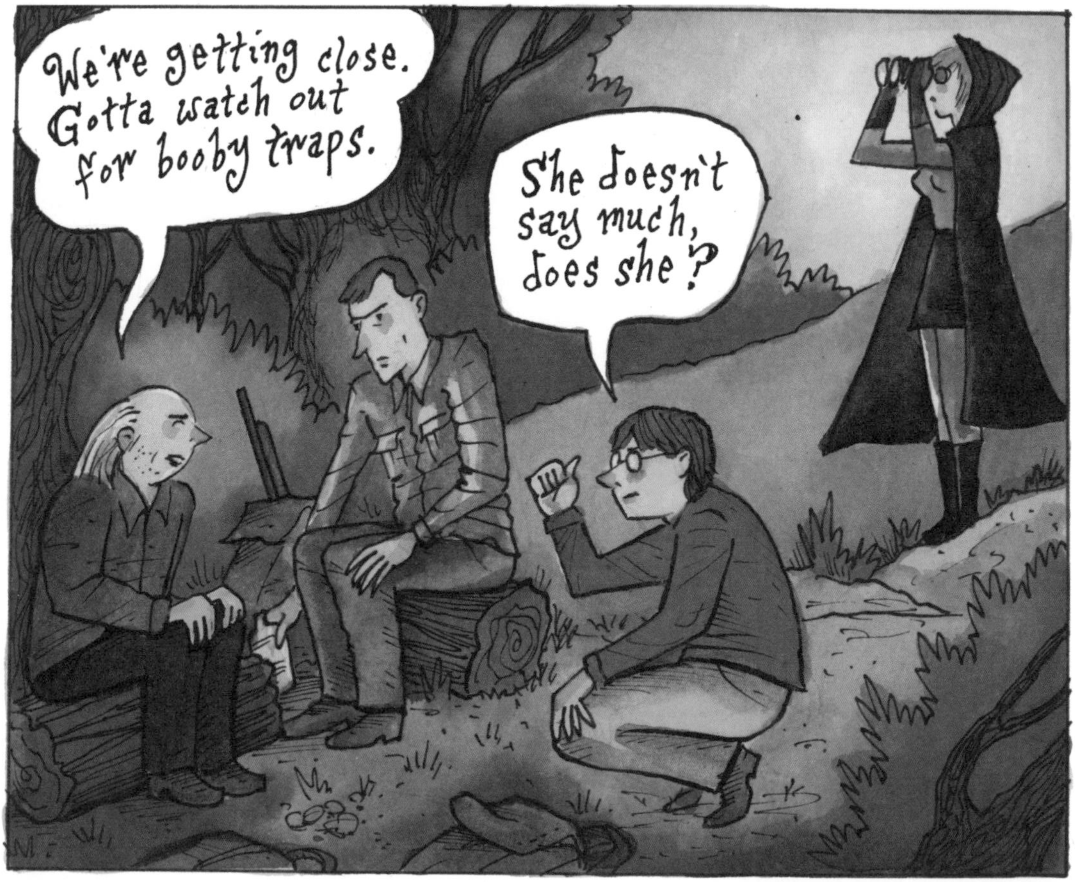
We're getting close. Gotta watch out for booby traps.
She doesn't say much, does she?

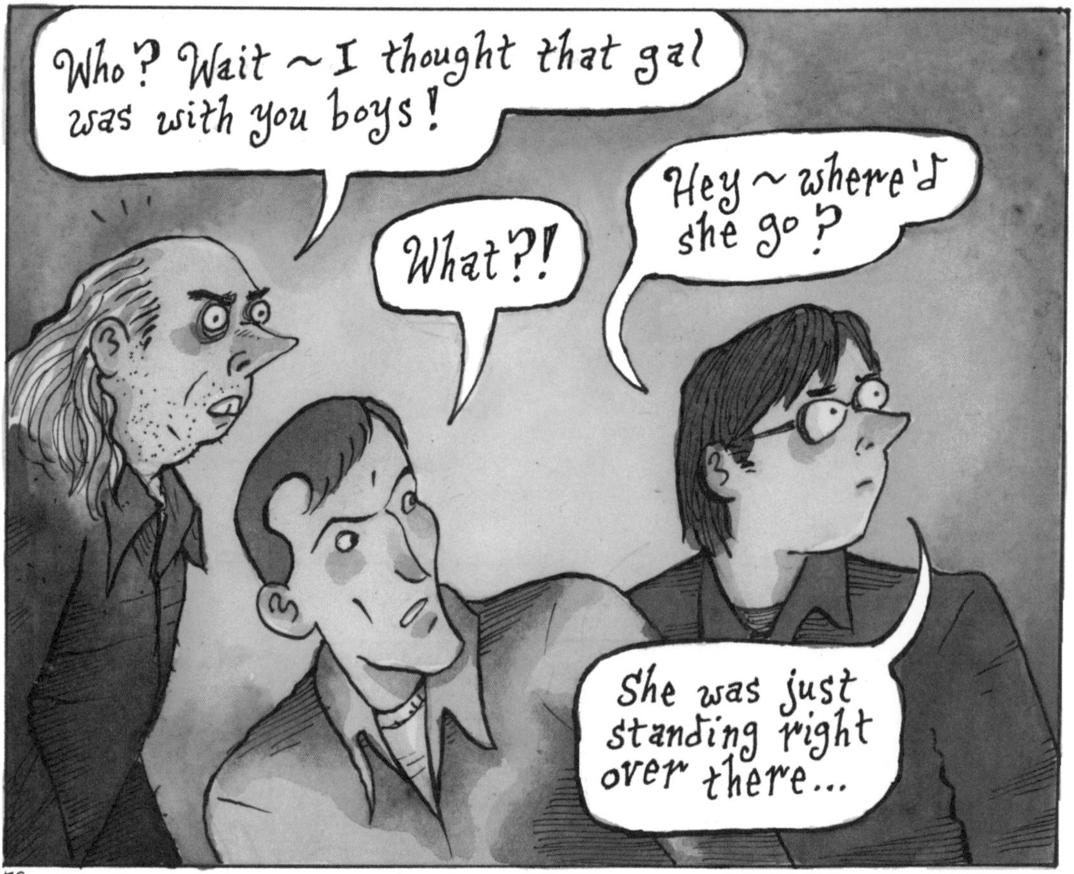
Who? Wait ~ I thought that gal was with you boys!
What?!
Hey ~ where'd she go?
She was just standing right over there...

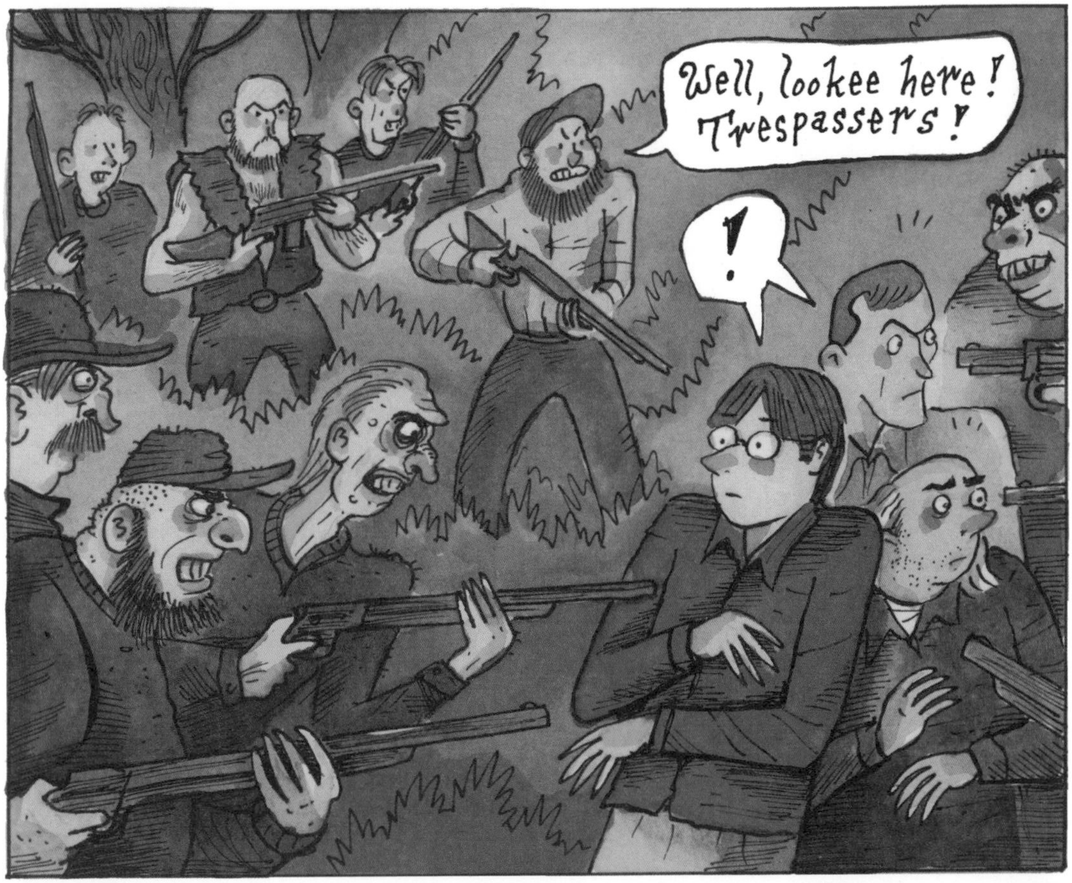
Well, lookee here! Trespassers!
!

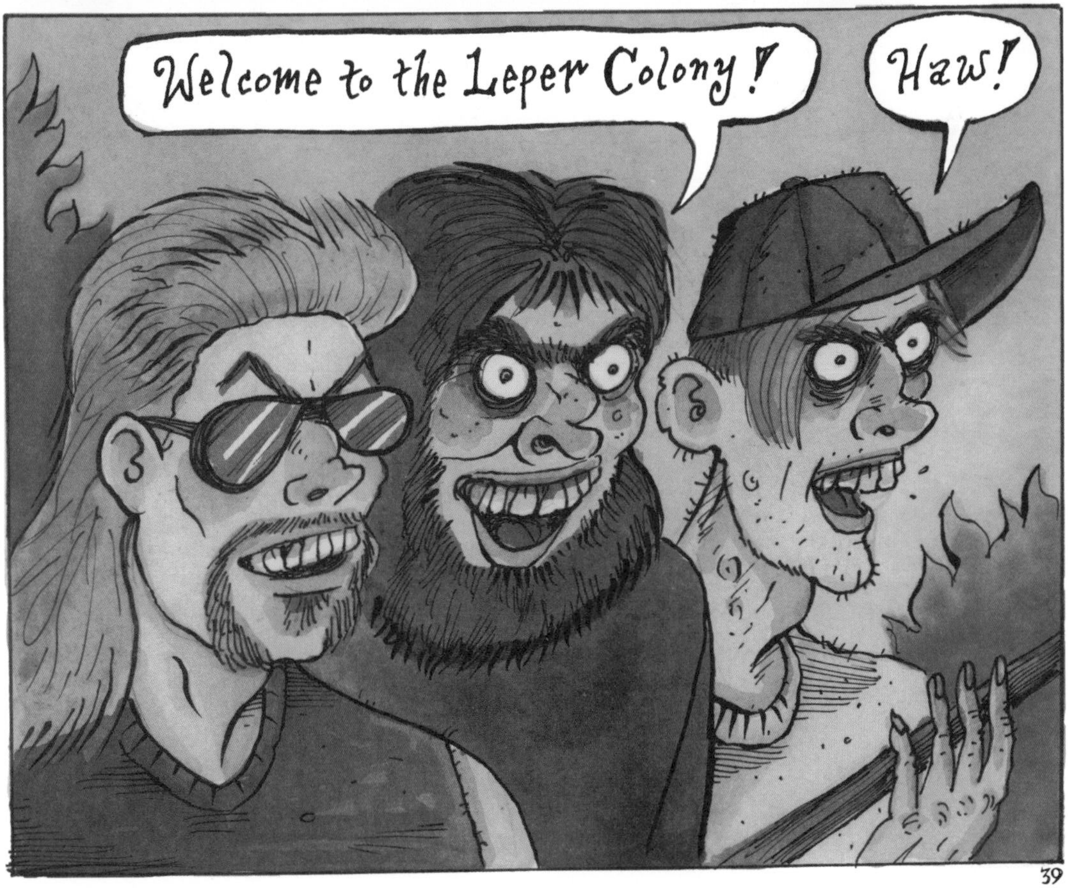
Welcome to the Leper Colony!
Haw!

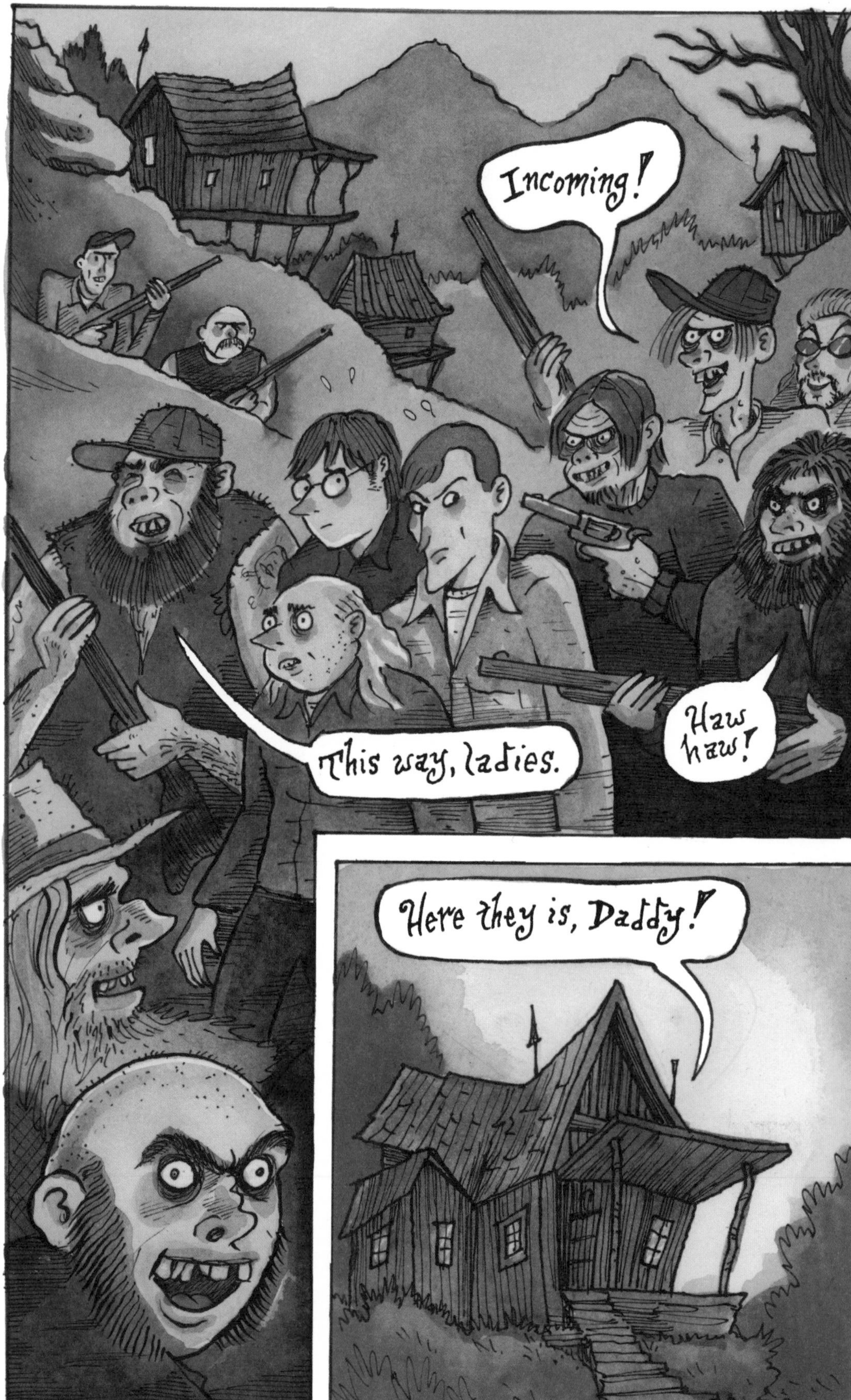
Incoming!
This way, ladies.
Haw haw!
Here they is, Daddy!

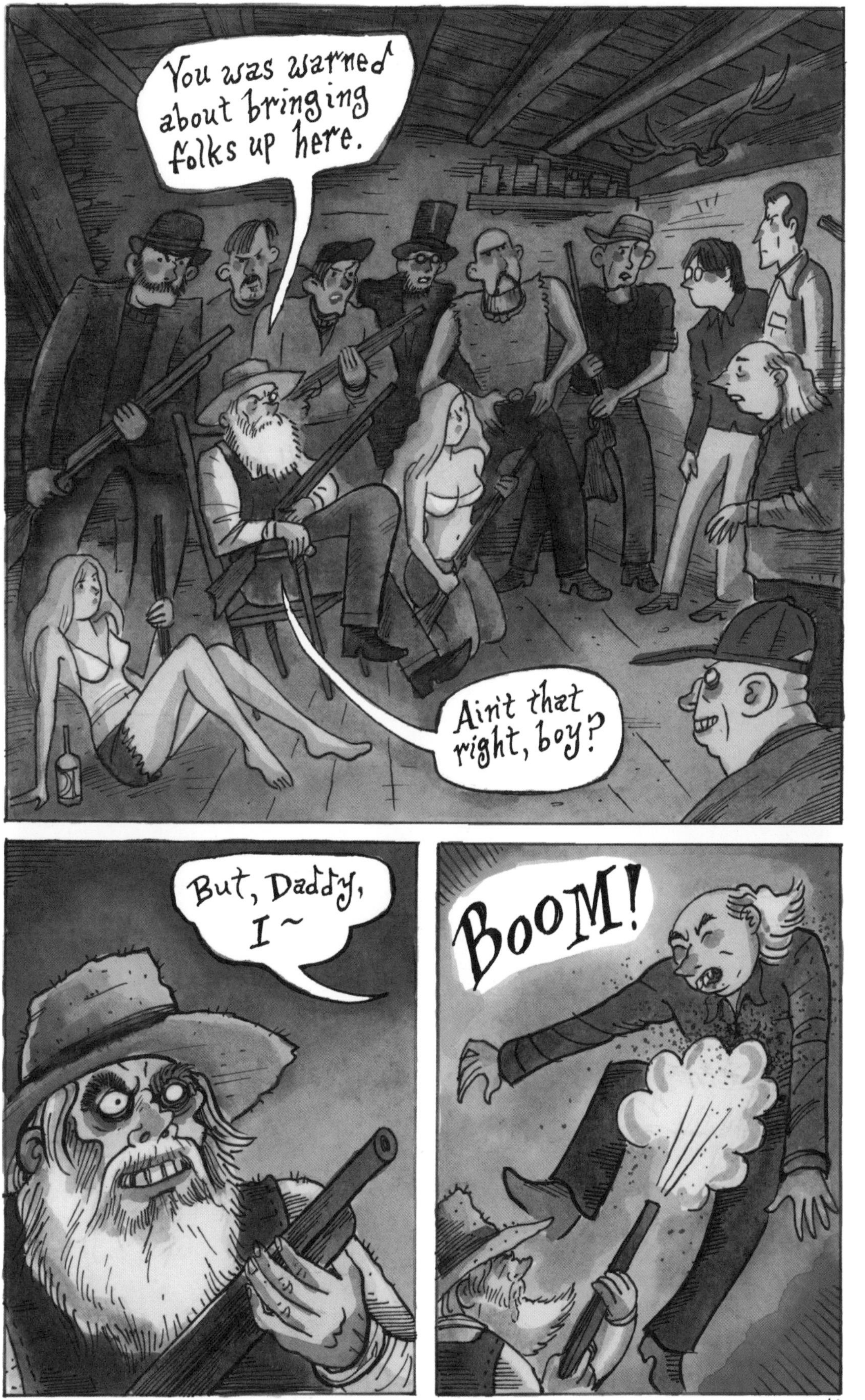
You was warned about bringing folks up here.
Ain't that right, boy?
But, Daddy, I~
BOOM!

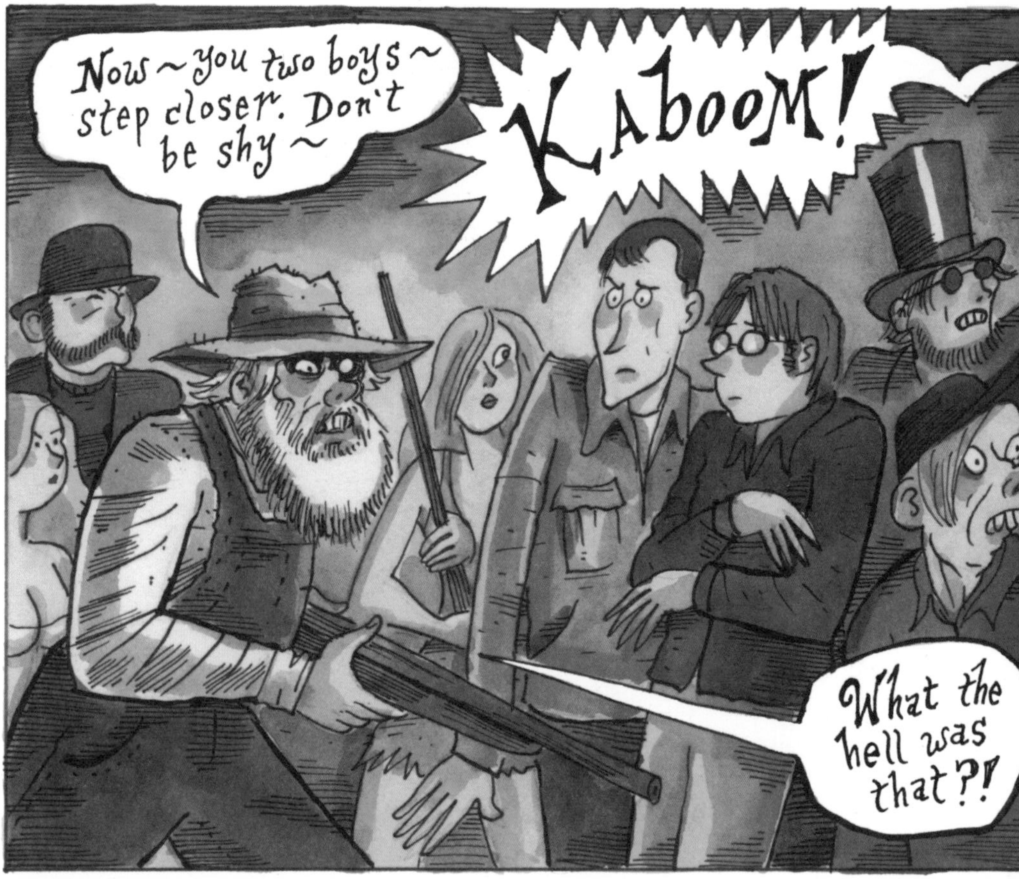
Now ~ you two boys ~ step closer. Don't be shy ~
KABOOM!
What the hell was that?!

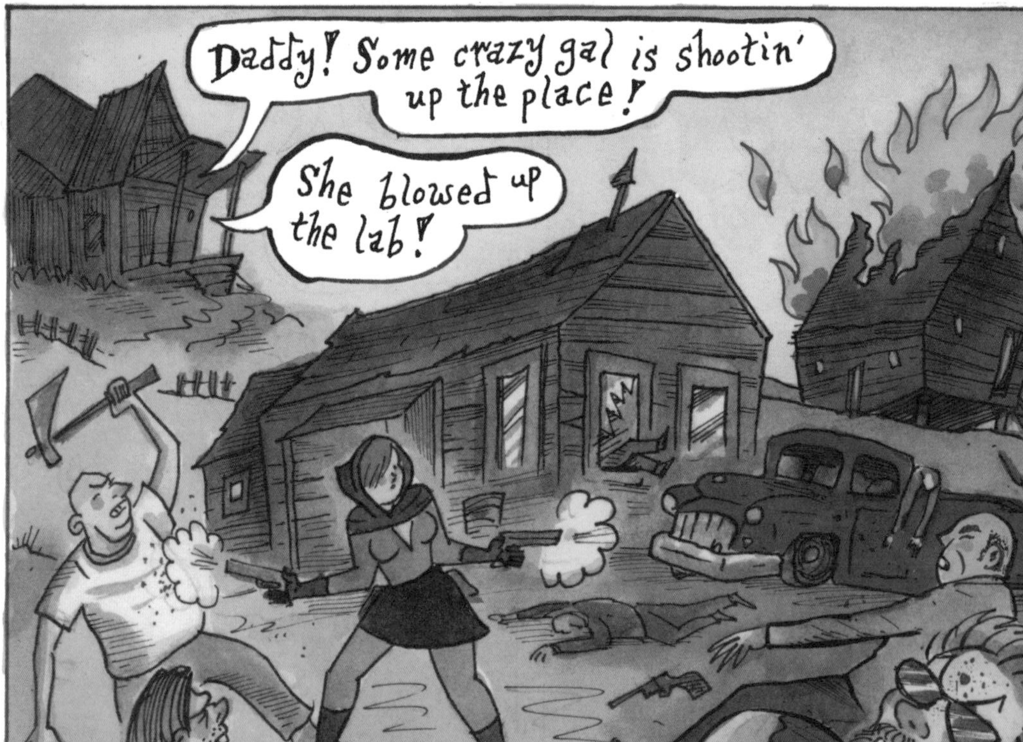
Daddy! Some crazy gal is shootin' up the place!
She blowed up the lab!

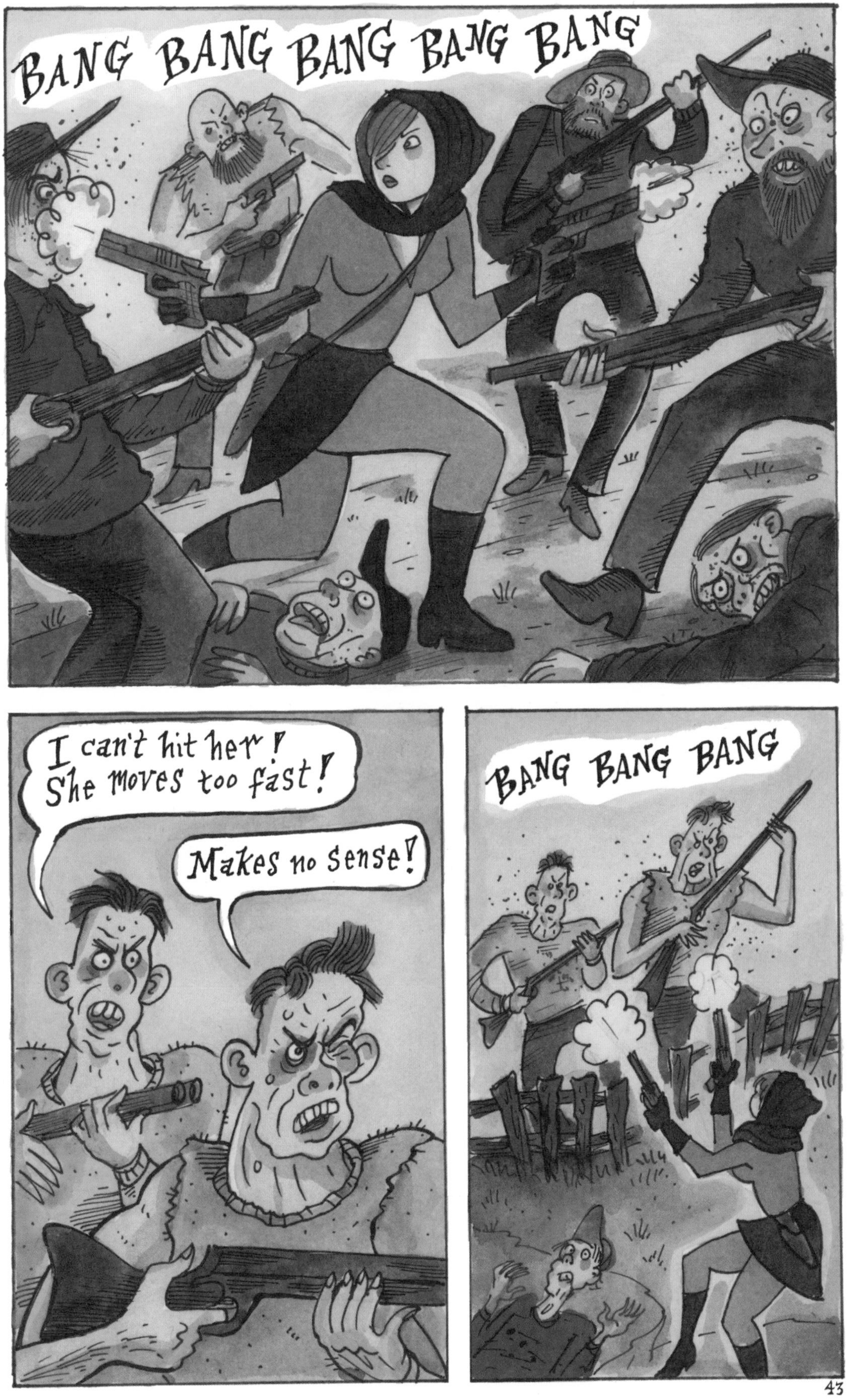
BANG BANG BANG BANG BANG
I can't hit her! She moves too fast!
Makes no sense!
BANG BANG BANG

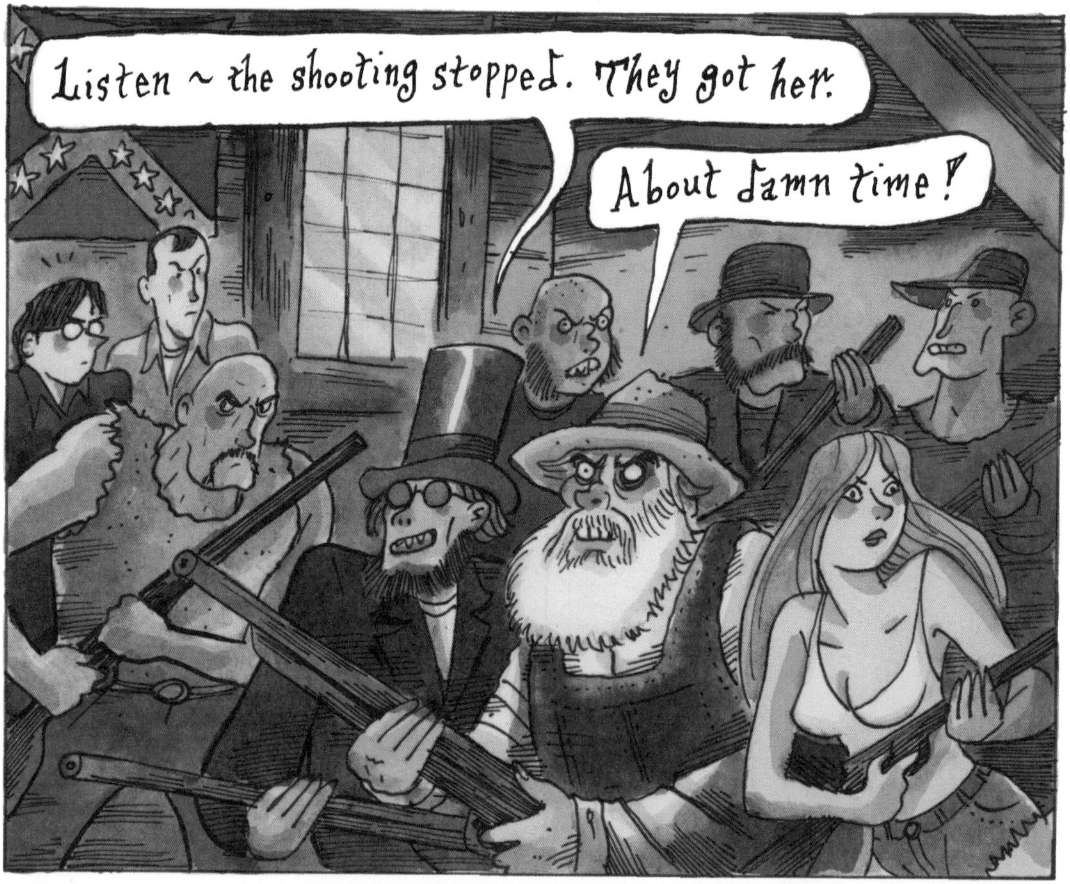
Listen ~ the shooting stopped. They got her.
About damn time!

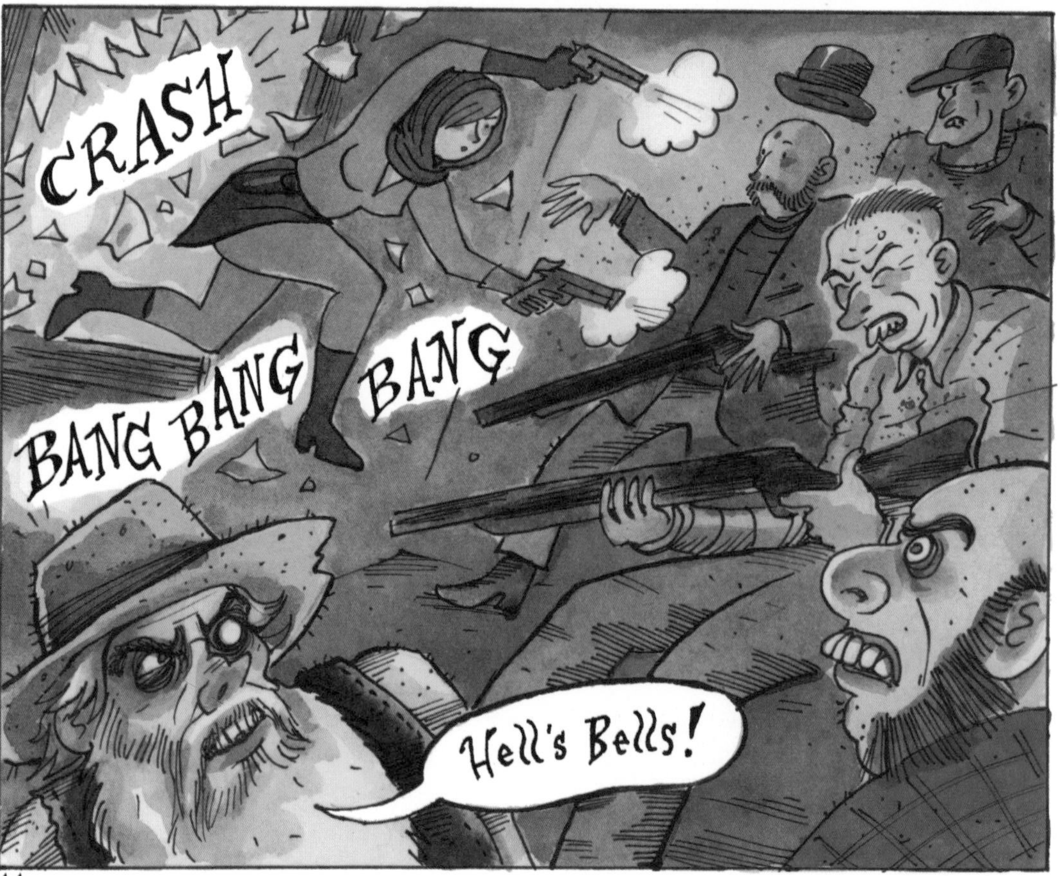
CRASH
BANG BANG BANG
Hell's Bells!

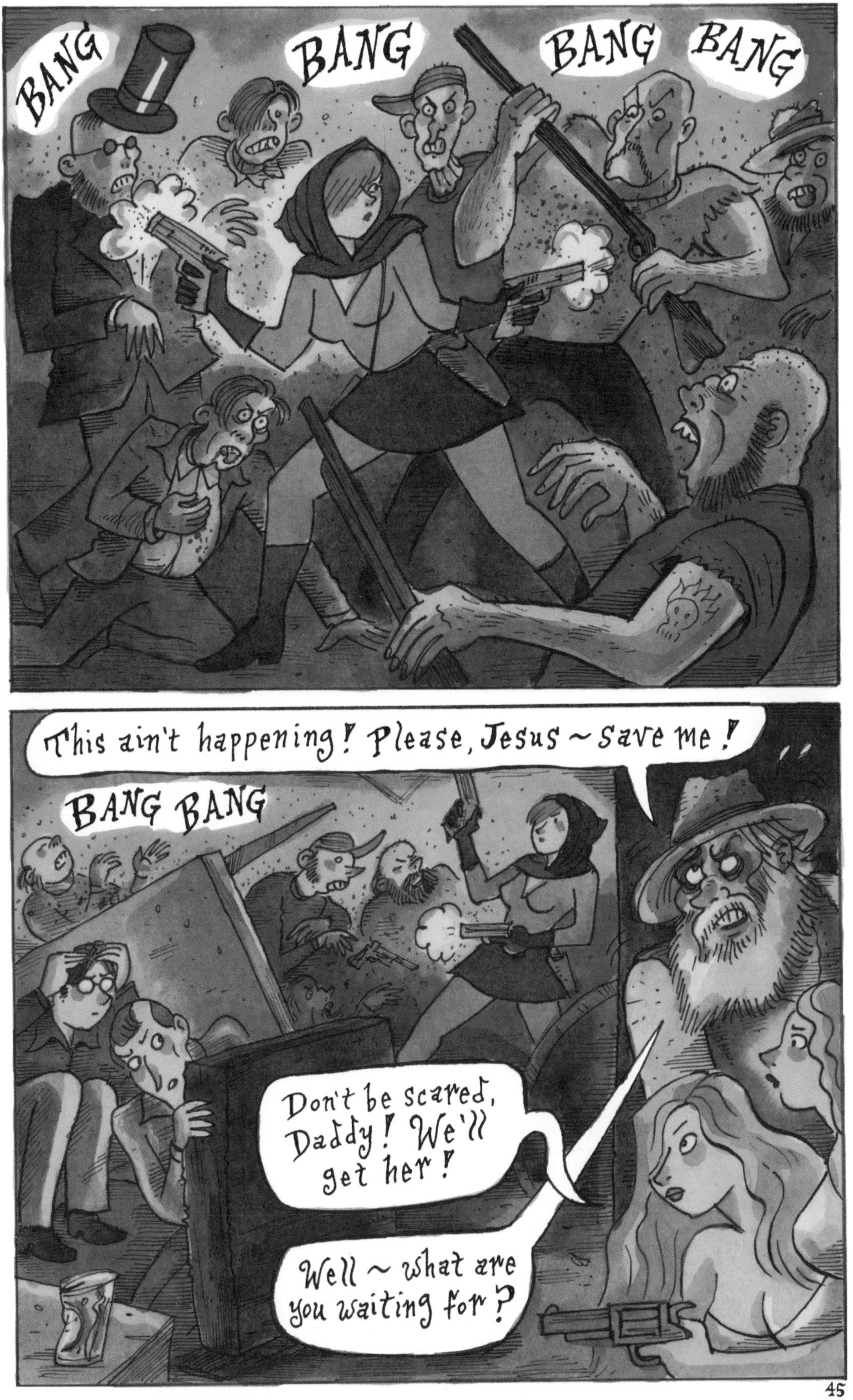
BANG
BANG
BANG
BANG
This ain't happening! Please, Jesus ~ save me!
BANG BANG
Don't be scared, Daddy! We'll get her!
Well ~ what are you waiting for?

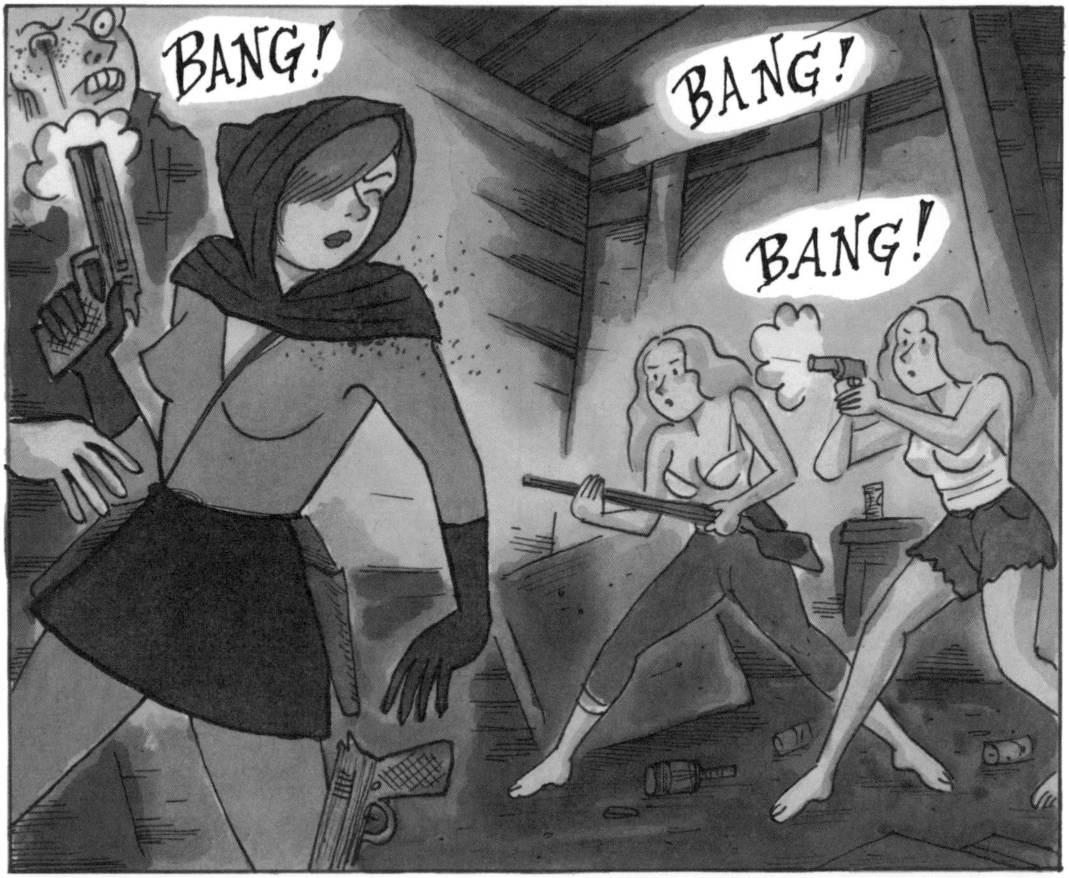
BANG!
BANG!
BANG!

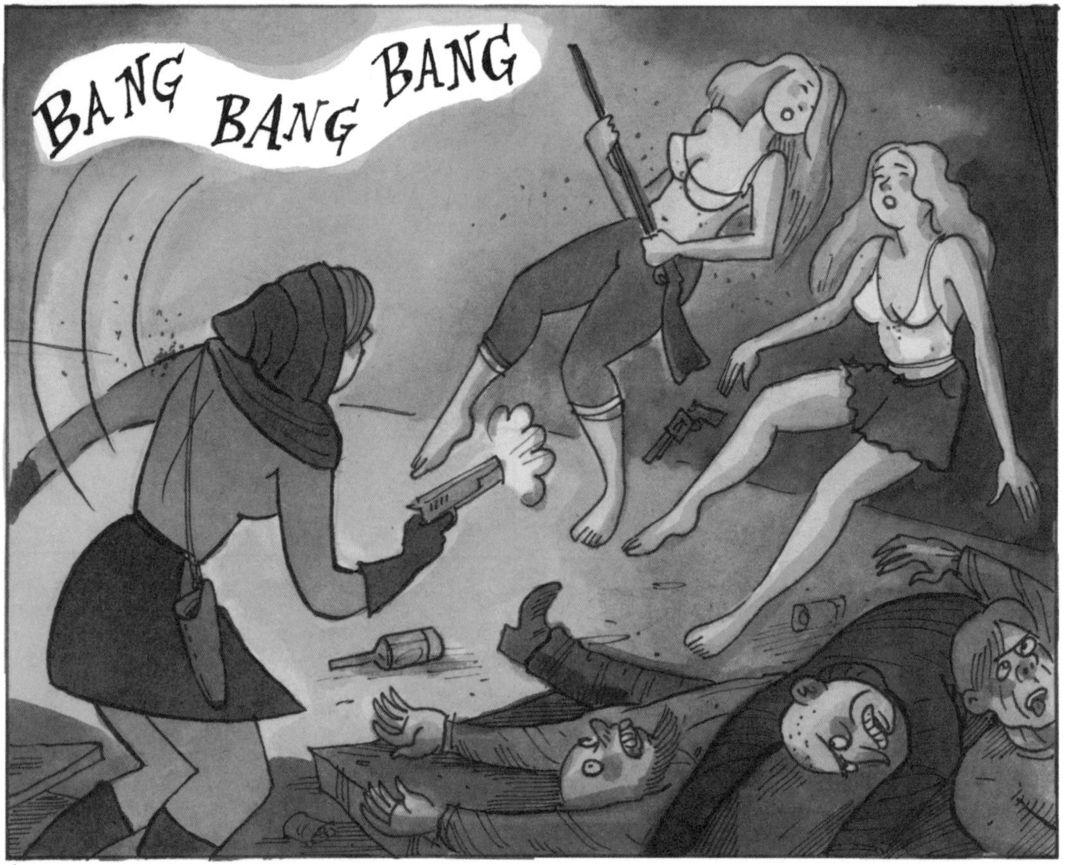
BANG BANG BANG

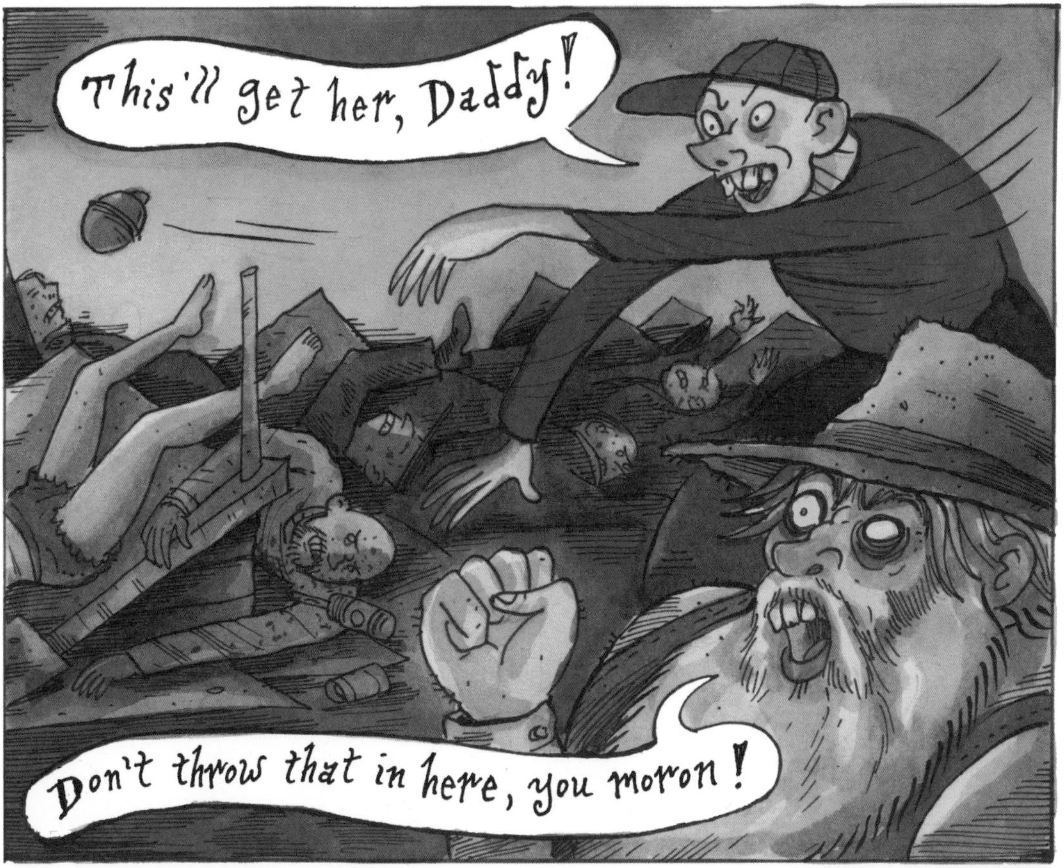
This'll get her, Daddy!
Don't throw that in here, you moron!

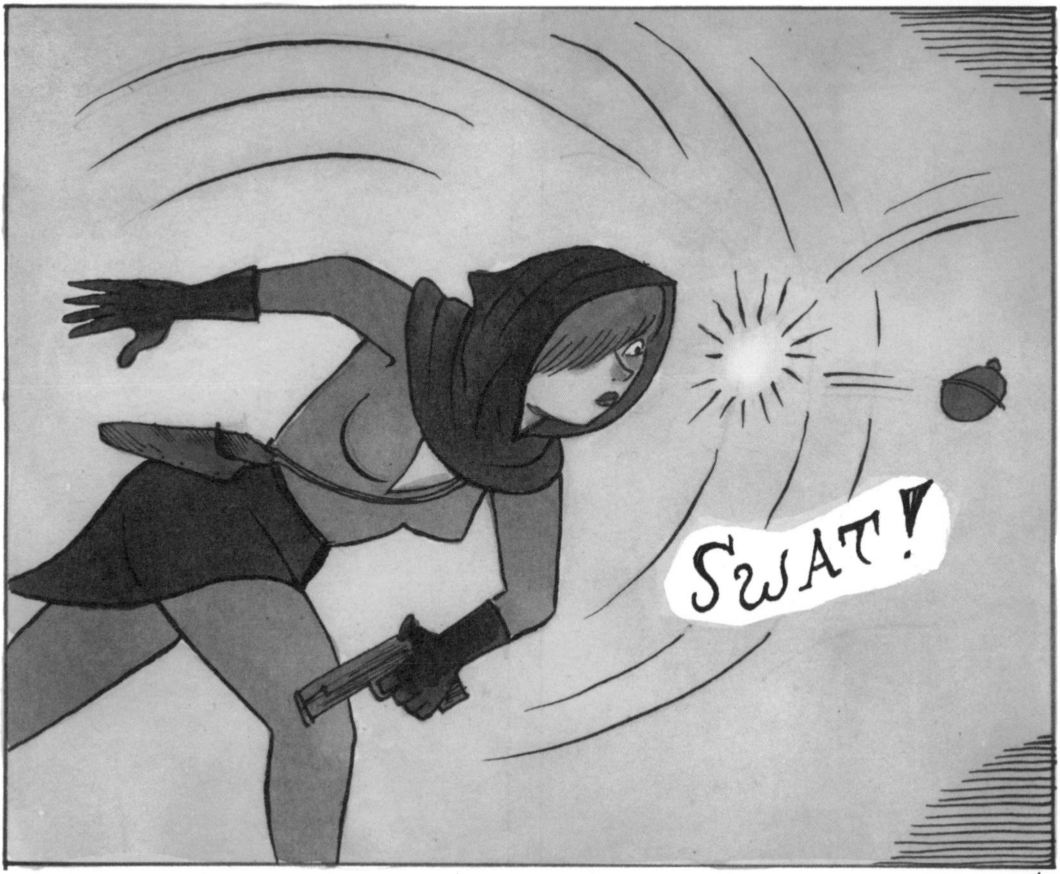
SWAT!

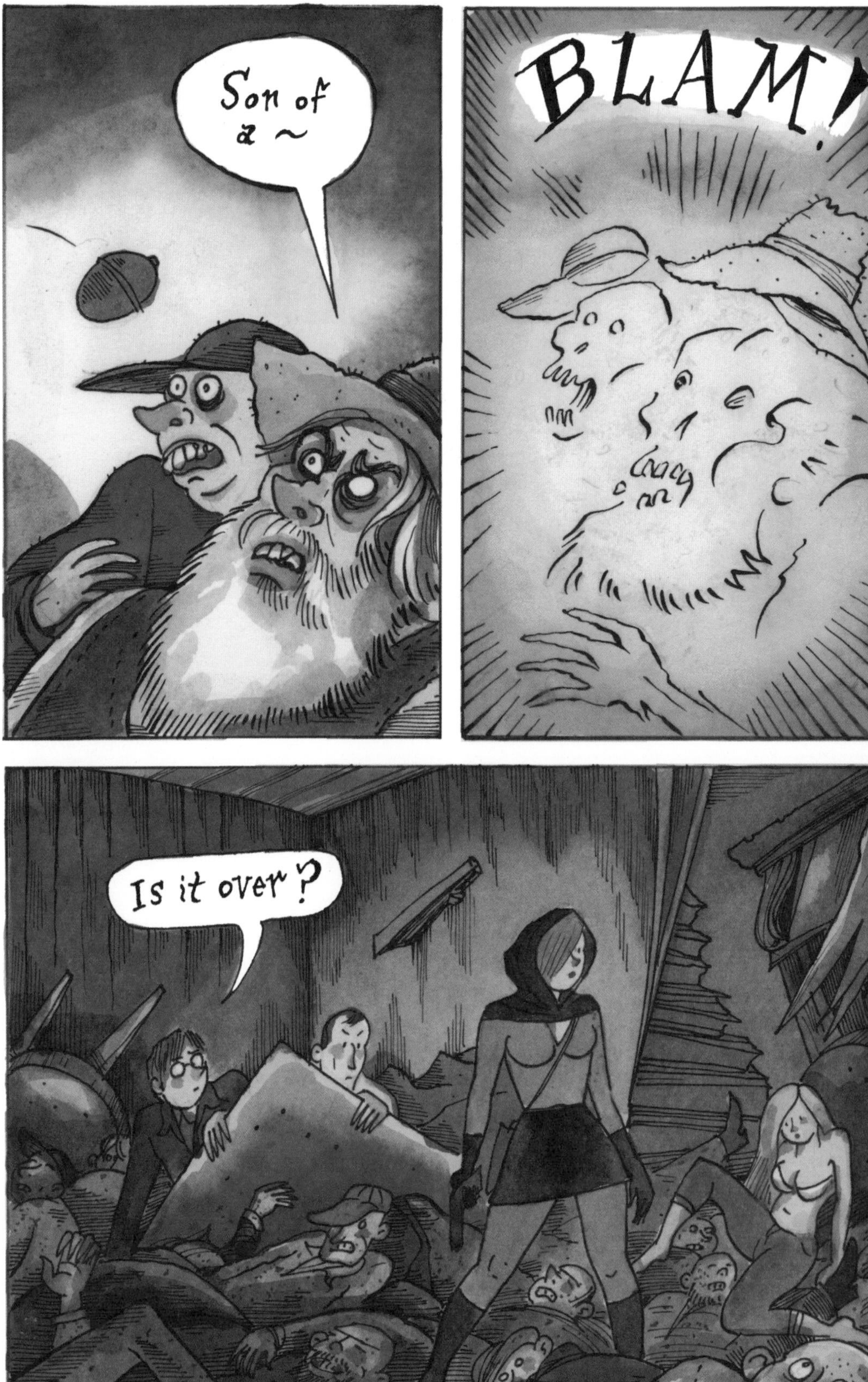
Son of a ~
BLAM!
Is it over?

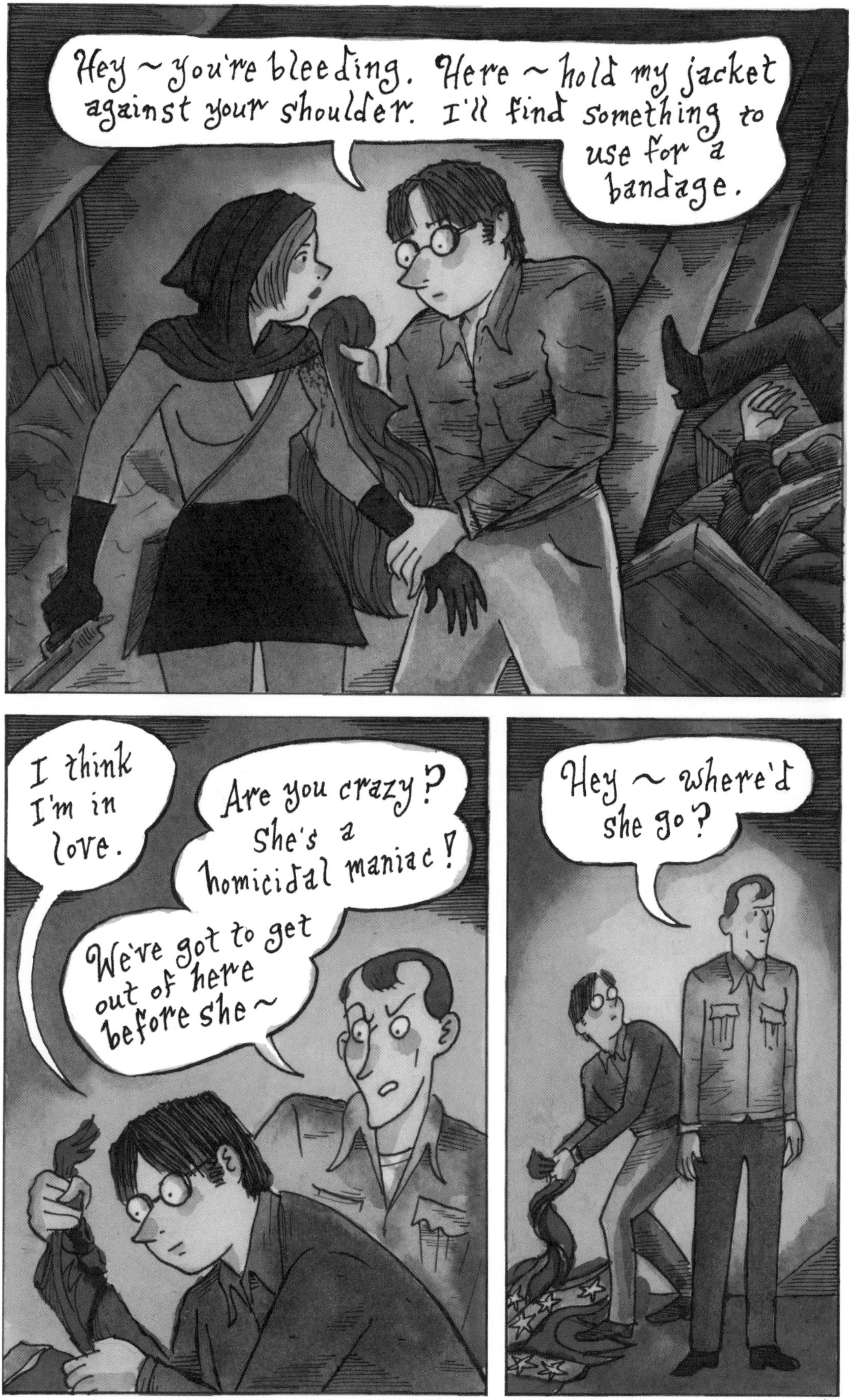
Hey ~ you're bleeding. Here ~ hold my jacket against your shoulder. I'll find something to use for a bandage.
I think I'm in love.
Are you crazy? She's a homicidal maniac!
We've got to get out of here before she ~
Hey ~ where'd she go?

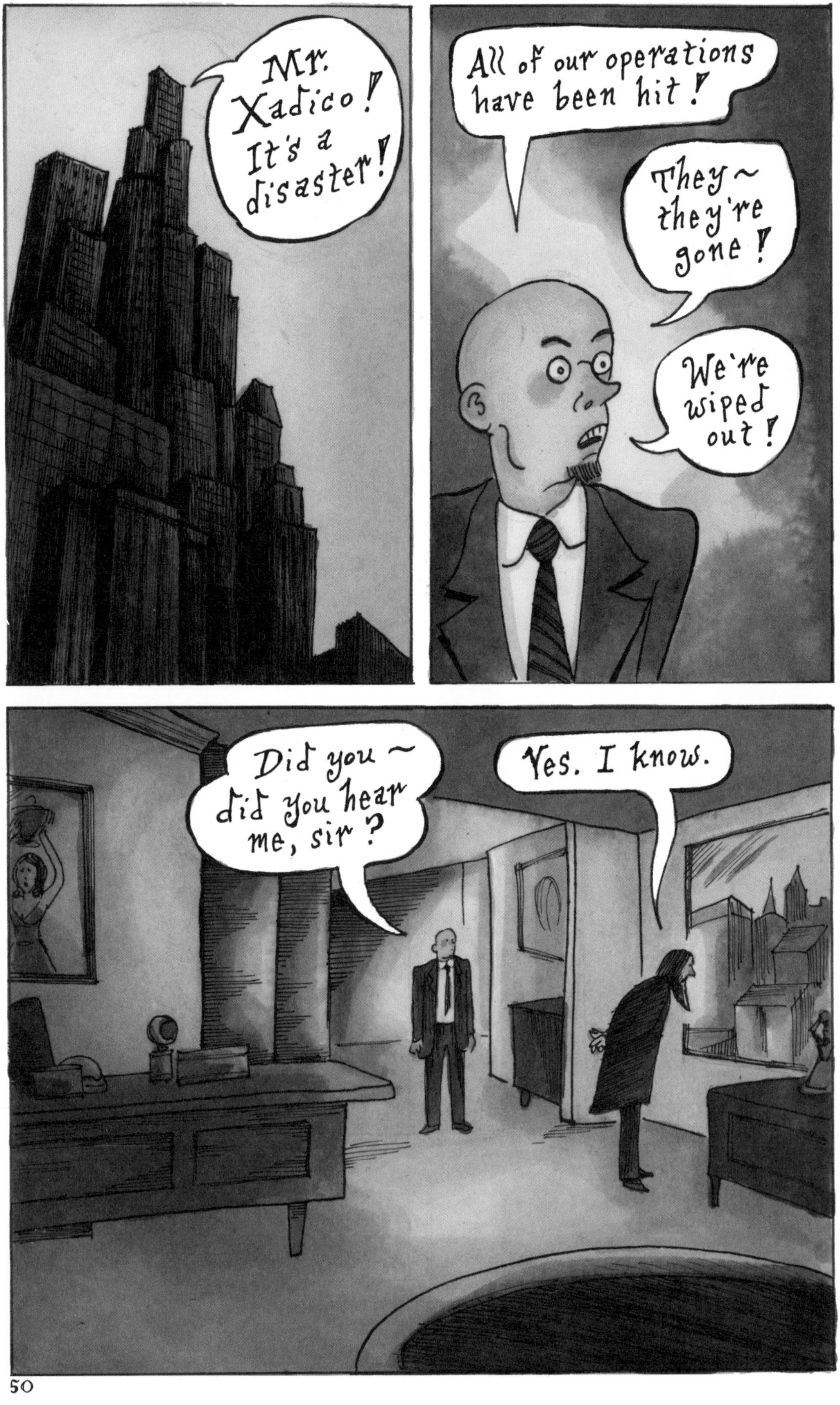
Mr. Xadico! It's a disaster!
All of our operations have been hit!
They~ they're gone!
We're wiped out!
Did you~ did you hear me, sir?
Yes. I know.

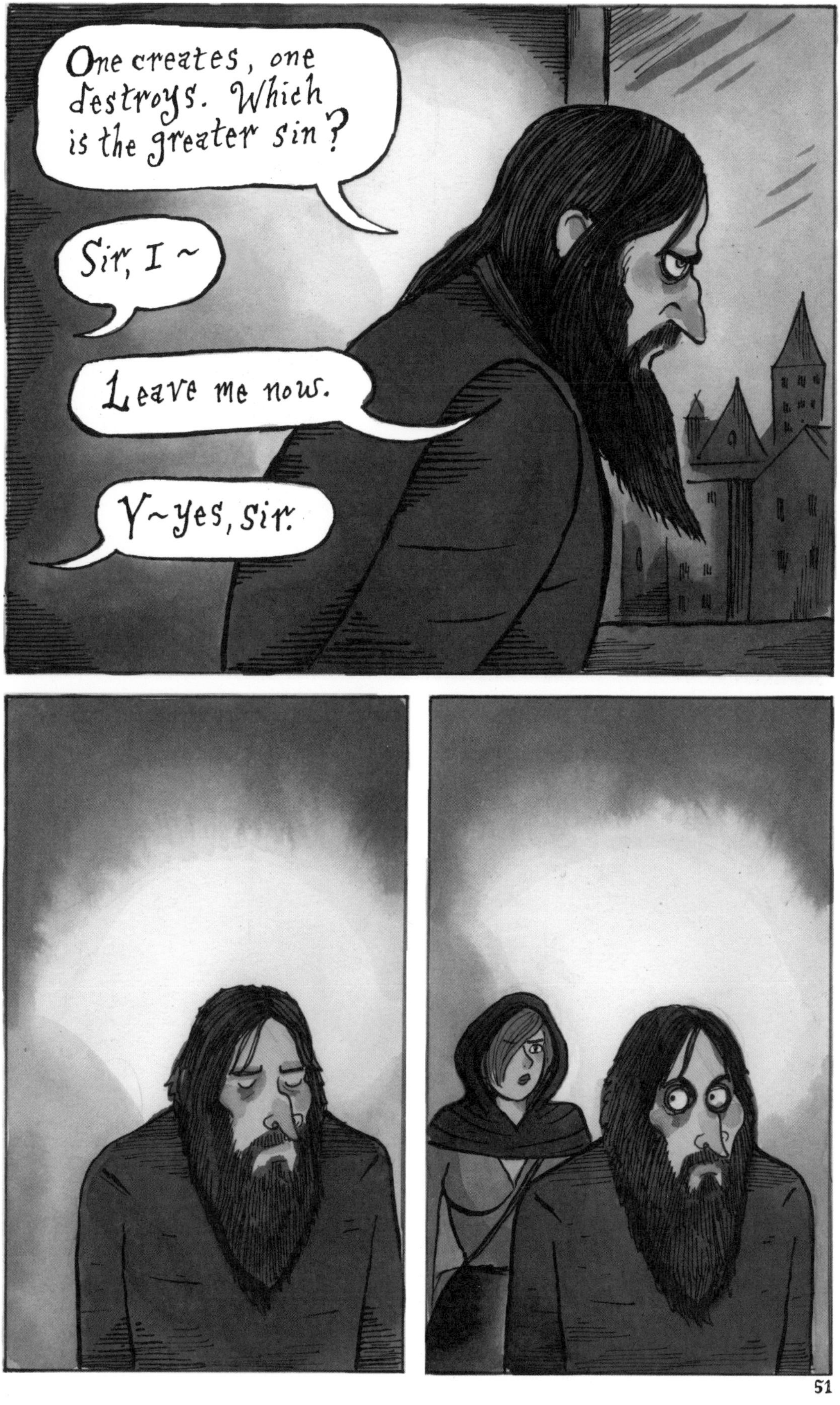
One creates, one destroys. Which is the greater sin?
Sir, I ~
Leave me now.
Y~yes, sir.

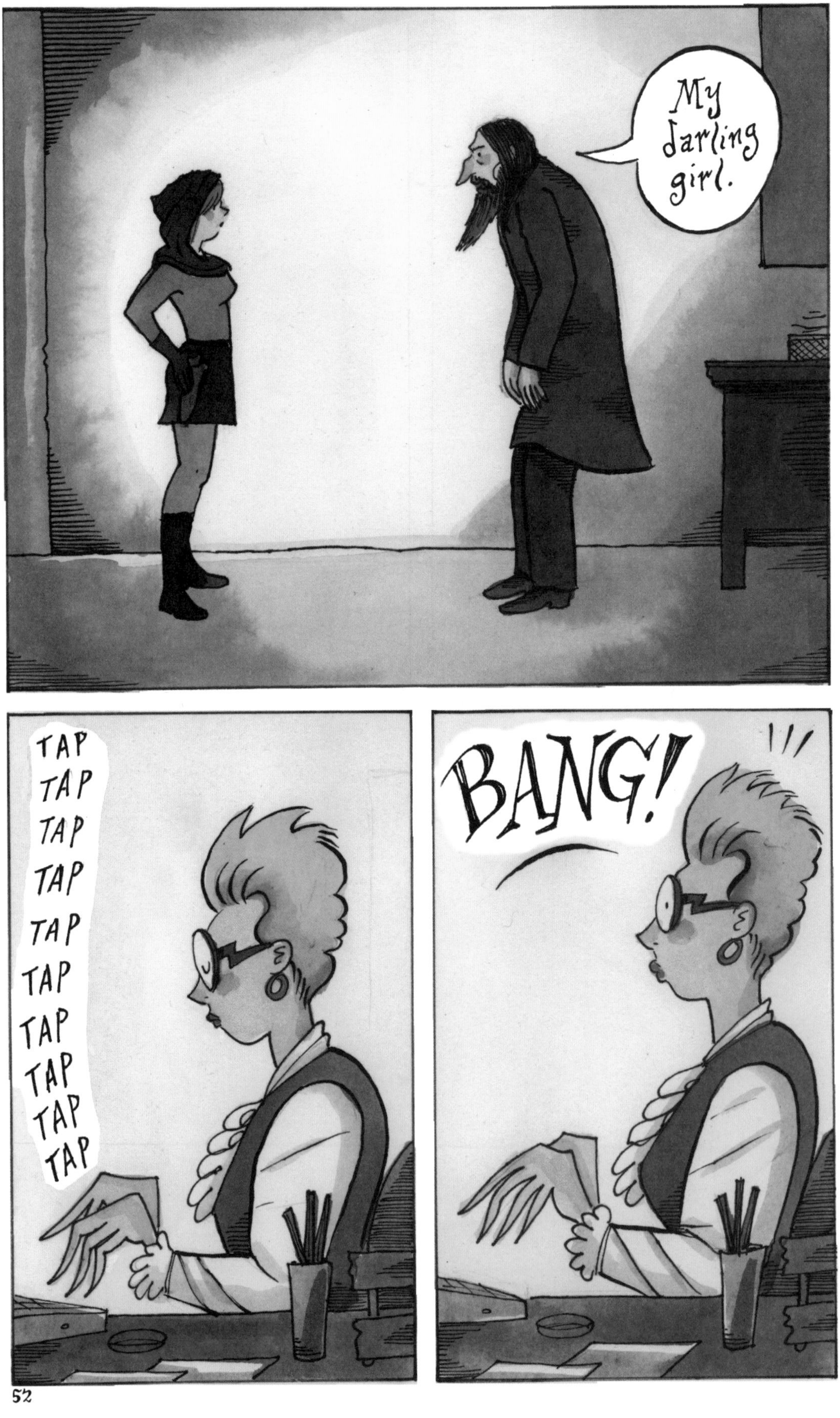
My darling girl.
TAP TAP TAP TAP TAP TAP TAP TAP TAP TAP
BANG!

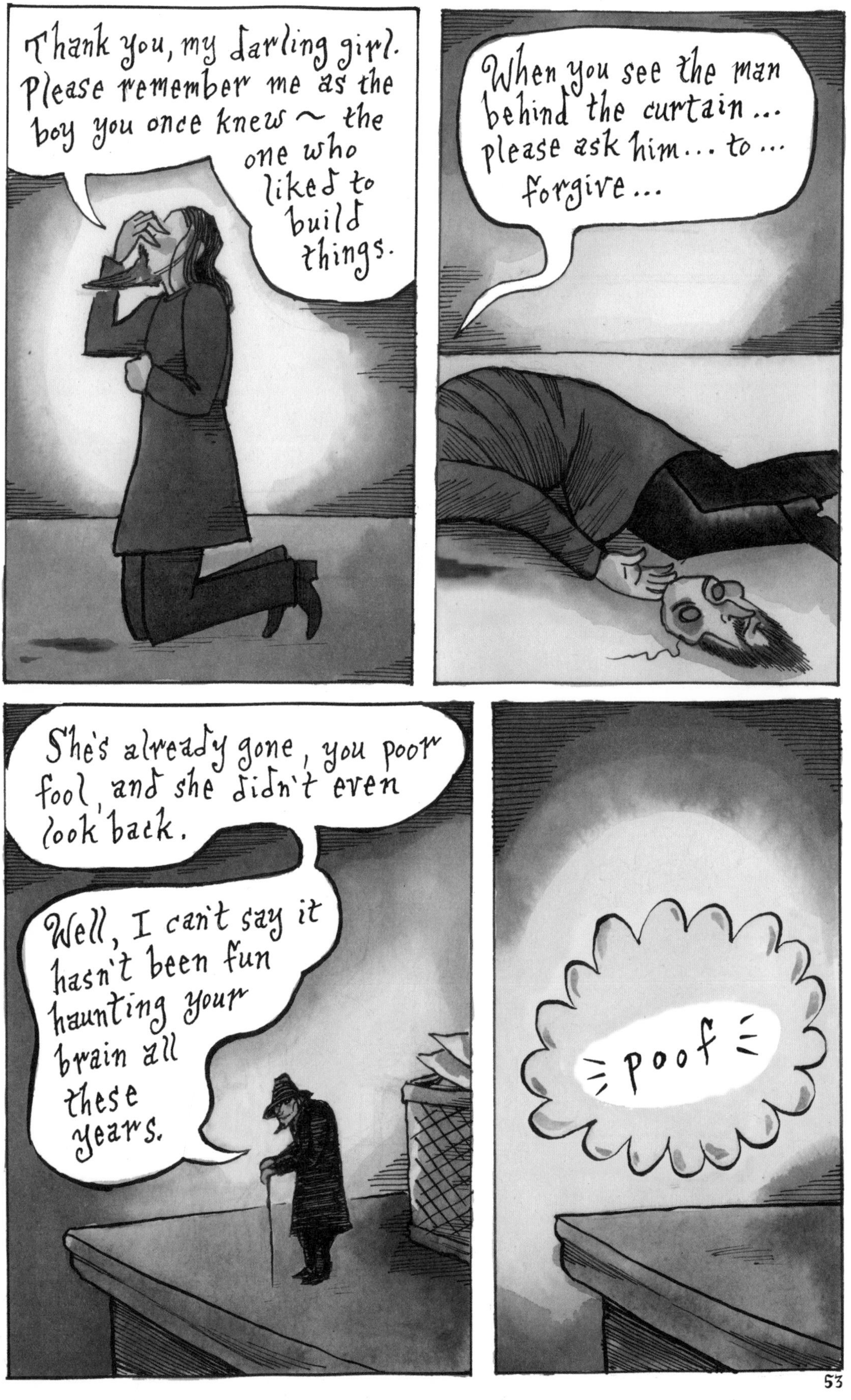
Thank you, my darling girl. Please remember me as the boy you once knew ~ the one who liked to build things.
When you see the man behind the curtain... please ask him... to... forgive...
She's already gone, you poor fool, and she didn't even look back.
Well, I can't say it hasn't been fun haunting your brain all these years.
poof

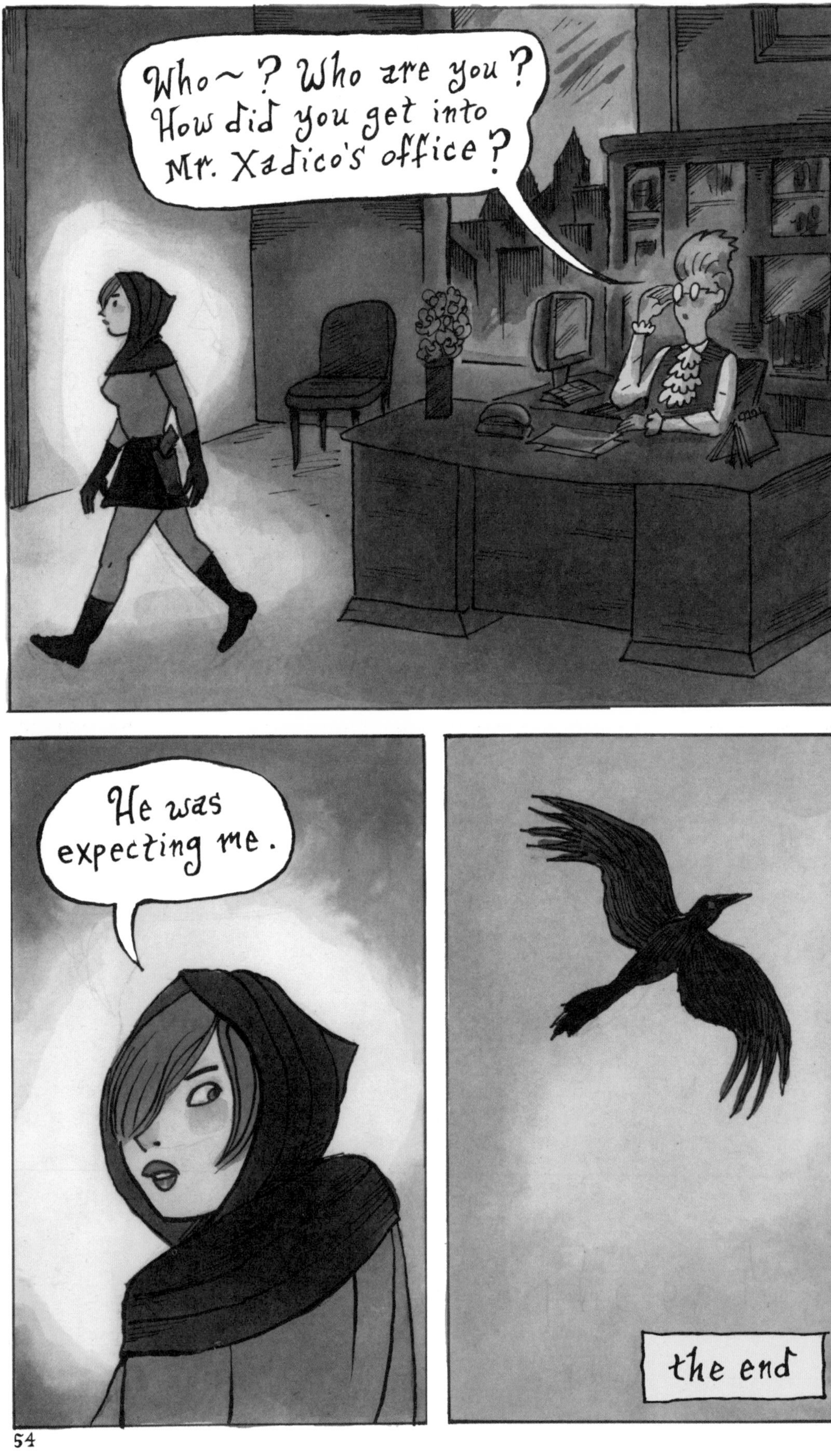
Who~? Who are you? How did you get into Mr. Xadico's office?
He was expecting me.
the end

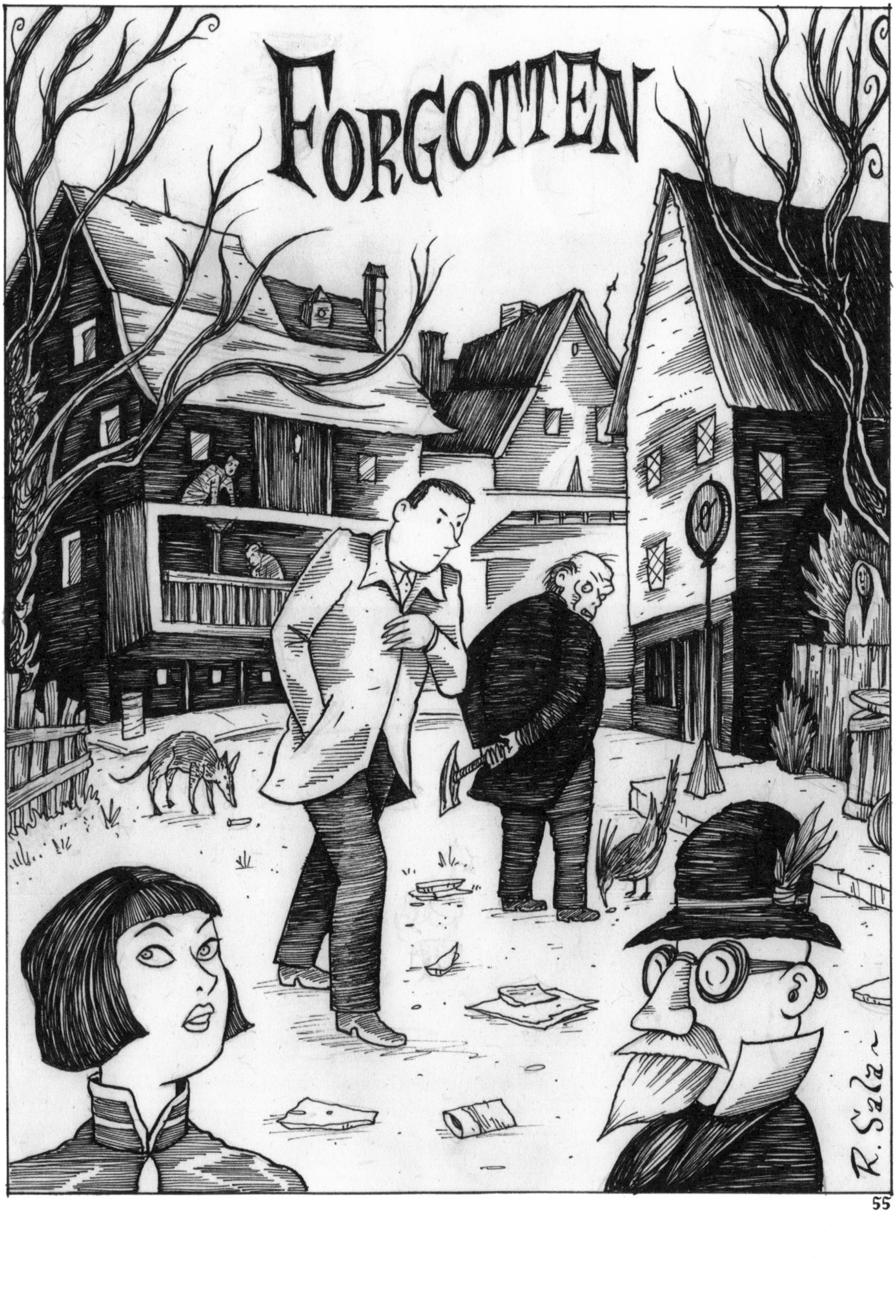
FORGOTTEN
R. Sala

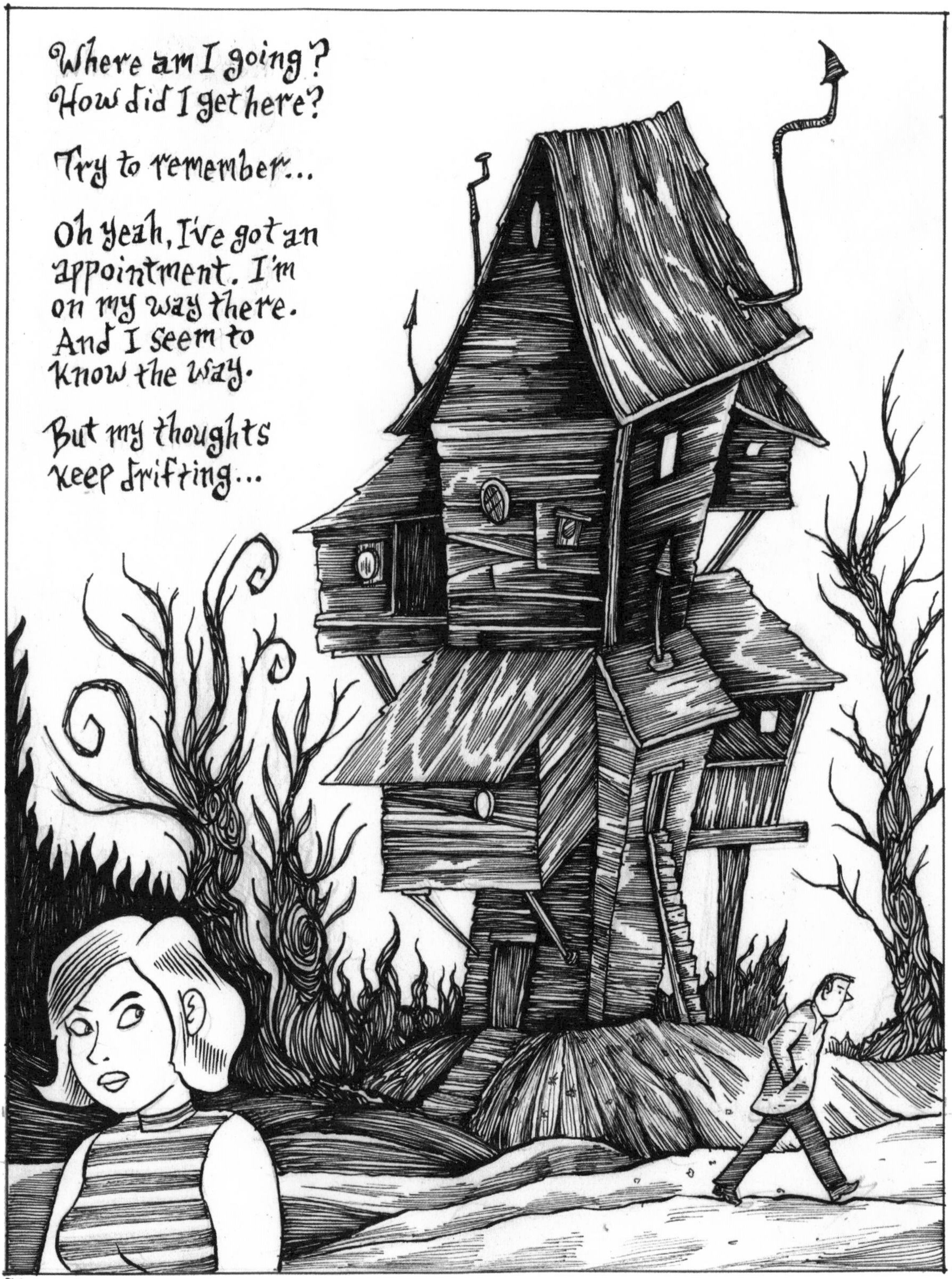
Where am I going?
How did I get here?
Try to remember...
Oh yeah, I've got an appointment. I'm on my way there. And I seem to know the way.
But my thoughts keep drifting...

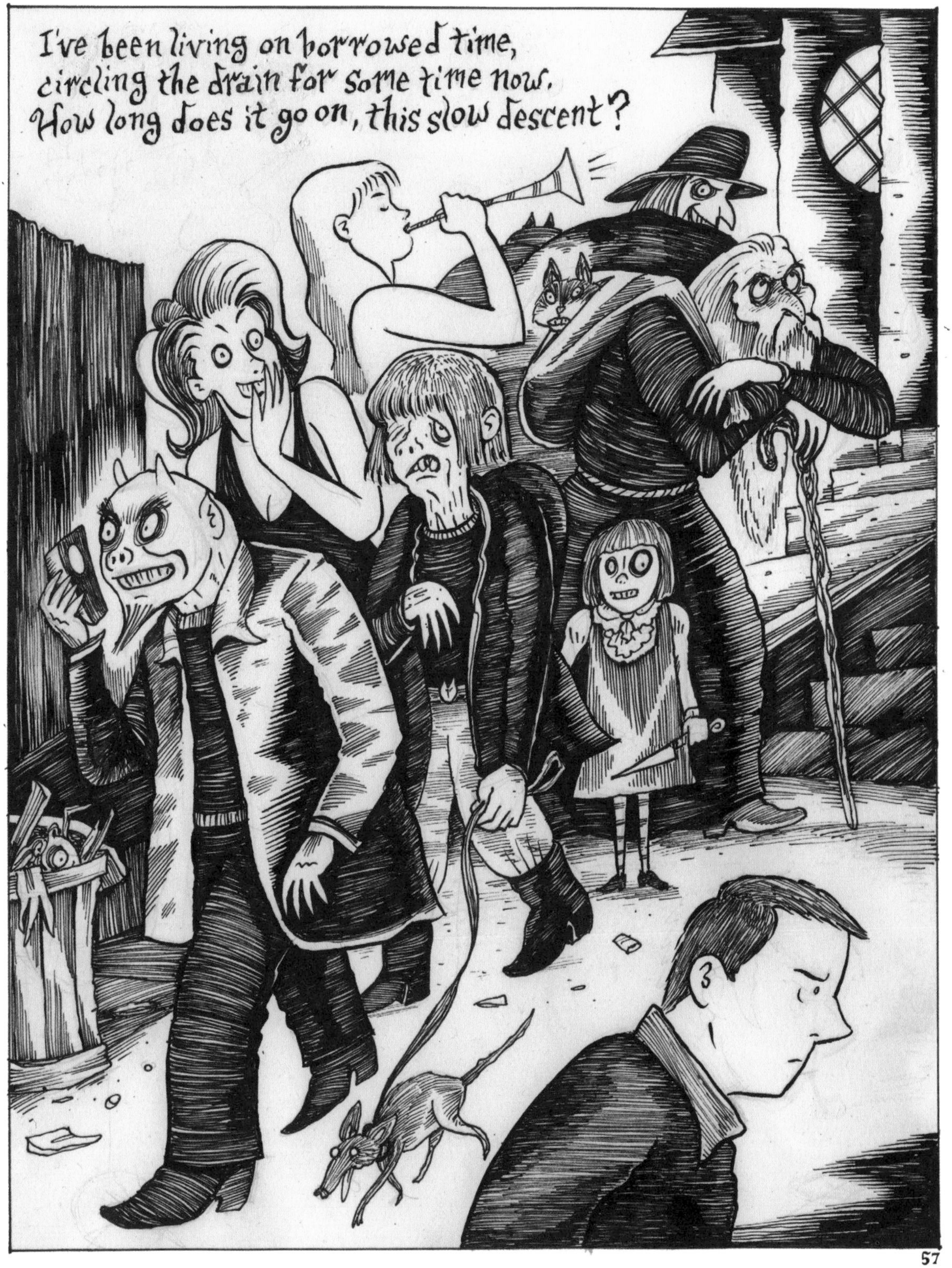
I've been living on borrowed time,
circling the drain for some time now.
How long does it go on, this slow descent?

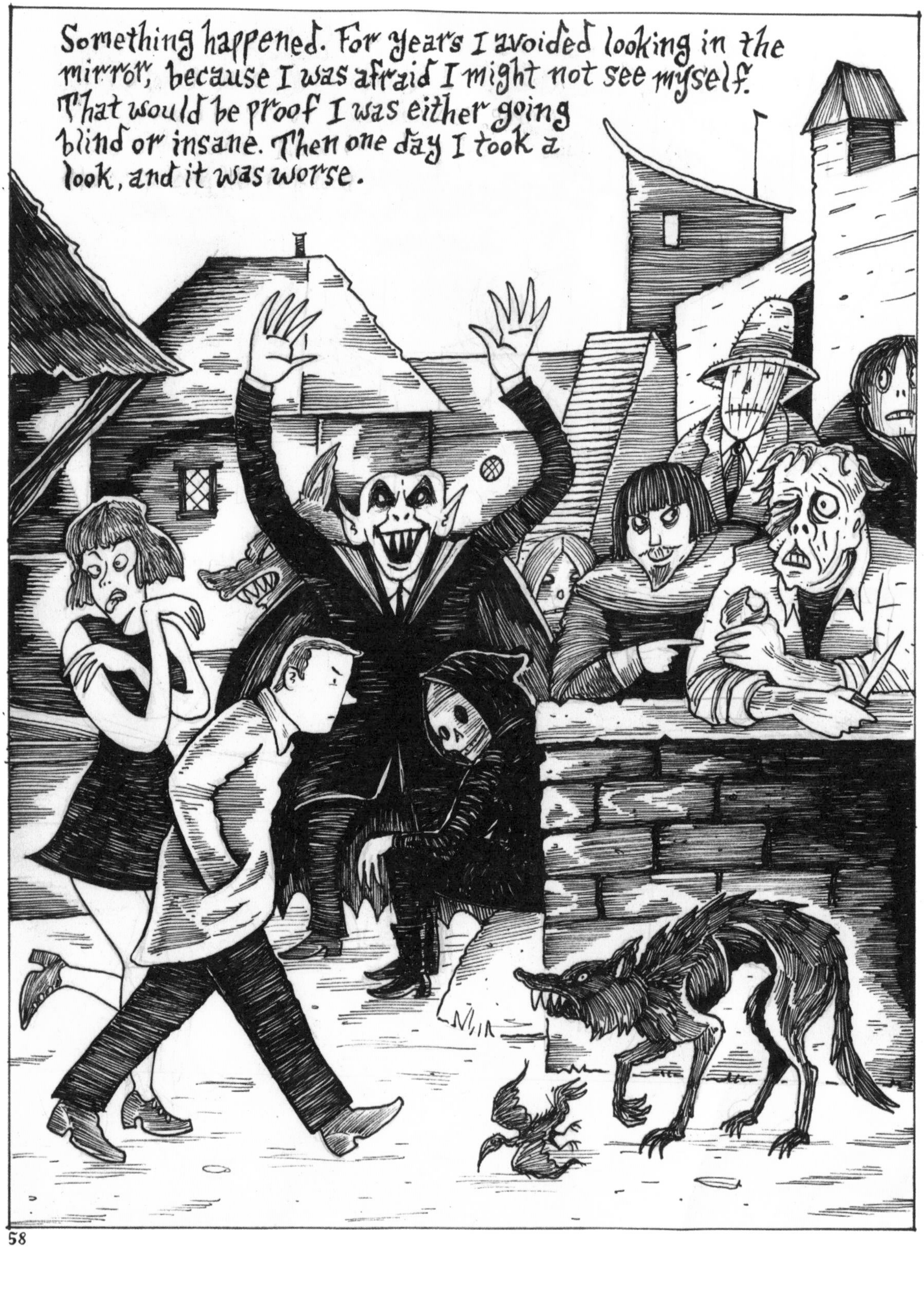
Something happened. For years I avoided looking in the mirror, because I was afraid I might not see myself. That would be proof I was either going blind or insane. Then one day I took a look, and it was worse.

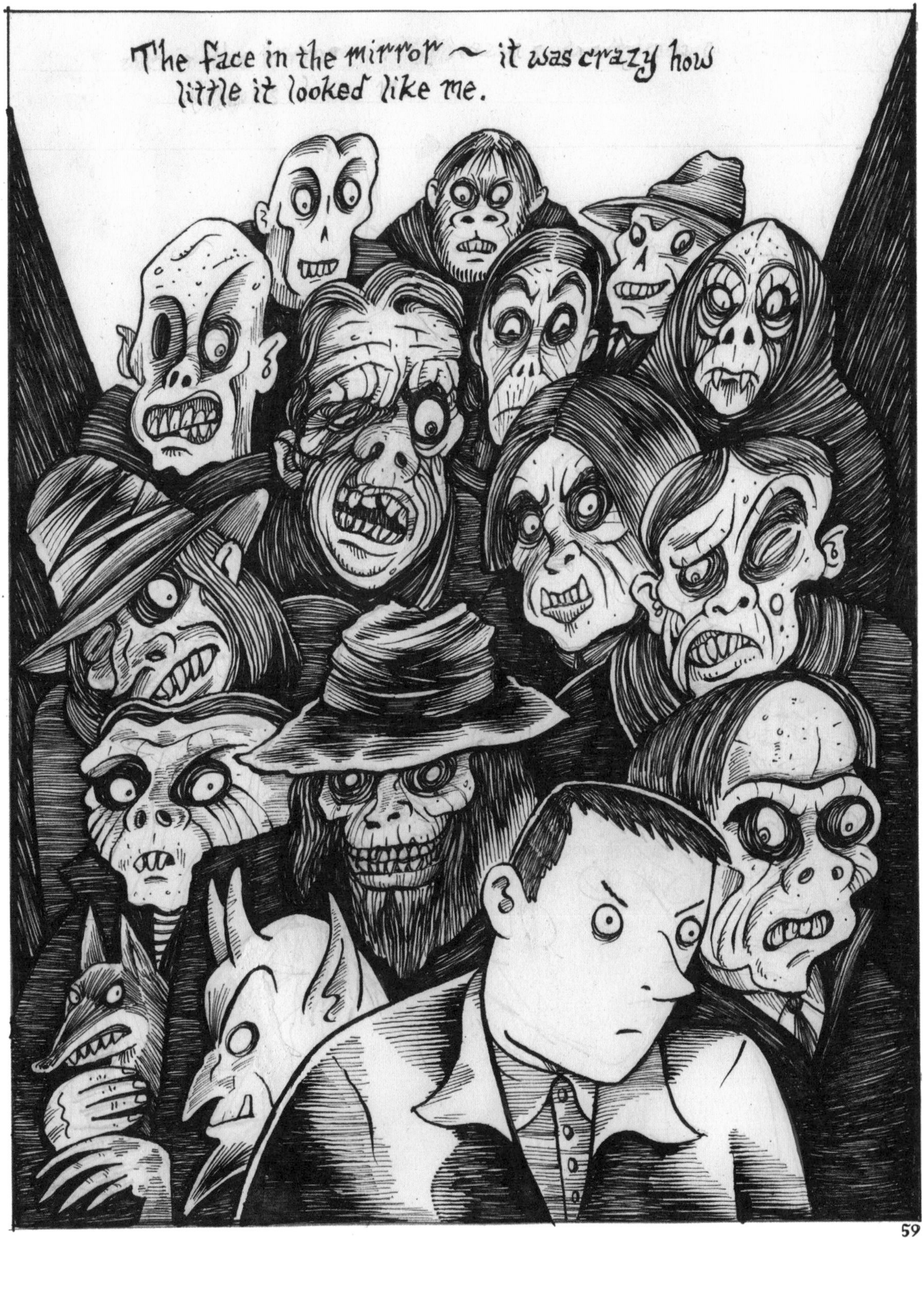
The face in the mirror ~ it was crazy how little it looked like me.

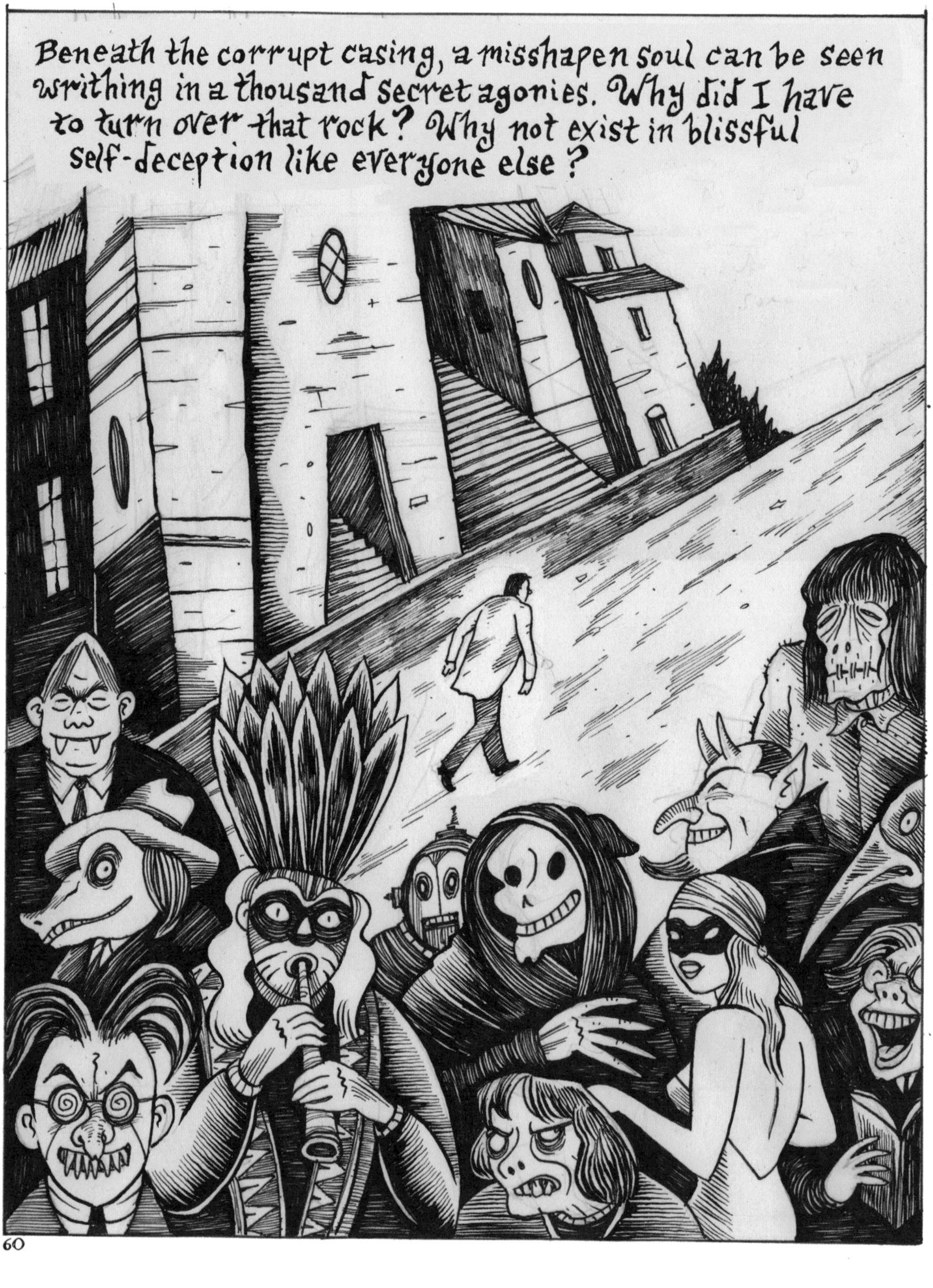
Beneath the corrupt casing, a misshapen soul can be seen writhing in a thousand secret agonies. Why did I have to turn over that rock? Why not exist in blissful self-deception like everyone else?

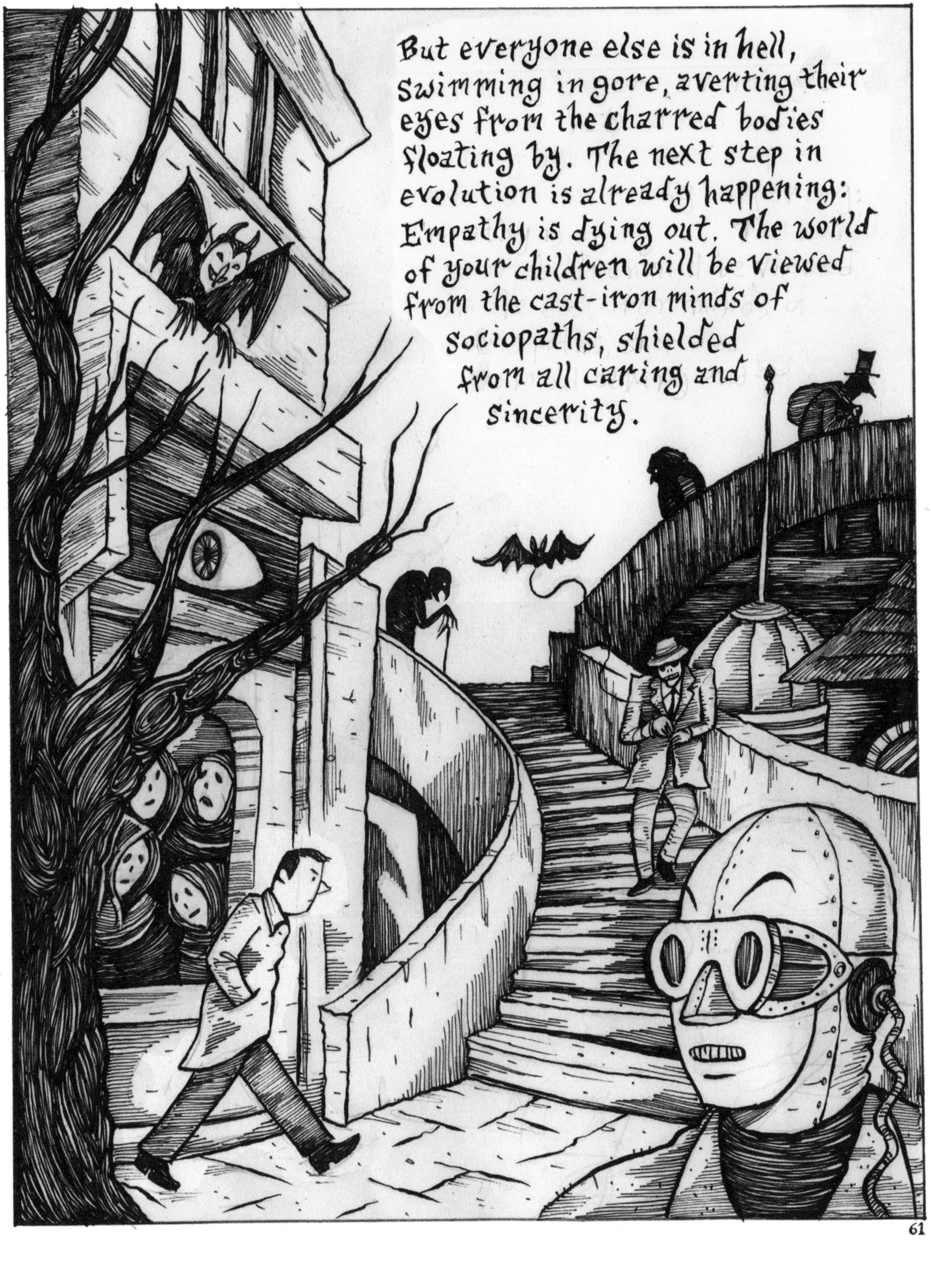
But everyone else is in hell, swimming in gore, averting their eyes from the charred bodies floating by. The next step in evolution is already happening: Empathy is dying out. The world of your children will be viewed from the cast-iron minds of sociopaths, shielded from all caring and sincerity.

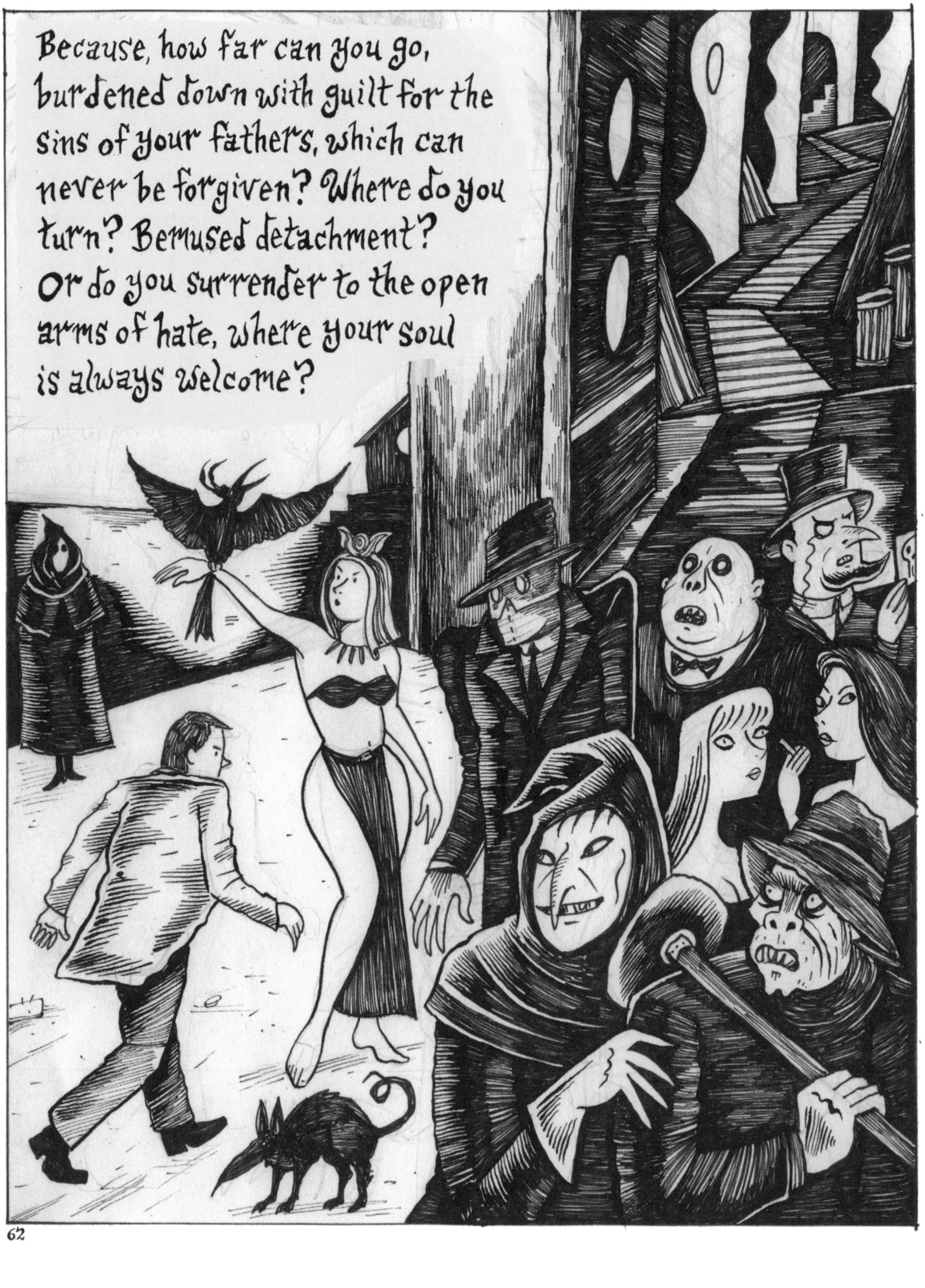
Because, how far can you go, burdened down with guilt for the sins of your fathers, which can never be forgiven? Where do you turn? Bemused detachment? Or do you surrender to the open arms of hate, where your soul is always welcome?

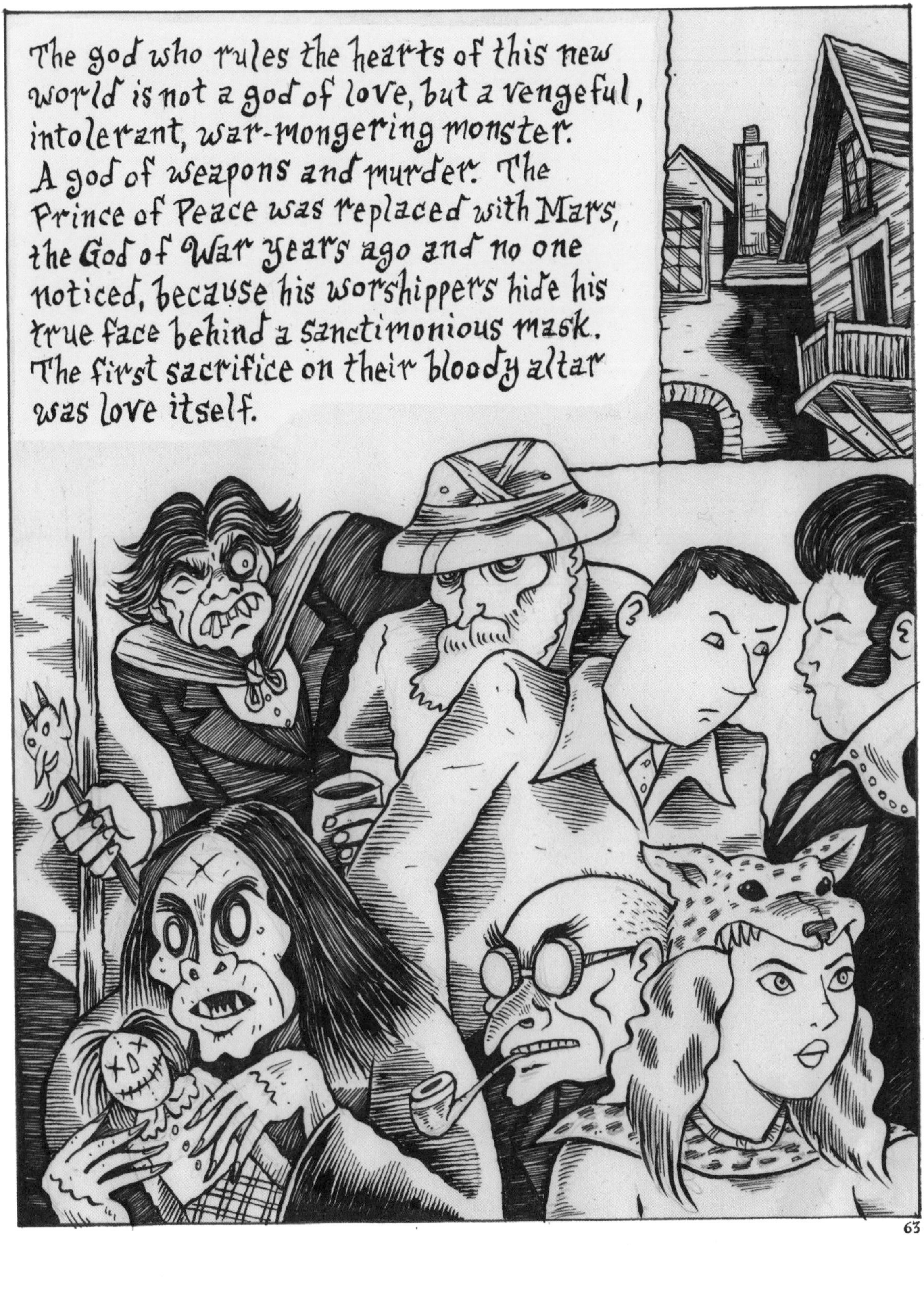
The god who rules the hearts of this new world is not a god of love, but a vengeful, intolerant, war-mongering monster. A god of weapons and murder. The Prince of Peace was replaced with Mars, the God of War years ago and no one noticed, because his worshippers hide his true face behind a sanctimonious mask. The first sacrifice on their bloody altar was love itself.

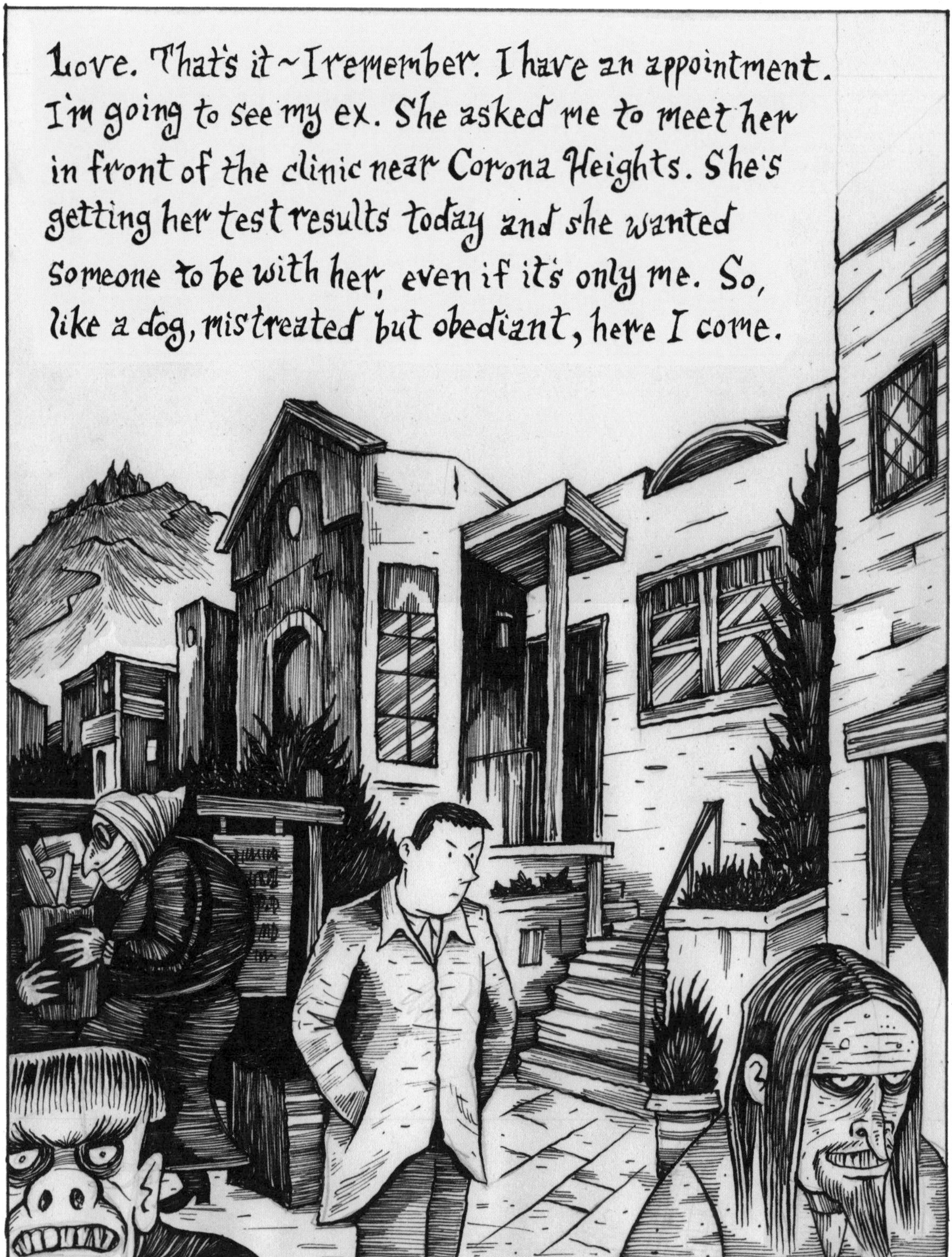
Love. That's it ~ I remember. I have an appointment. I'm going to see my ex. She asked me to meet her in front of the clinic near Corona Heights. She's getting her test results today and she wanted someone to be with her, even if it's only me. So, like a dog, mistreated but obediant, here I come.

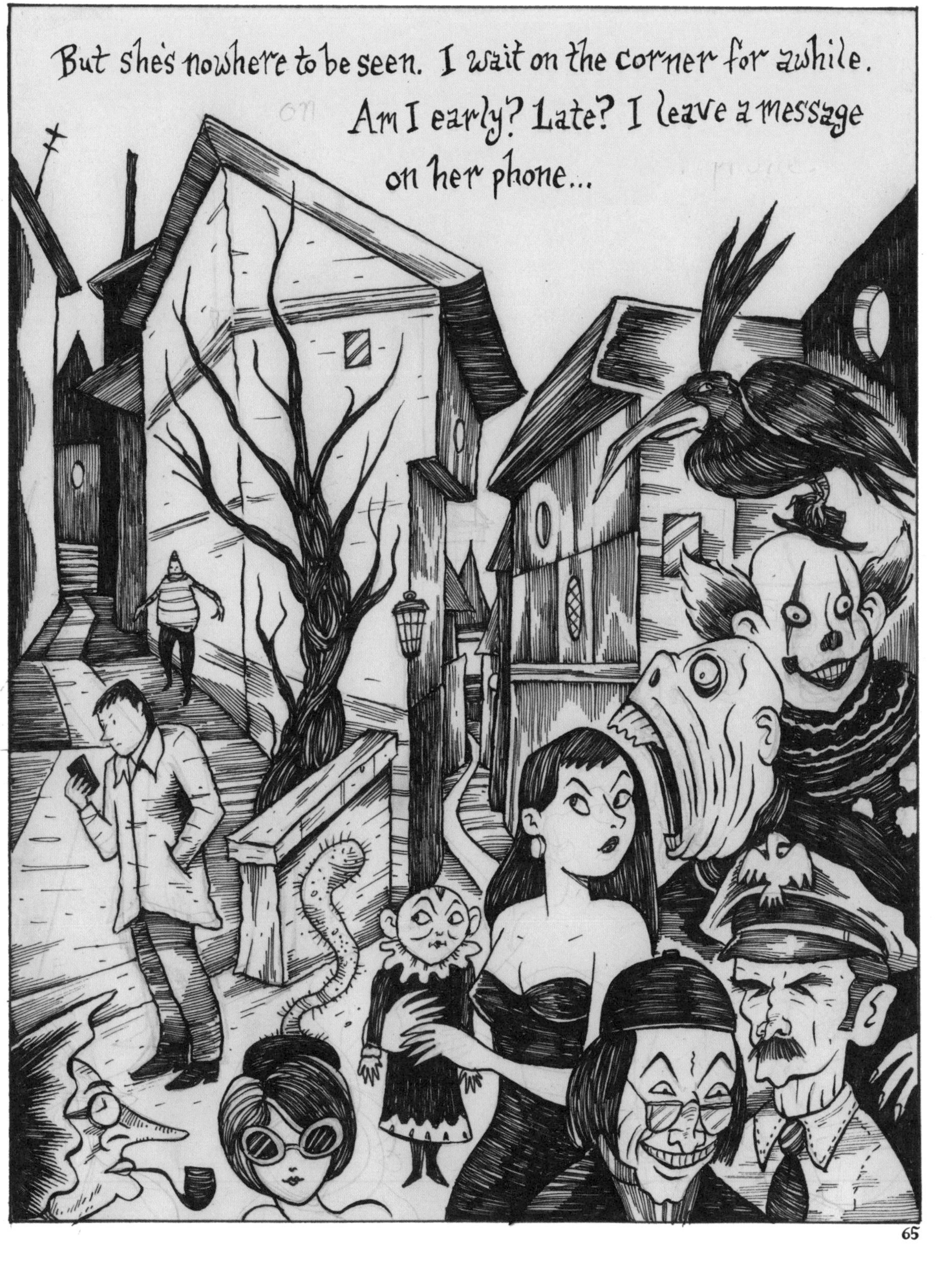
But she's nowhere to be seen. I wait on the corner for awhile.
Am I early? Late? I leave a message
on her phone...

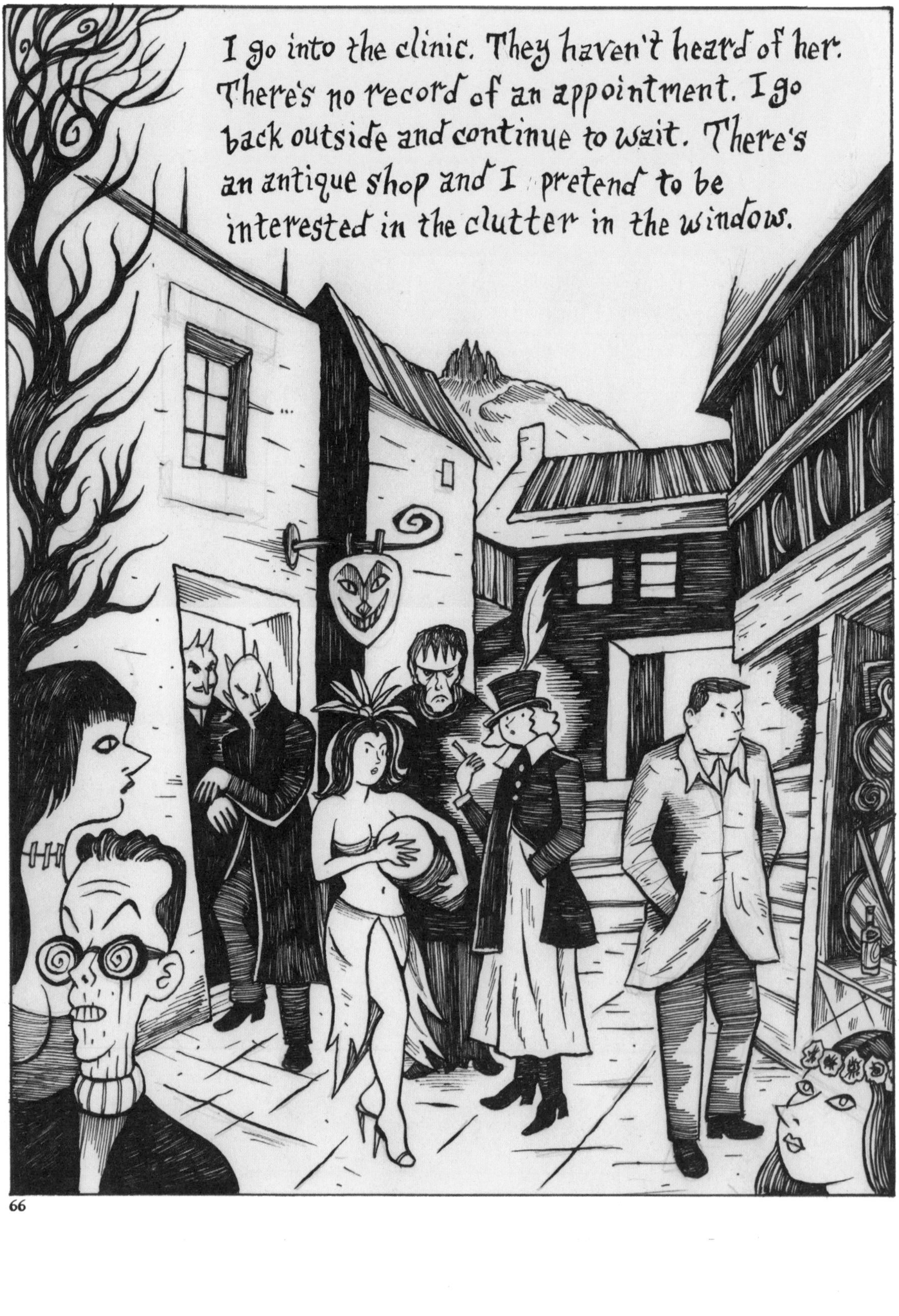
I go into the clinic. They haven't heard of her. There's no record of an appointment. I go back outside and continue to wait. There's an antique shop and I pretend to be interested in the clutter in the window.

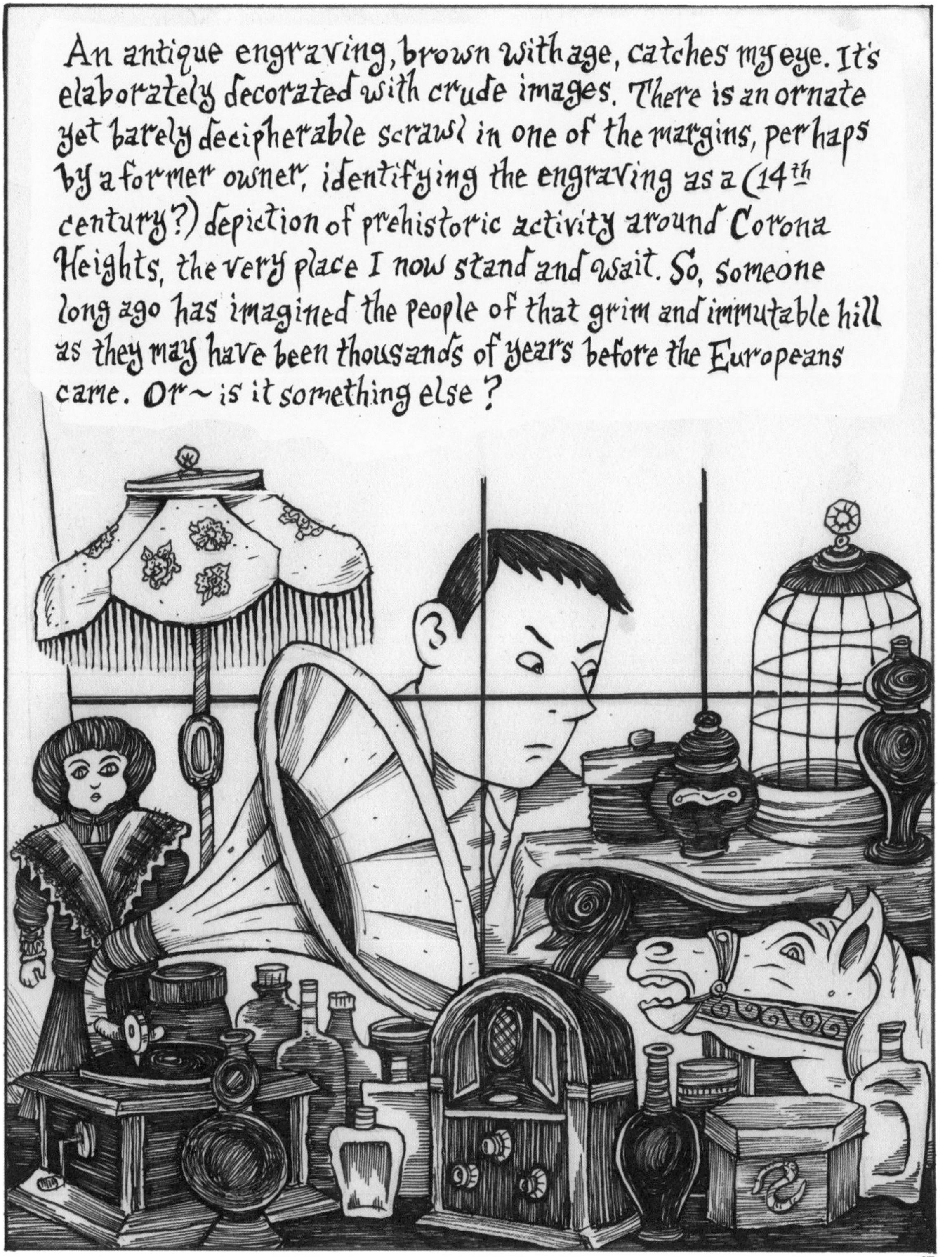
An antique engraving, brown with age, catches my eye. It's elaborately decorated with crude images. There is an ornate yet barely decipherable scrawl in one of the margins, perhaps by a former owner, identifying the engraving as a (14th century?) depiction of prehistoric activity around Corona Heights, the very place I now stand and wait. So, someone long ago has imagined the people of that grim and immutable hill as they may have been thousands of years before the Europeans came. Or ~ is it something else?

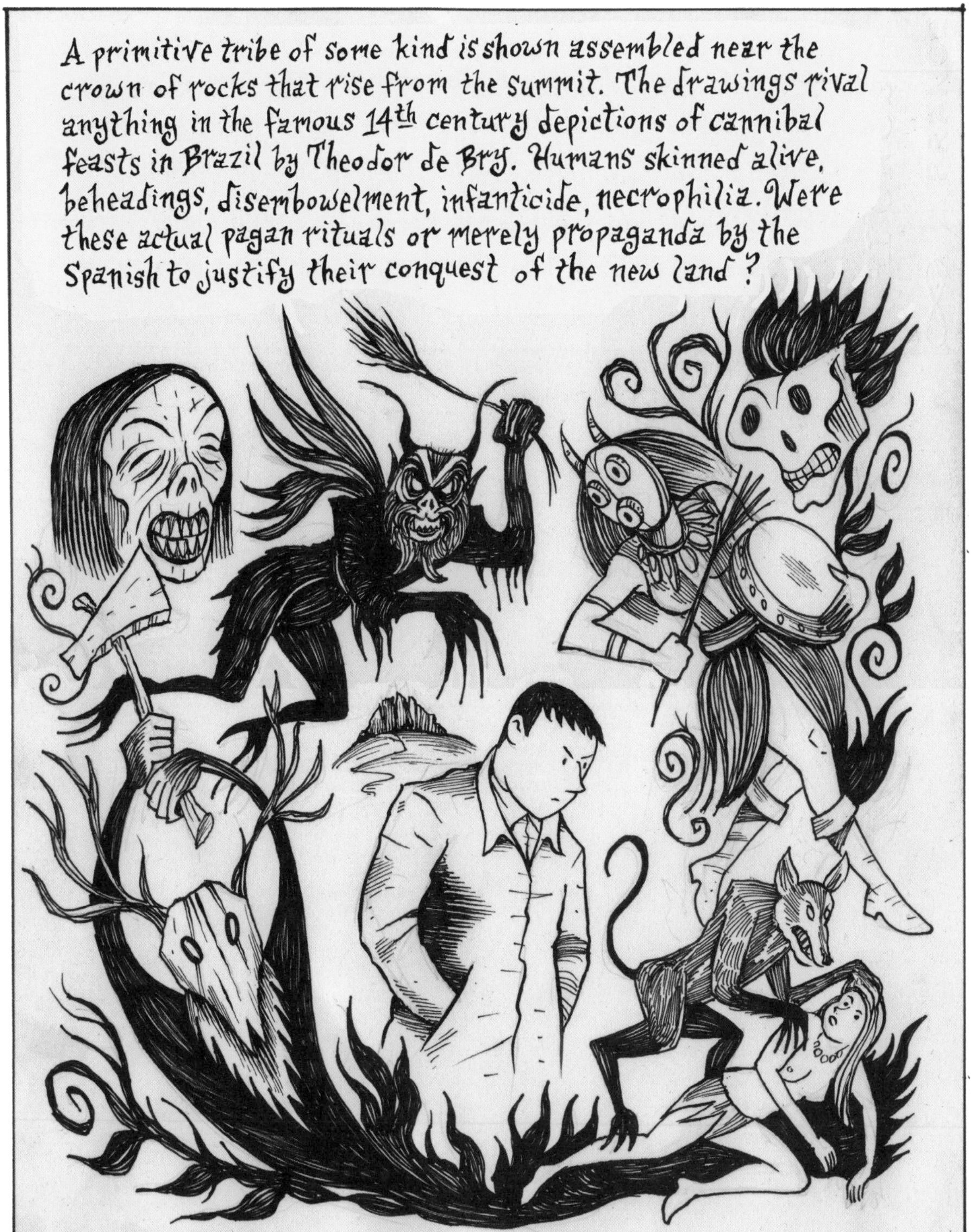
A primitive tribe of some kind is shown assembled near the crown of rocks that rise from the summit. The drawings rival anything in the famous 14th century depictions of cannibal feasts in Brazil by Theodor de Bry. Humans skinned alive, beheadings, disembowelment, infanticide, necrophilia. Were these actual pagan rituals or merely propaganda by the Spanish to justify their conquest of the new land?

"Primitive," "pagan" ~ terms now considered inappropriate in these more enlightened times. But how enlightened are we? In the drawing, creatures with talons, wings and nightmarish faces dance with and slaughter tribespeople with equal glee. These images came from twisted minds no different from those still among us today.

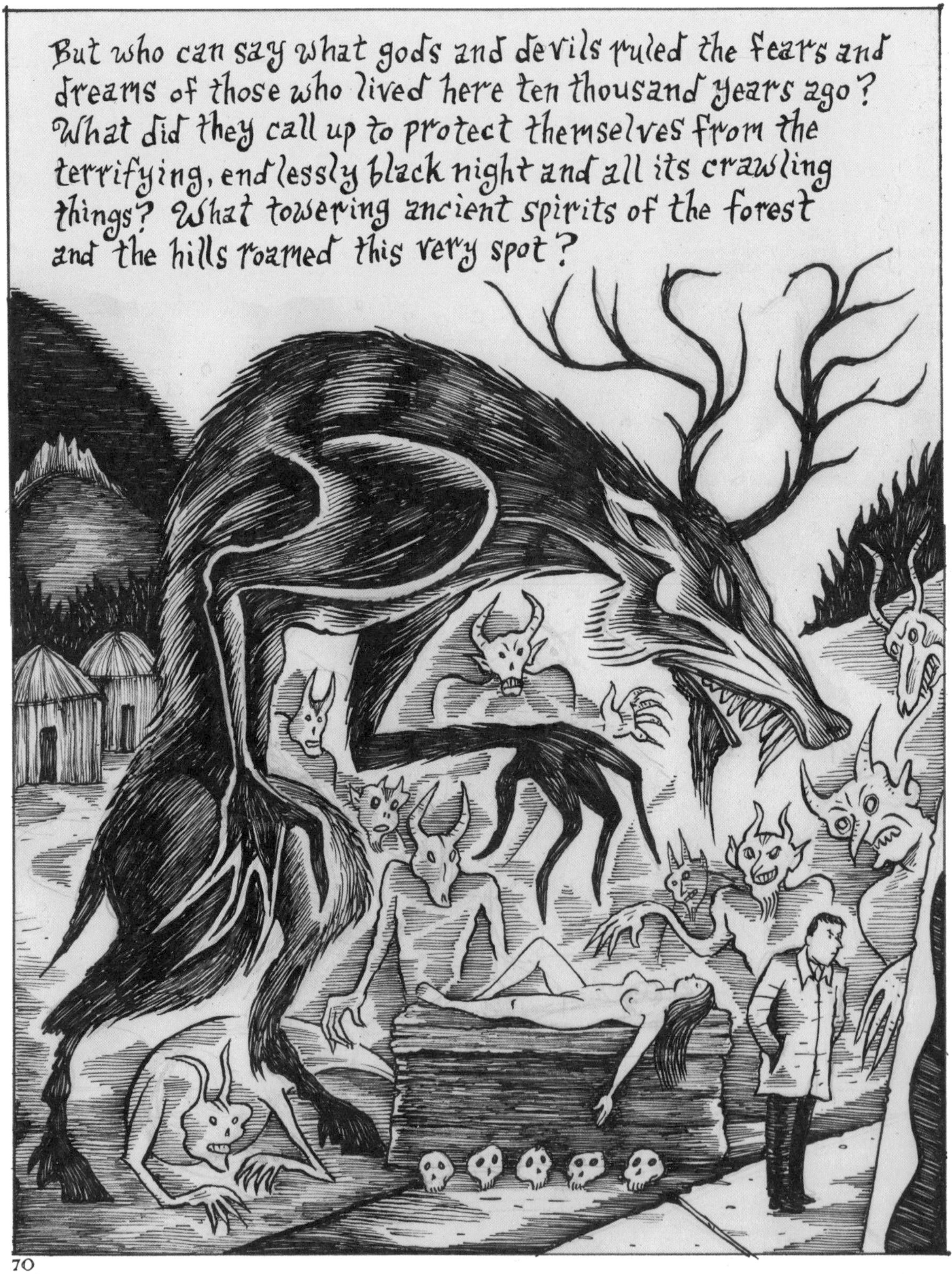
But who can say what gods and devils ruled the fears and dreams of those who lived here ten thousand years ago? What did they call up to protect themselves from the terrifying, endlessly black night and all its crawling things? What towering ancient spirits of the forest and the hills roamed this very spot?

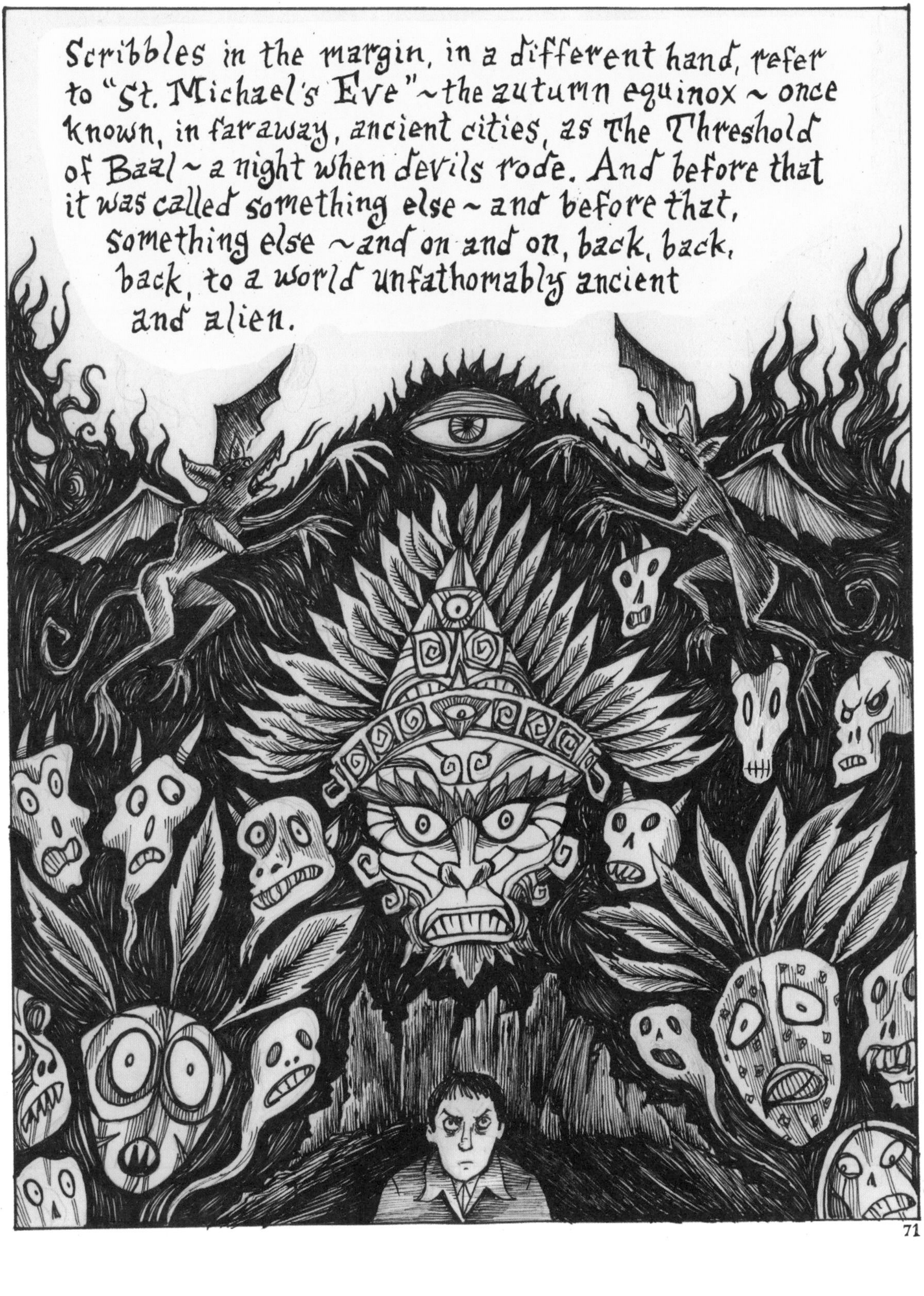
Scribbles in the margin, in a different hand, refer to "St. Michael's Eve" ~ the autumn equinox ~ once known, in faraway, ancient cities, as The Threshold of Baal ~ a night when devils rode. And before that it was called something else ~ and before that, something else ~ and on and on, back, back, back, to a world unfathomably ancient and alien.

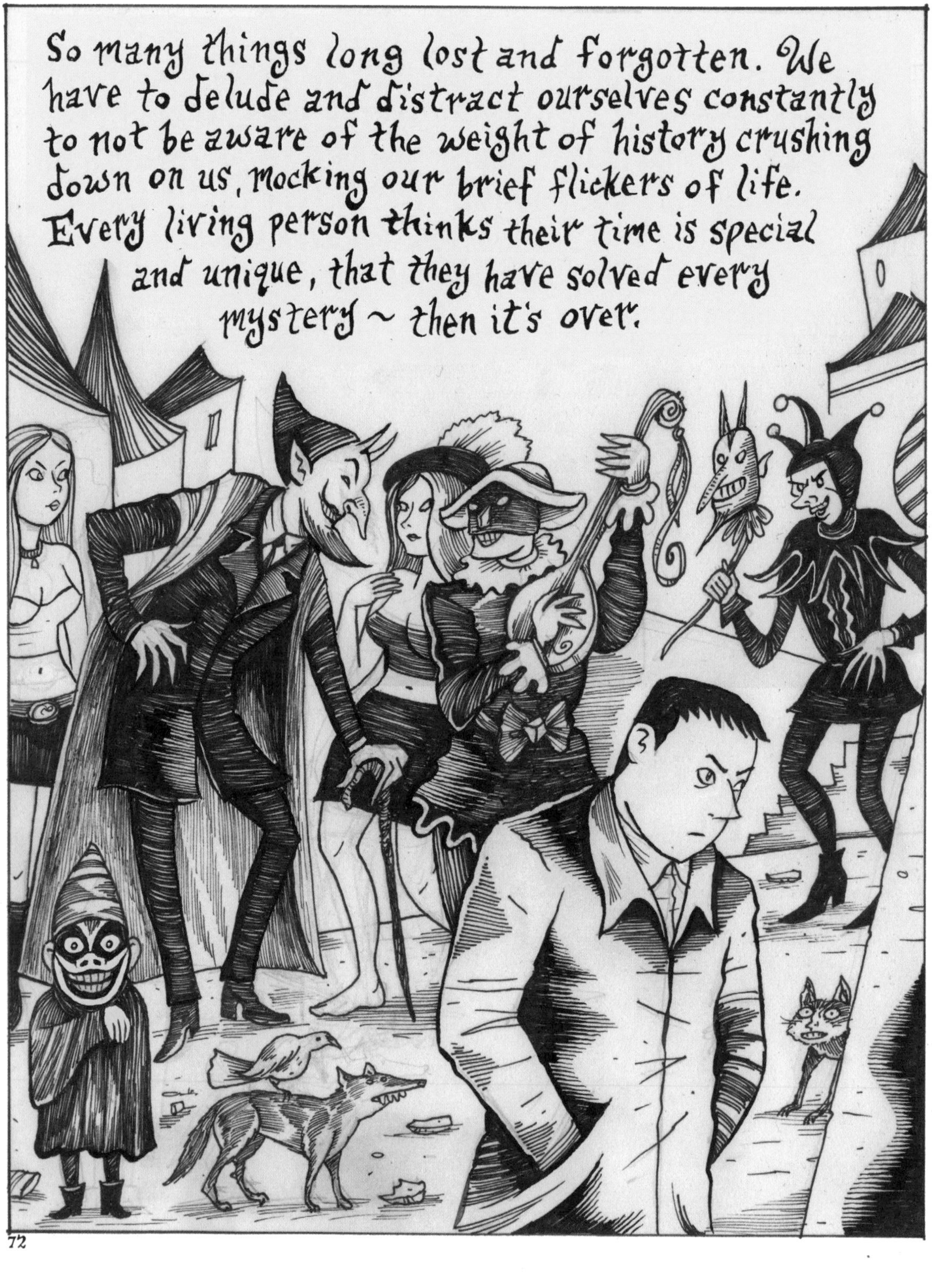
So many things long lost and forgotten. We have to delude and distract ourselves constantly to not be aware of the weight of history crushing down on us, mocking our brief flickers of life. Every living person thinks their time is special and unique, that they have solved every mystery ~ then it's over.

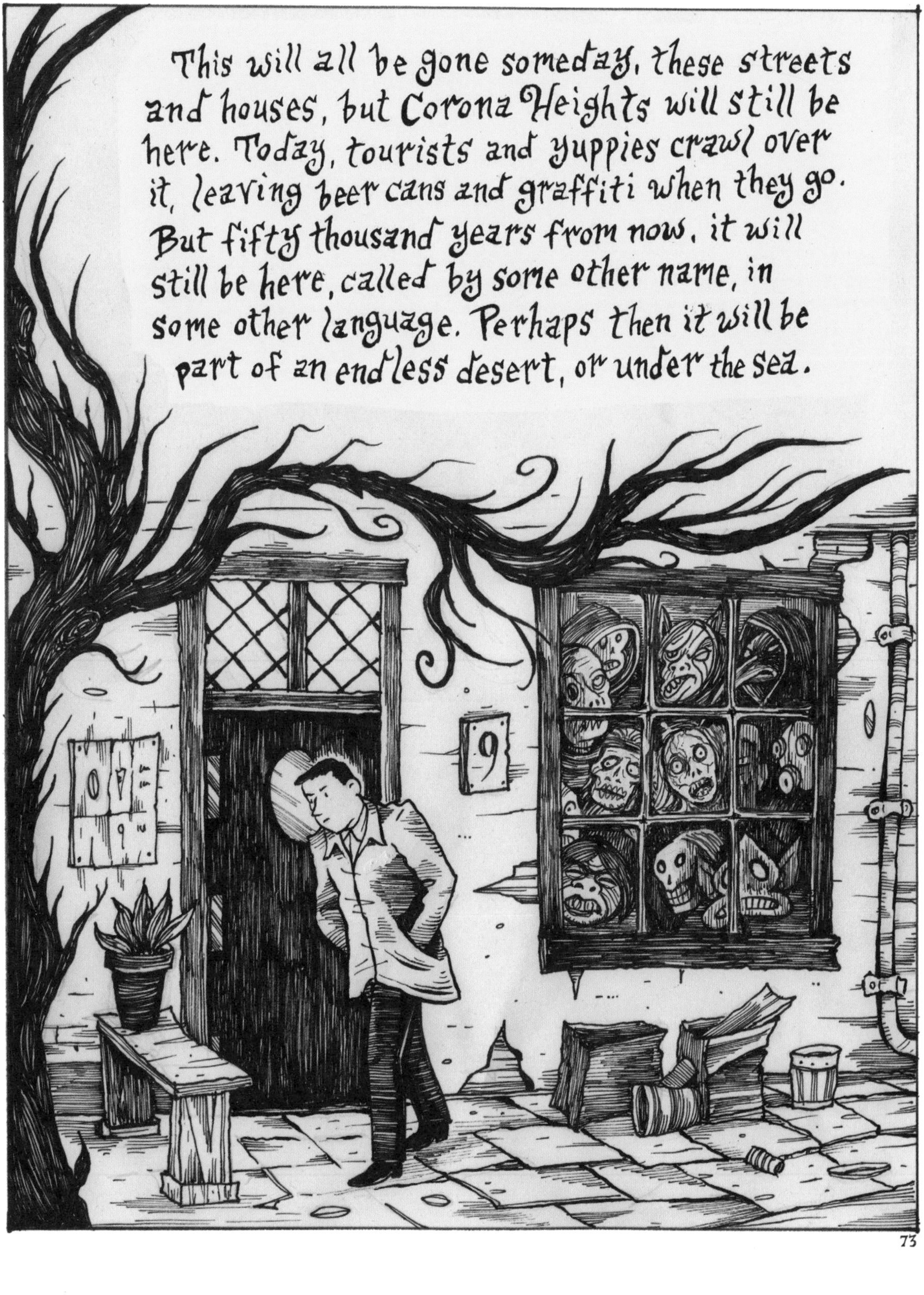
This will all be gone someday, these streets and houses, but Corona Heights will still be here. Today, tourists and yuppies crawl over it, leaving beer cans and graffiti when they go. But fifty thousand years from now, it will still be here, called by some other name, in some other language. Perhaps then it will be part of an endless desert, or under the sea.
9

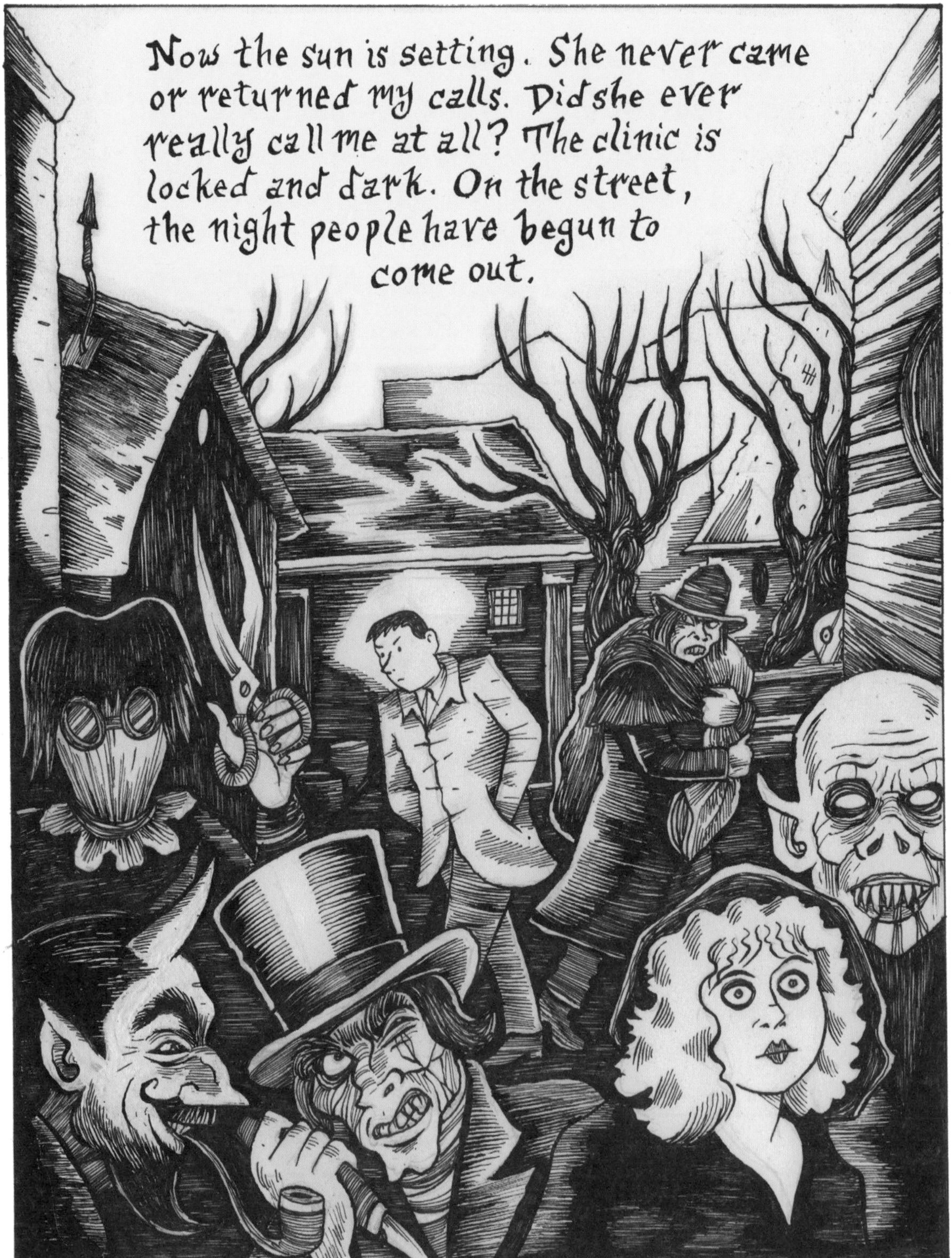
Now the sun is setting. She never came or returned my calls. Did she ever really call me at all? The clinic is locked and dark. On the street, the night people have begun to come out.

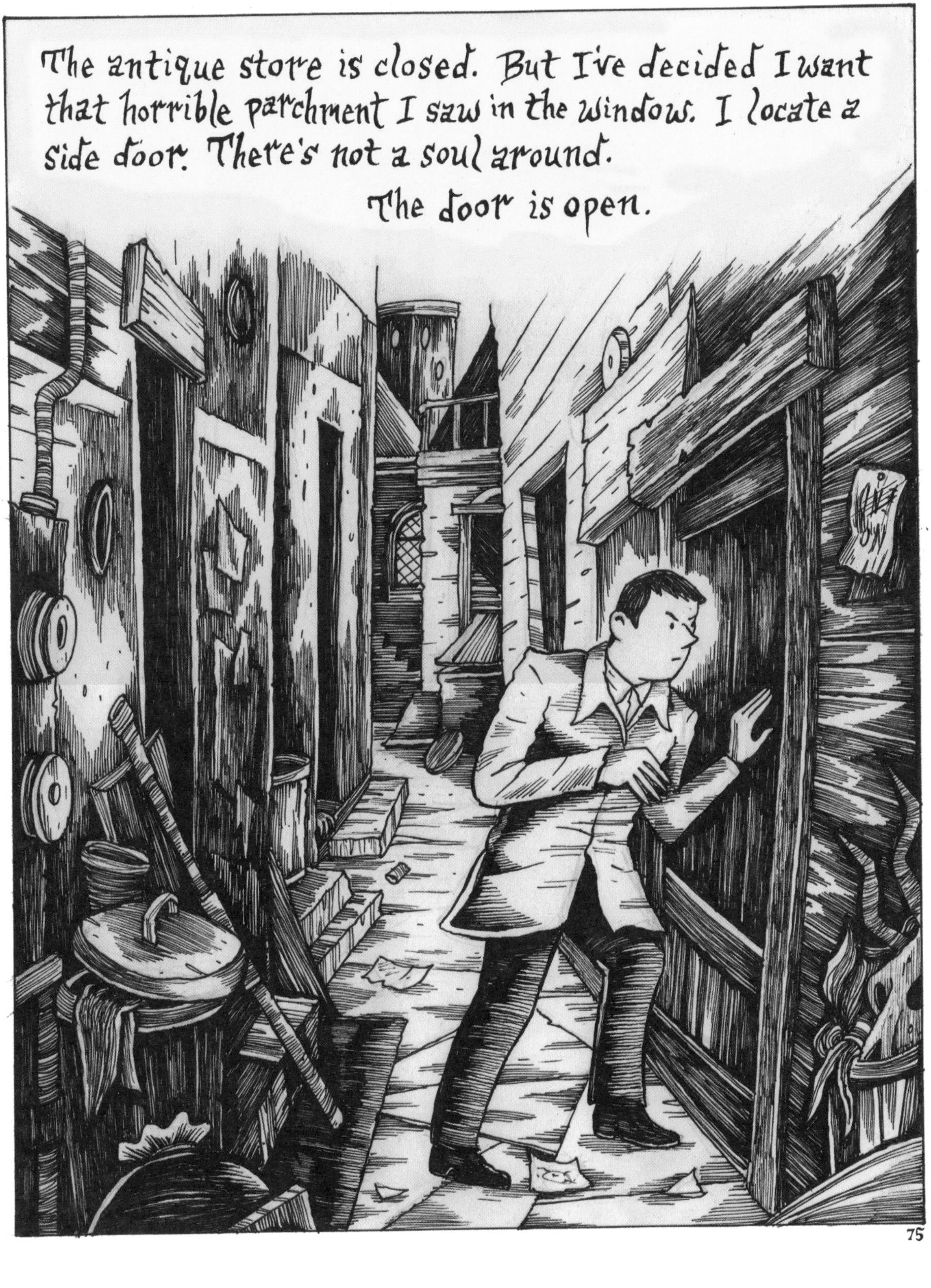
The antique store is closed. But I've decided I want that horrible parchment I saw in the window. I locate a side door. There's not a soul around.
The door is open.

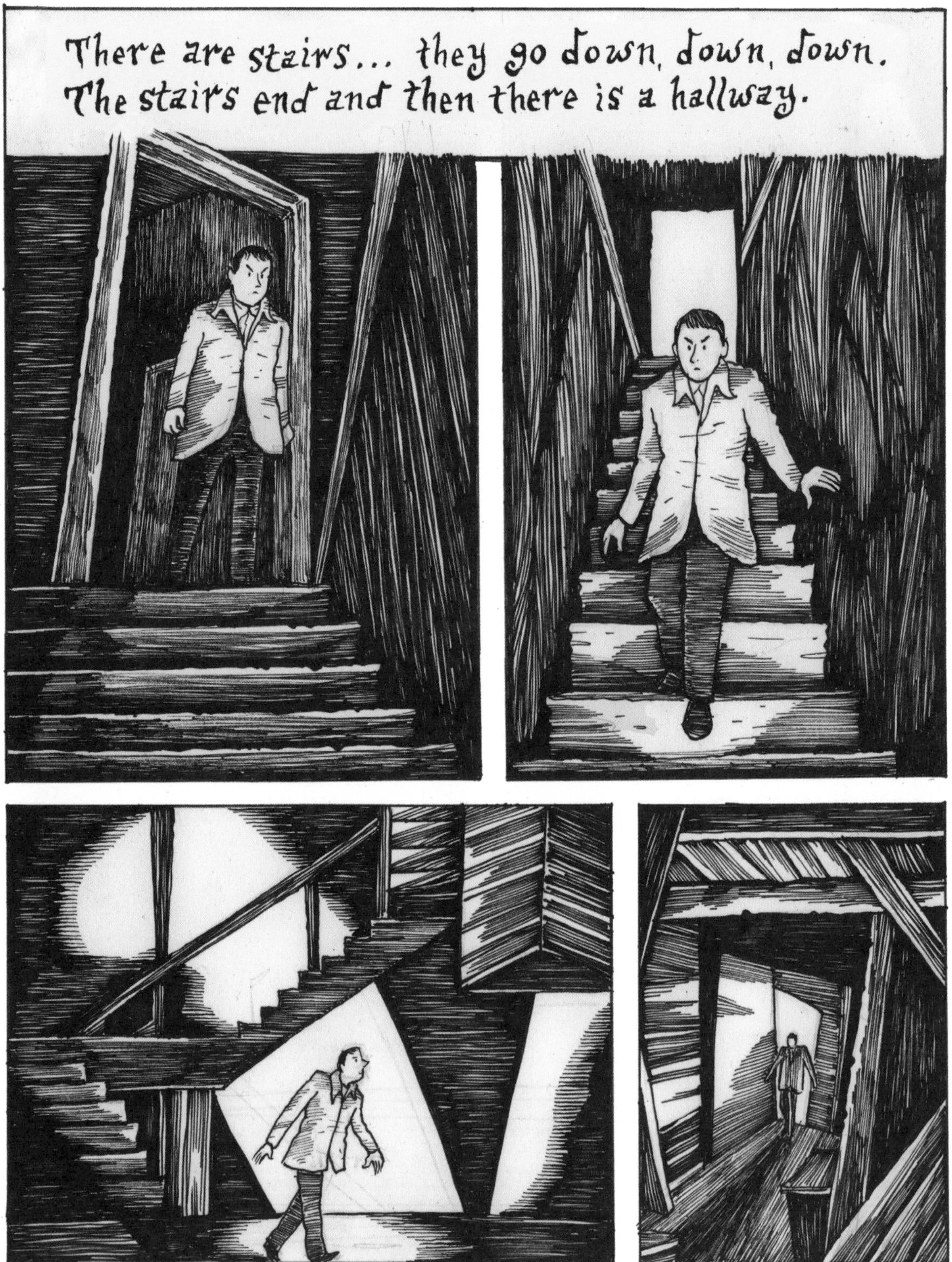
There are stairs... they go down, down, down.
The stairs end and then there is a hallway.

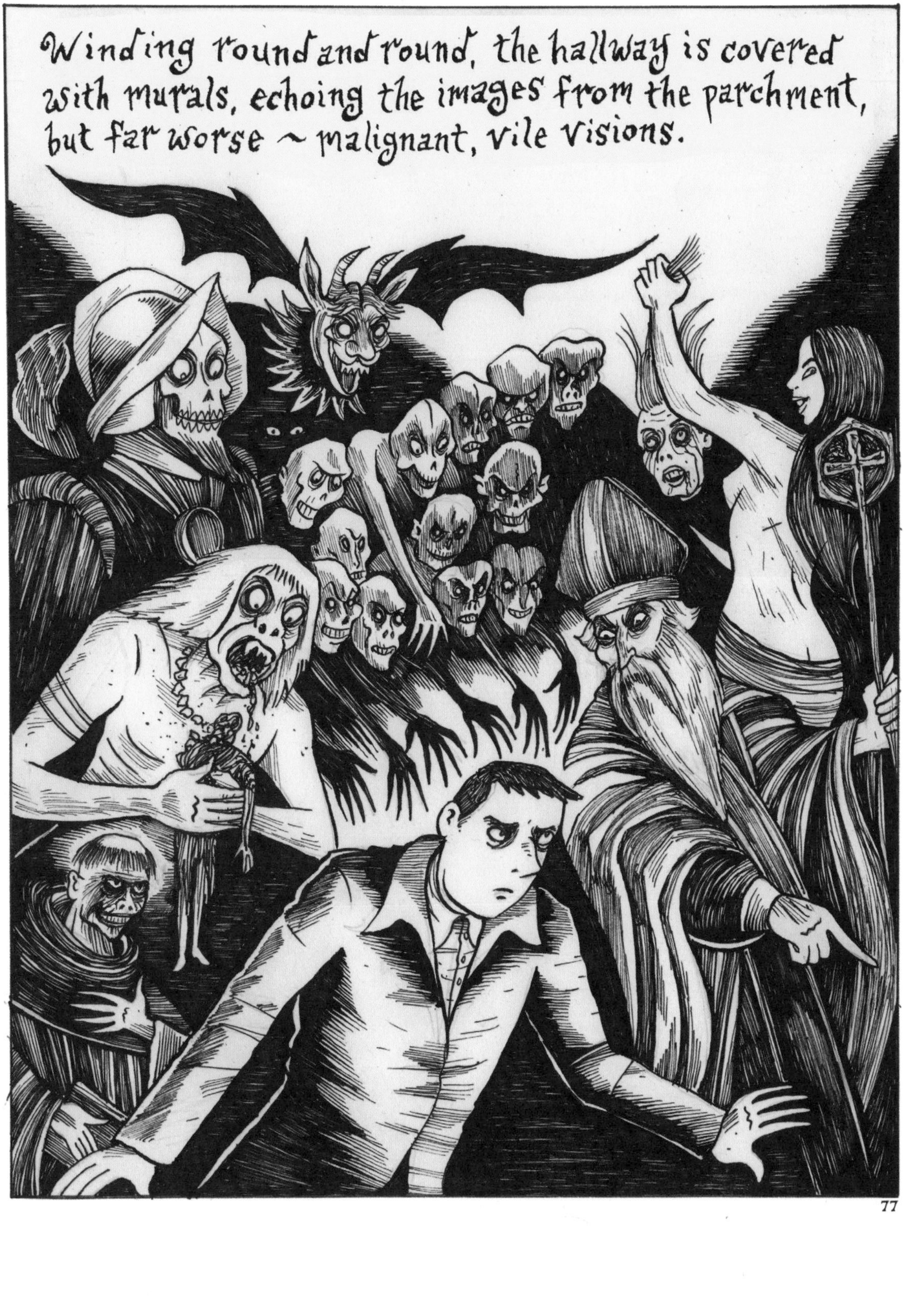
Winding round and round, the hallway is covered with murals, echoing the images from the parchment, but far worse ~ malignant, vile visions.

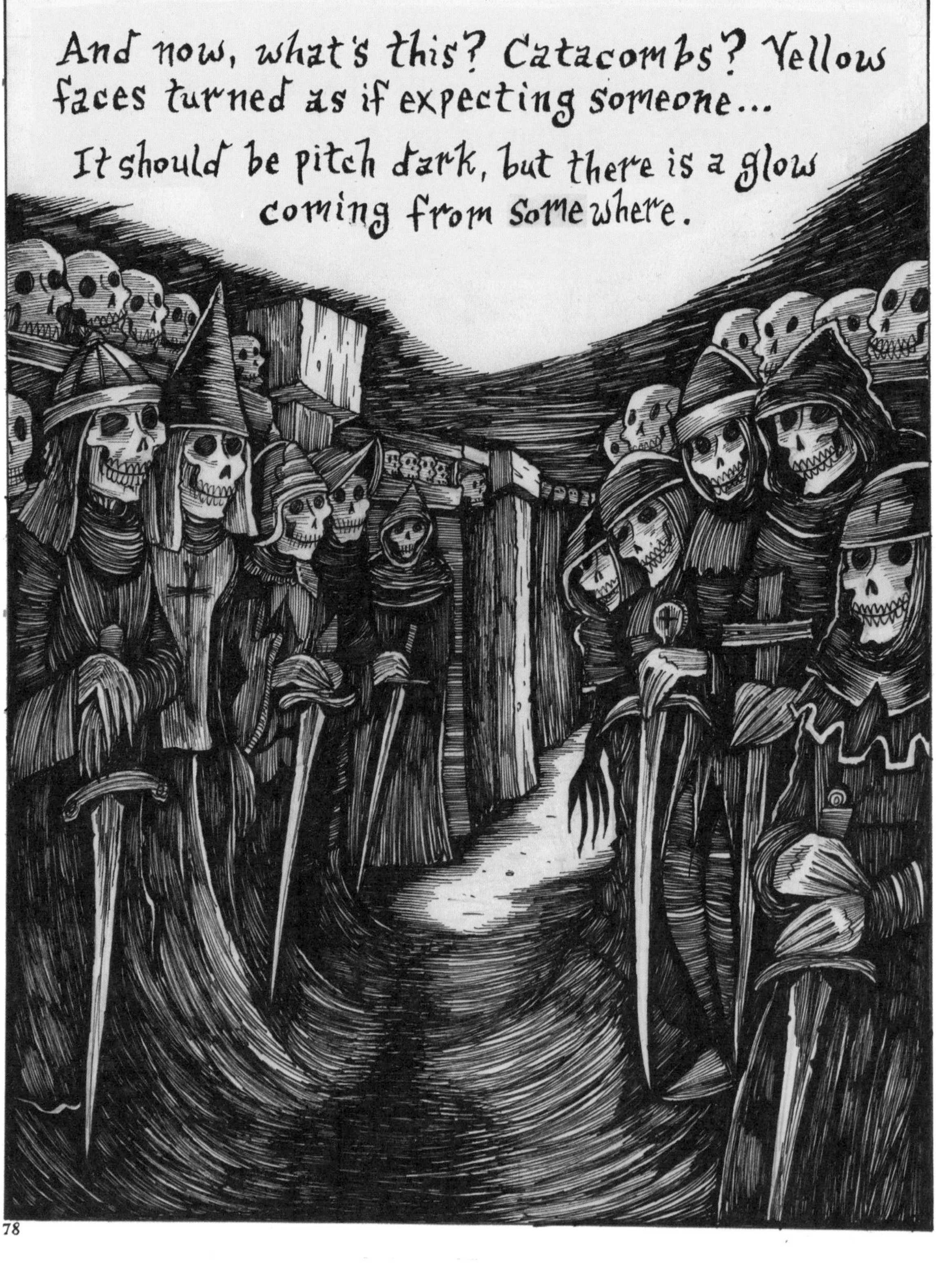
And now, what's this? Catacombs? Yellow faces turned as if expecting someone...
It should be pitch dark, but there is a glow coming from somewhere.

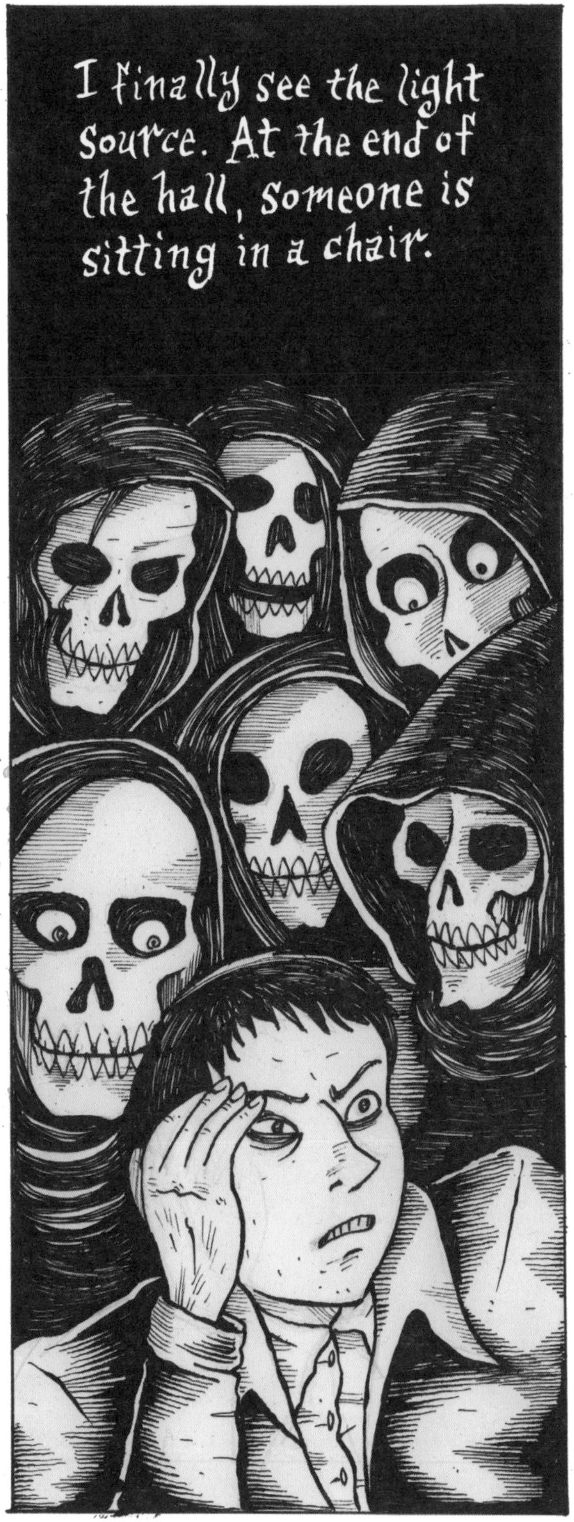
I finally see the light source. At the end of the hall, someone is sitting in a chair.

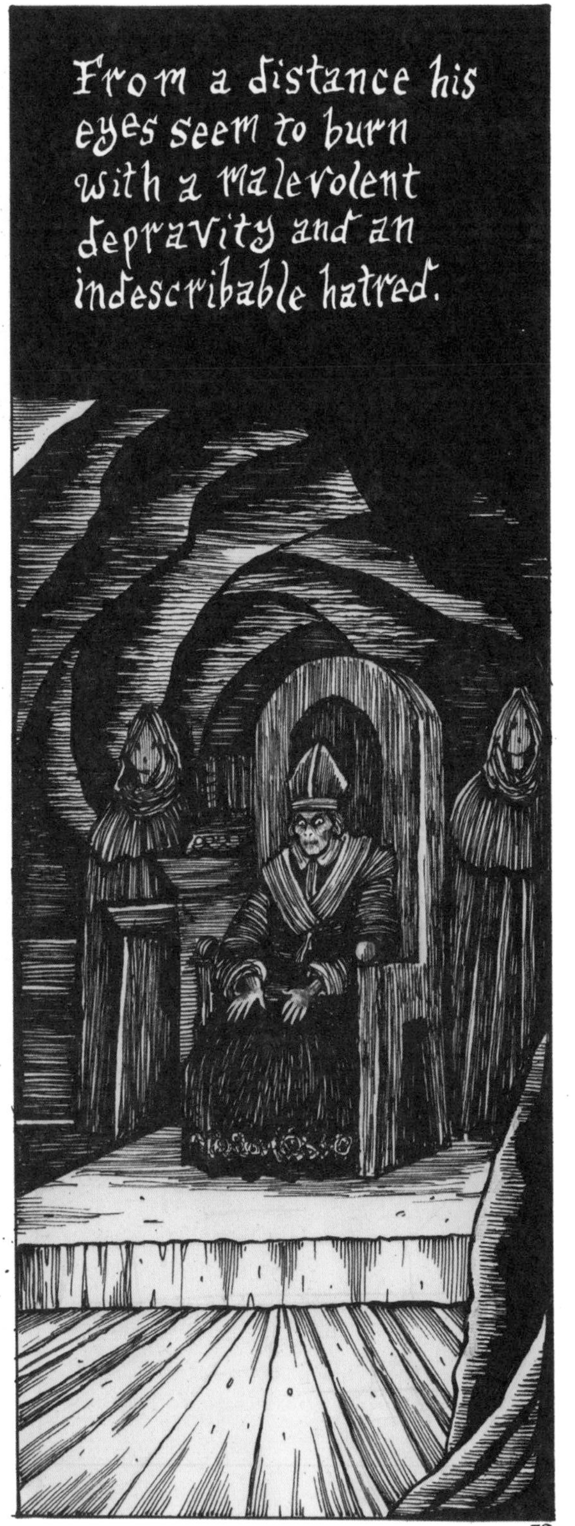
From a distance his eyes seem to burn with a malevolent depravity and an indescribable hatred.

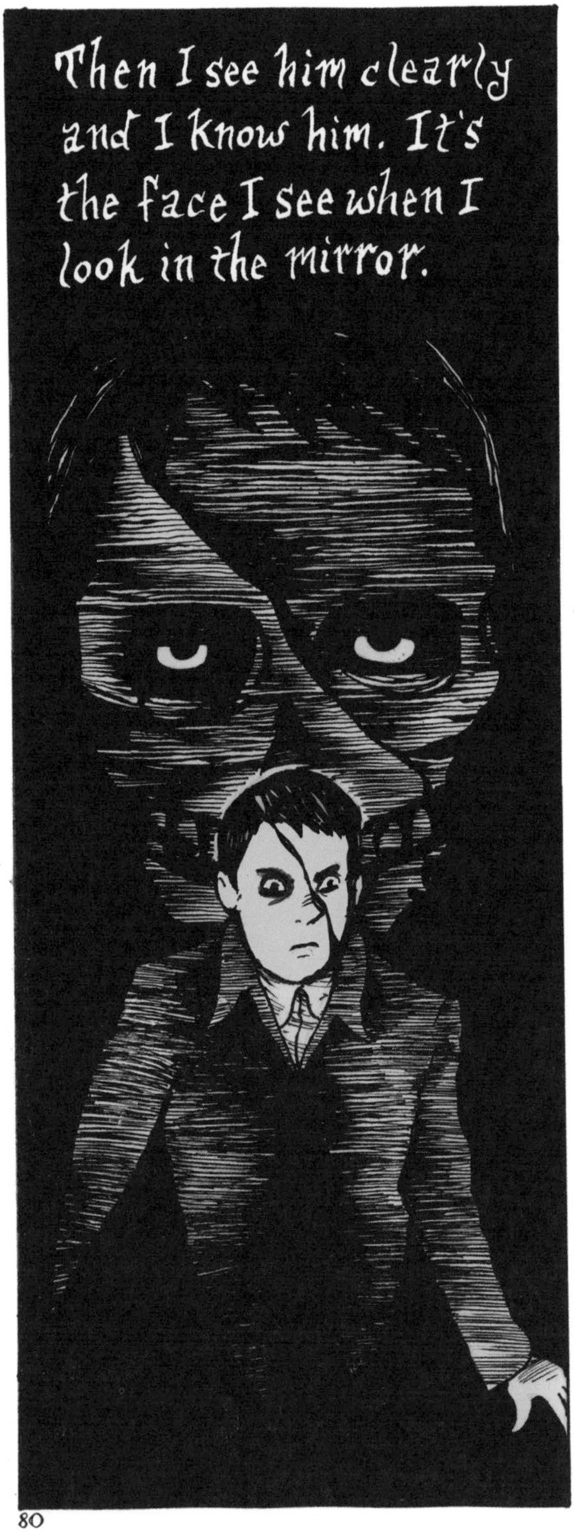
Then I see him clearly and I know him. It's the face I see when I look in the mirror.

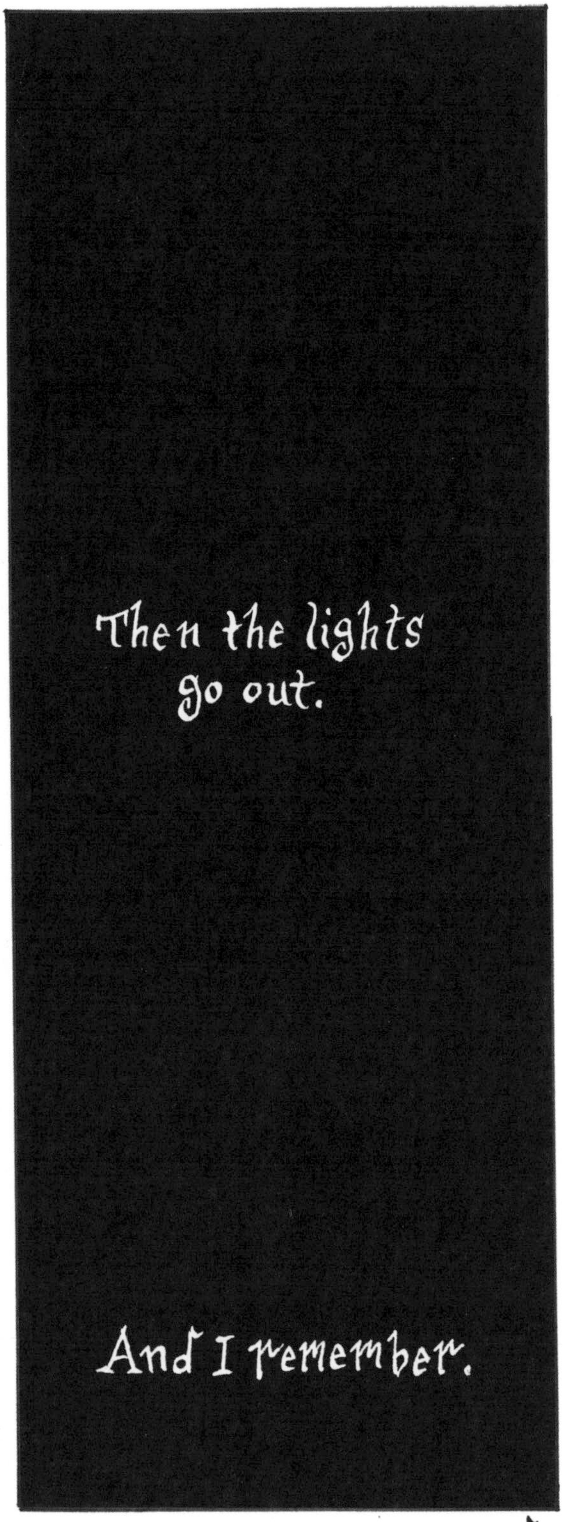
Then the lights go out.
And I remember.

end

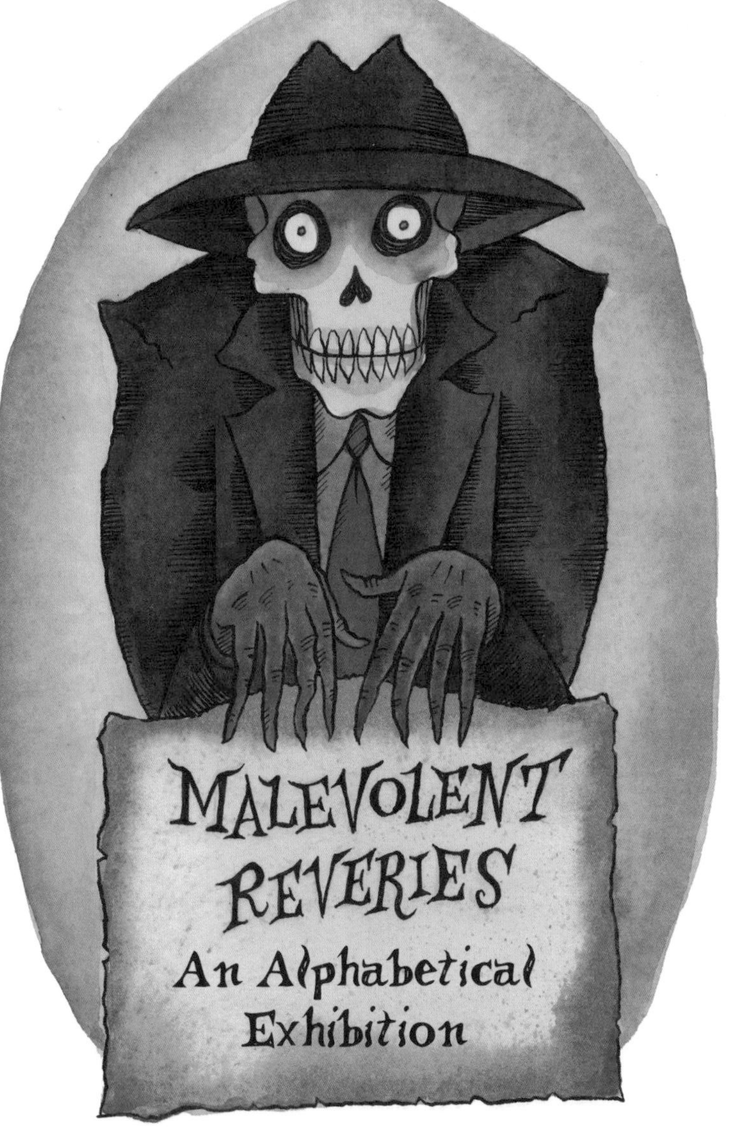
MALEVOLENT
REVERIES
An Alphabetical
Exhibition

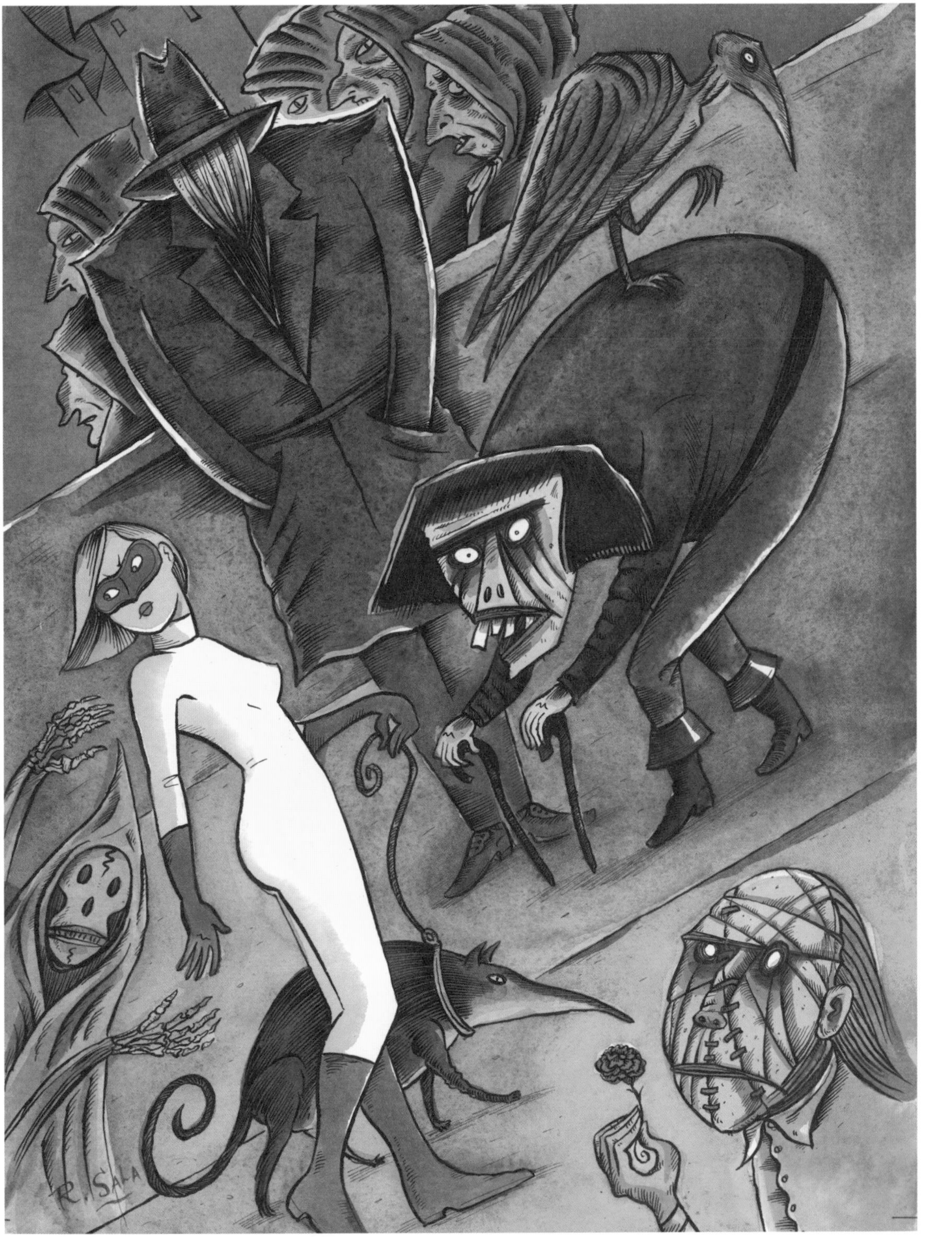
R. SALA

An Afternoon of Appalling Apparitions

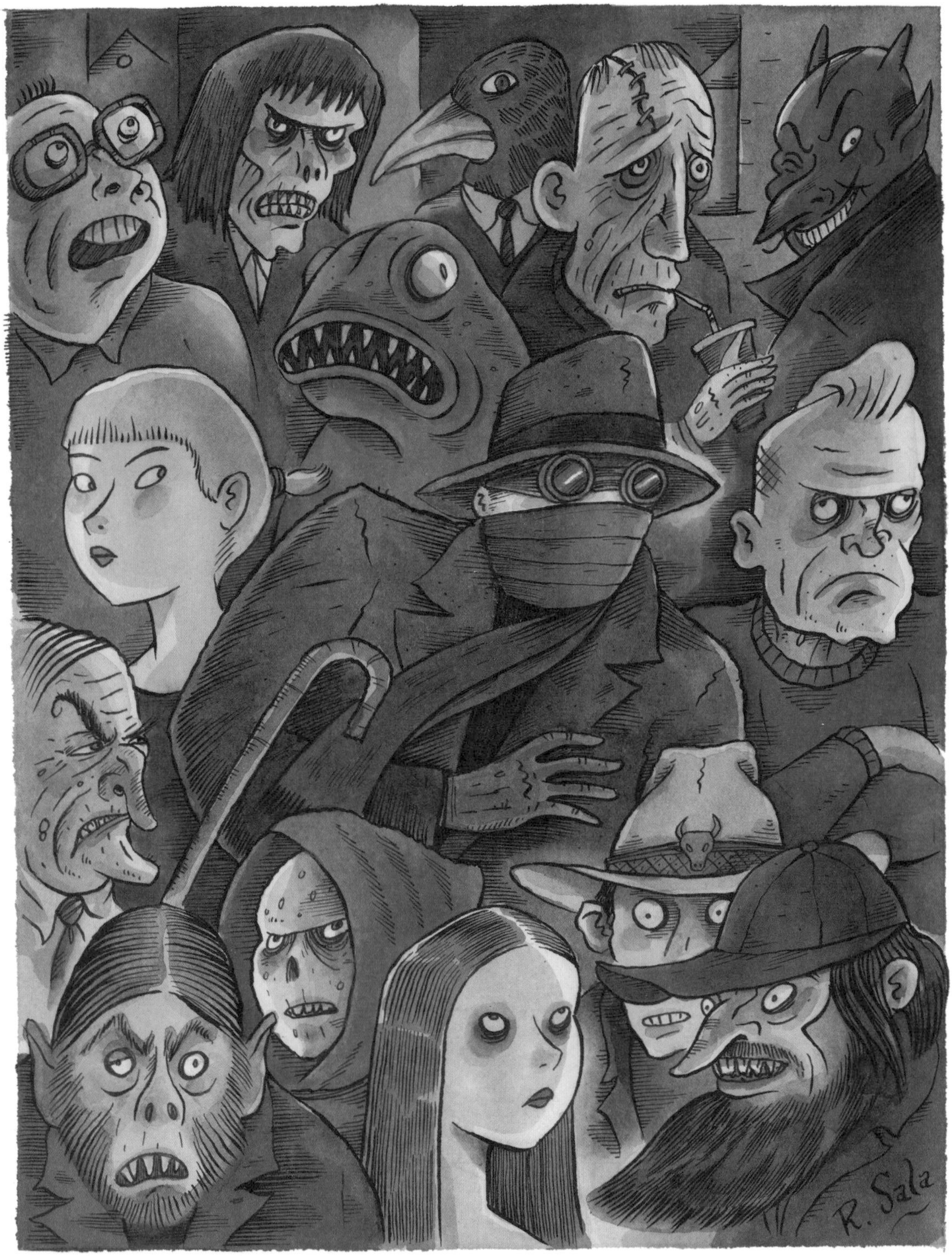
R. Sala
Bad Business Brewing

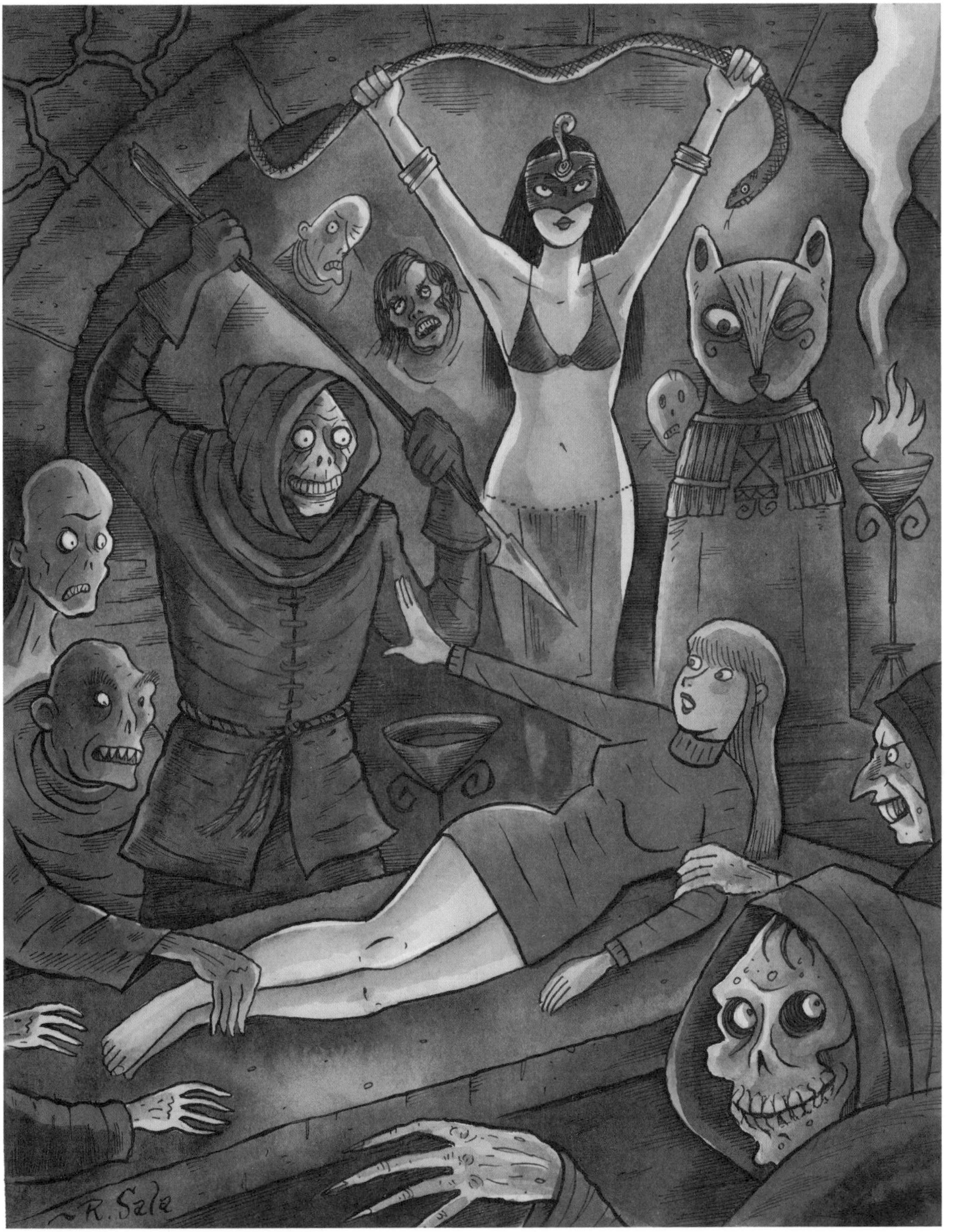
R. Sala

Cult of the Cyclopean Cat

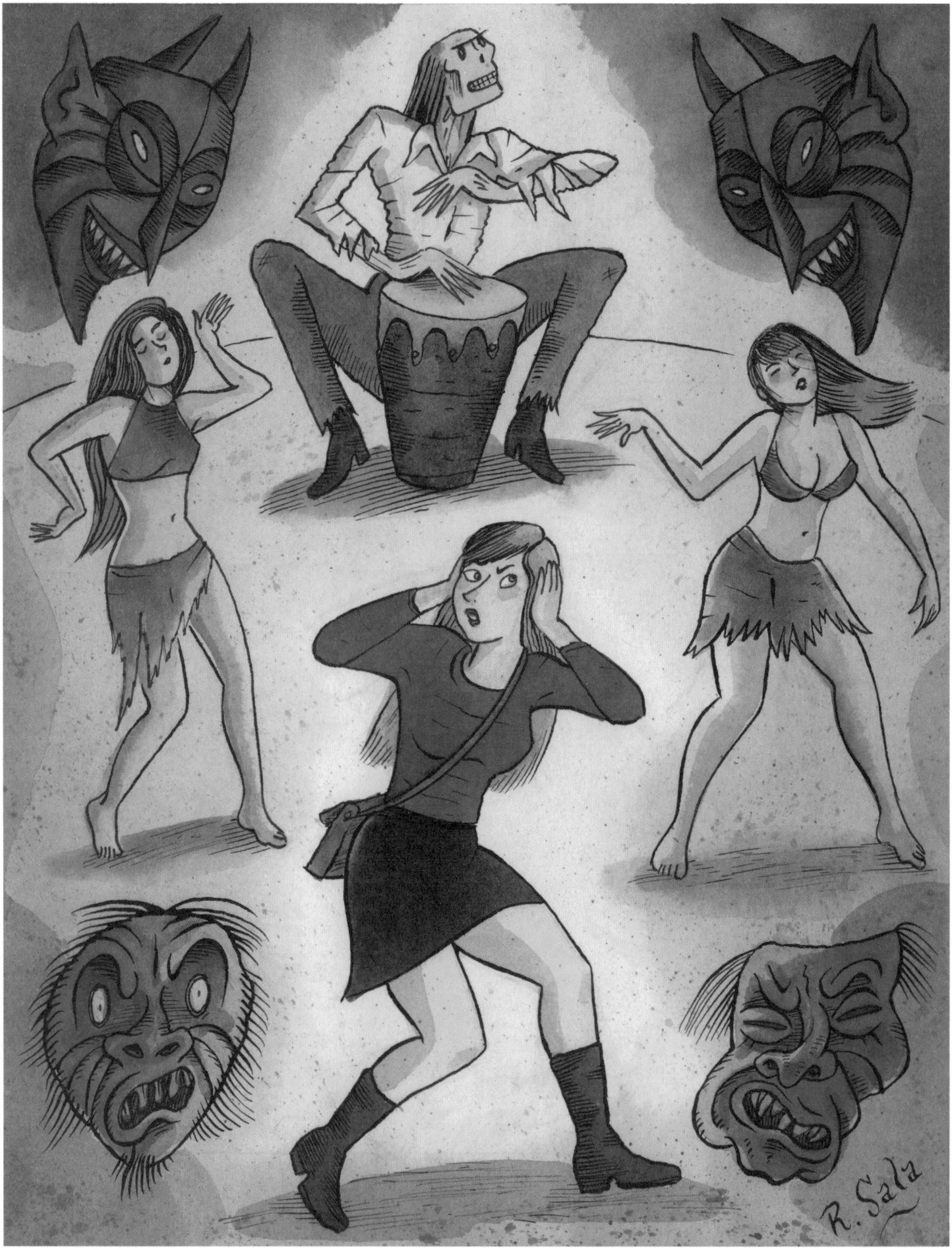
R. Sala

The Devil's Drum

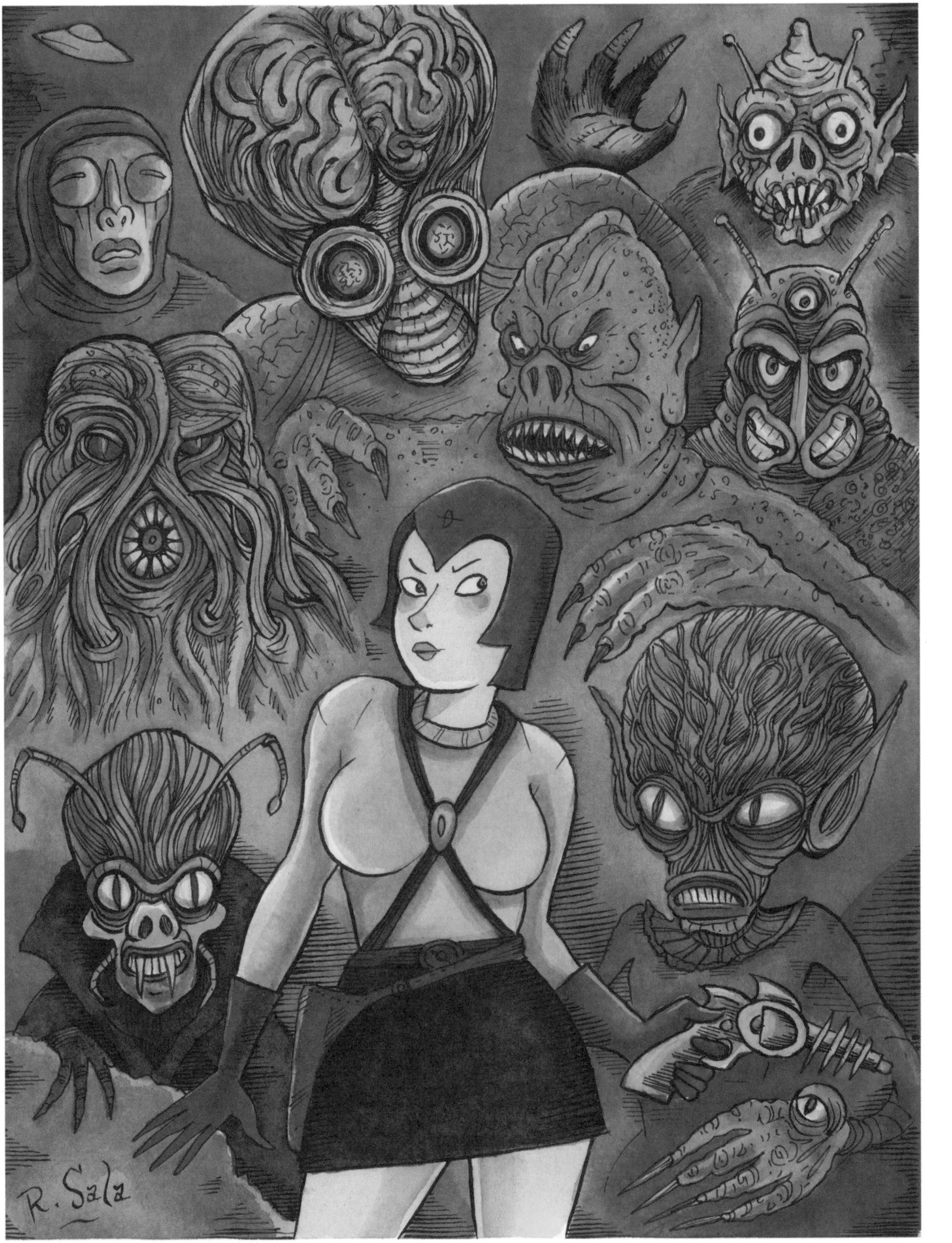
R. Sala
Extraterrestrials Everywhere

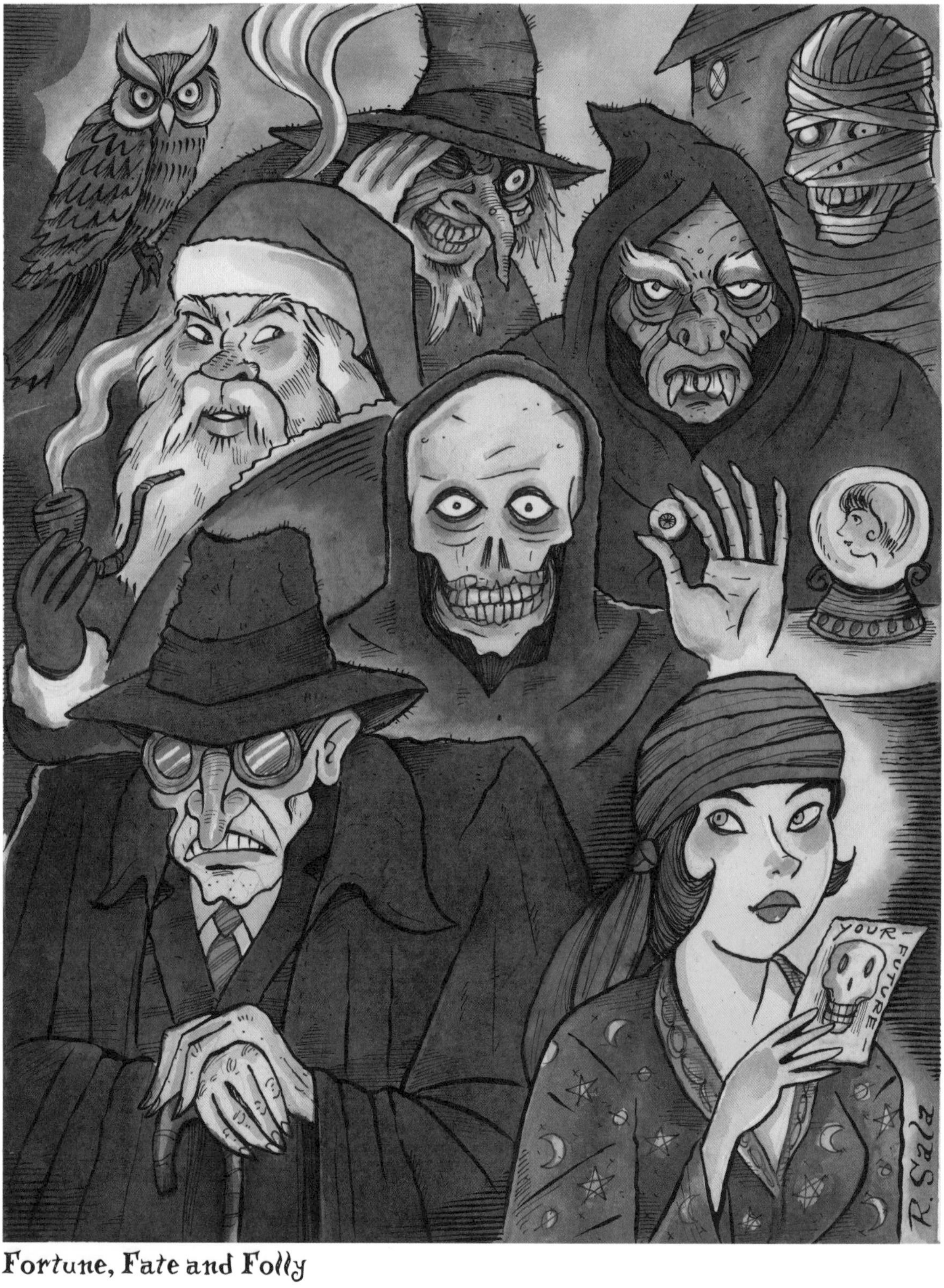
YOUR FUTURE
R. Sala

Fortune, Fate and Folly

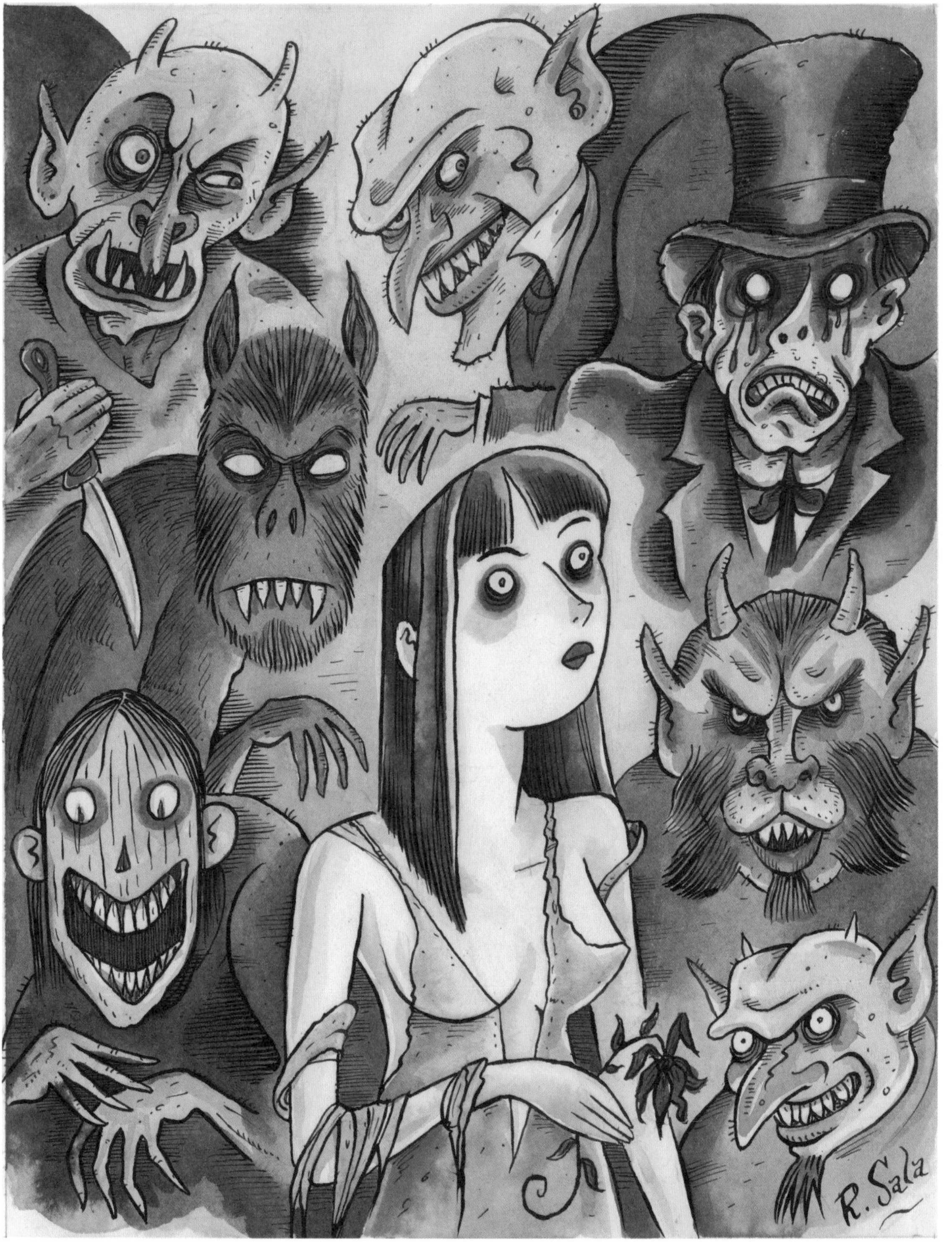
R. Sala

Gargoyles, Goblins and Ghosts

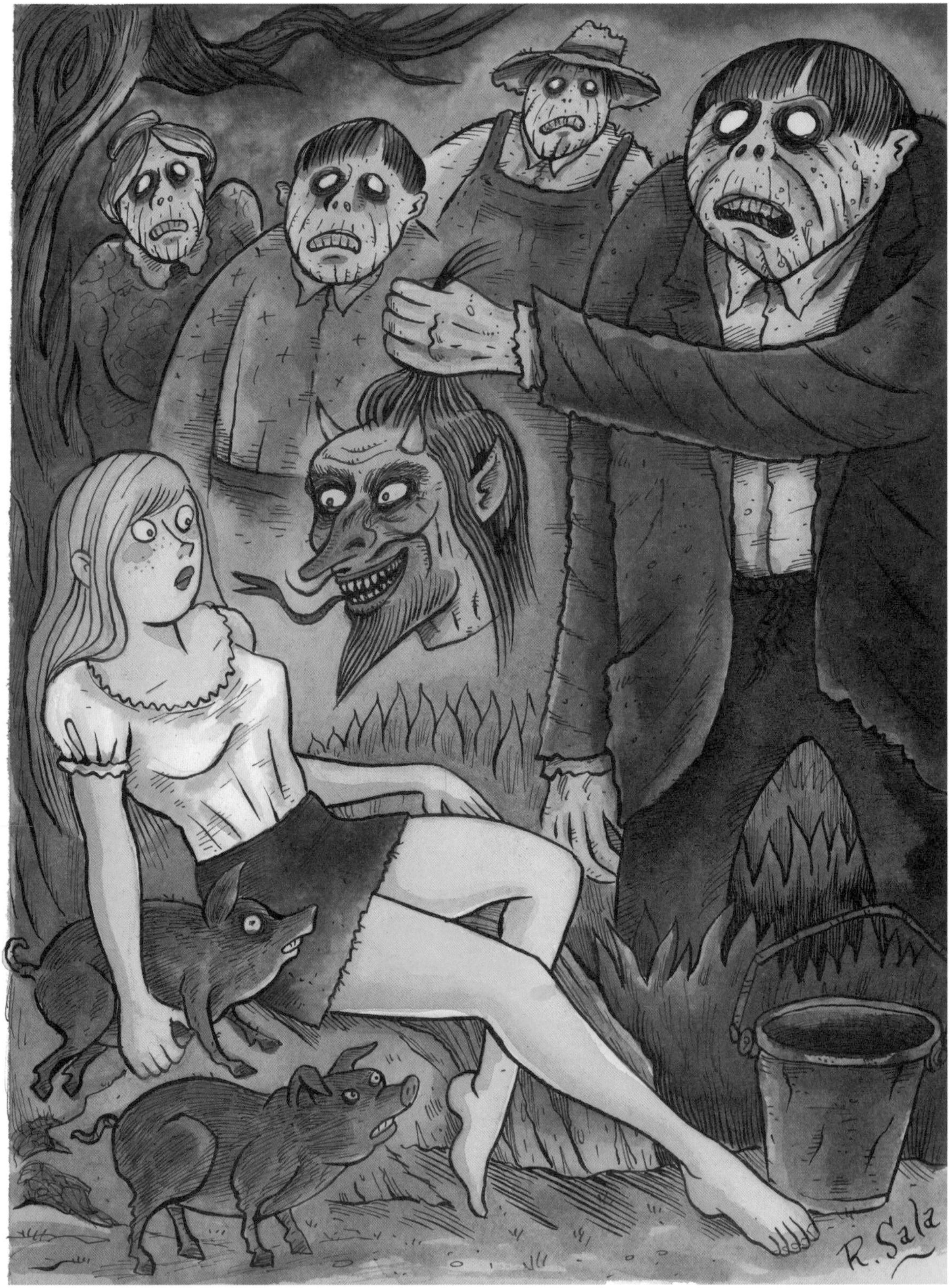
R. Sala
The Horrible Head of Hickory Hollow

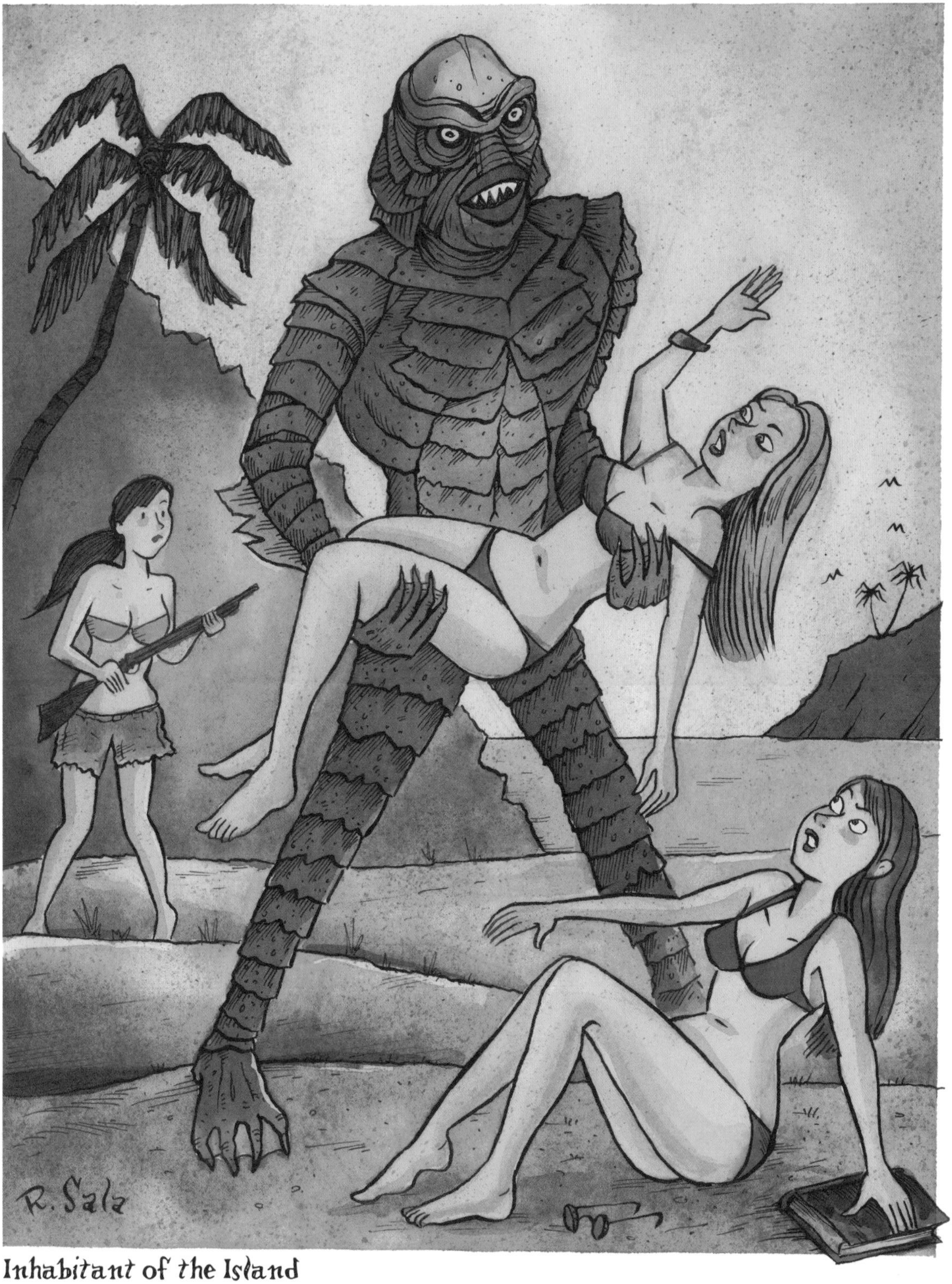
R. Sala

Inhabitant of the Island

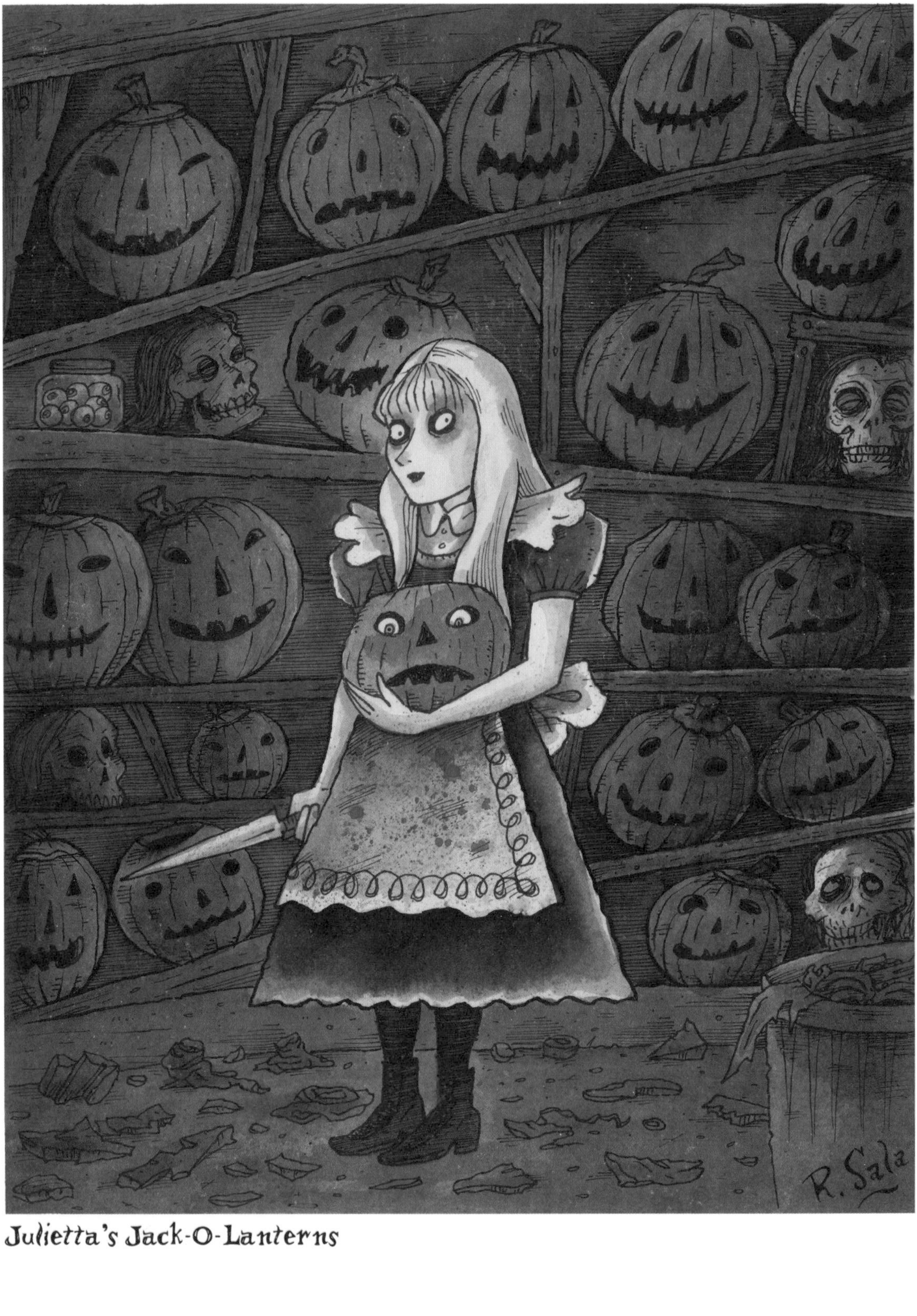
R. Sala

Julietta's Jack-O-Lanterns

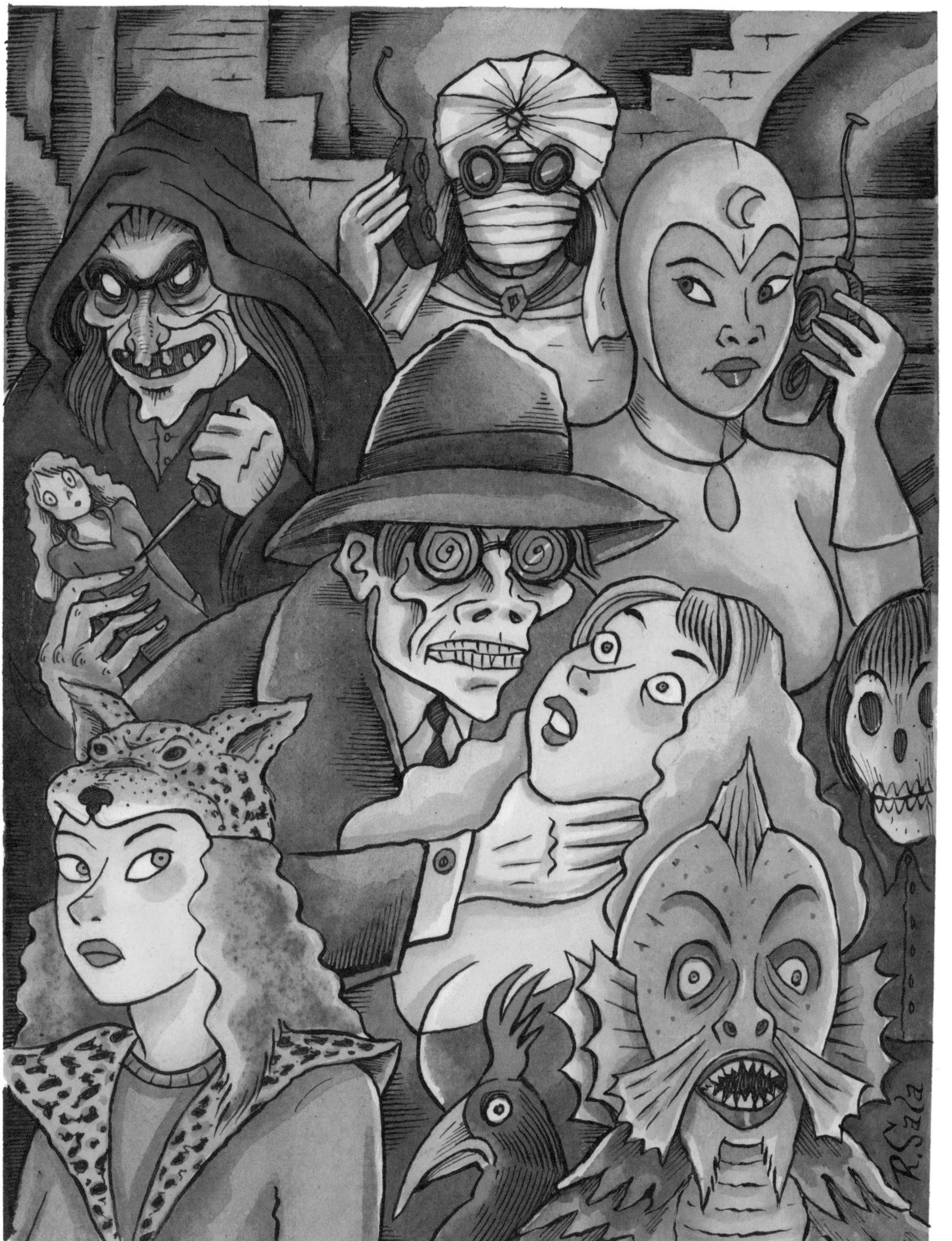
R. Sala
Killer with the Kaleidoscope Eyes

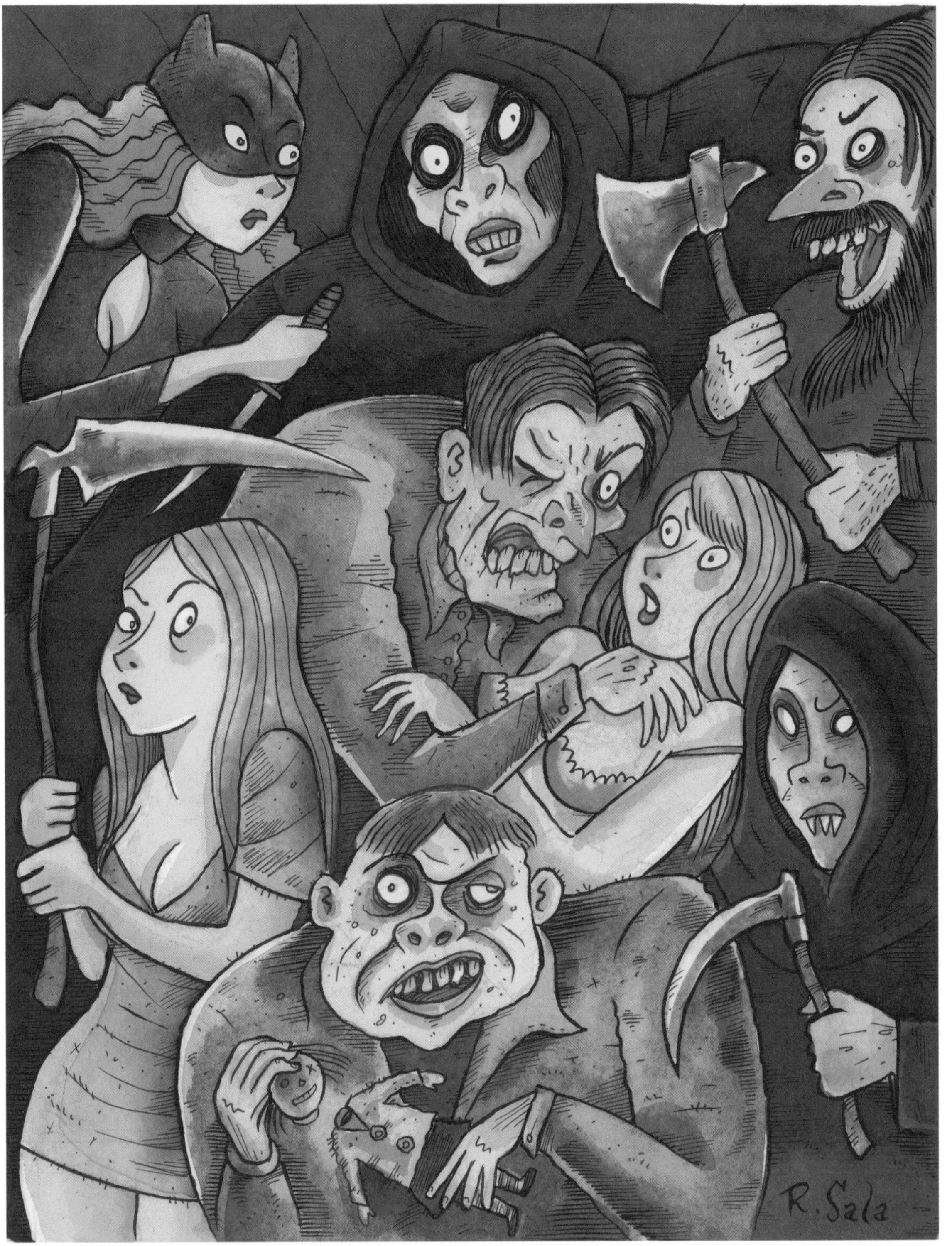
R. Sala
Labyrinth of Lunatics

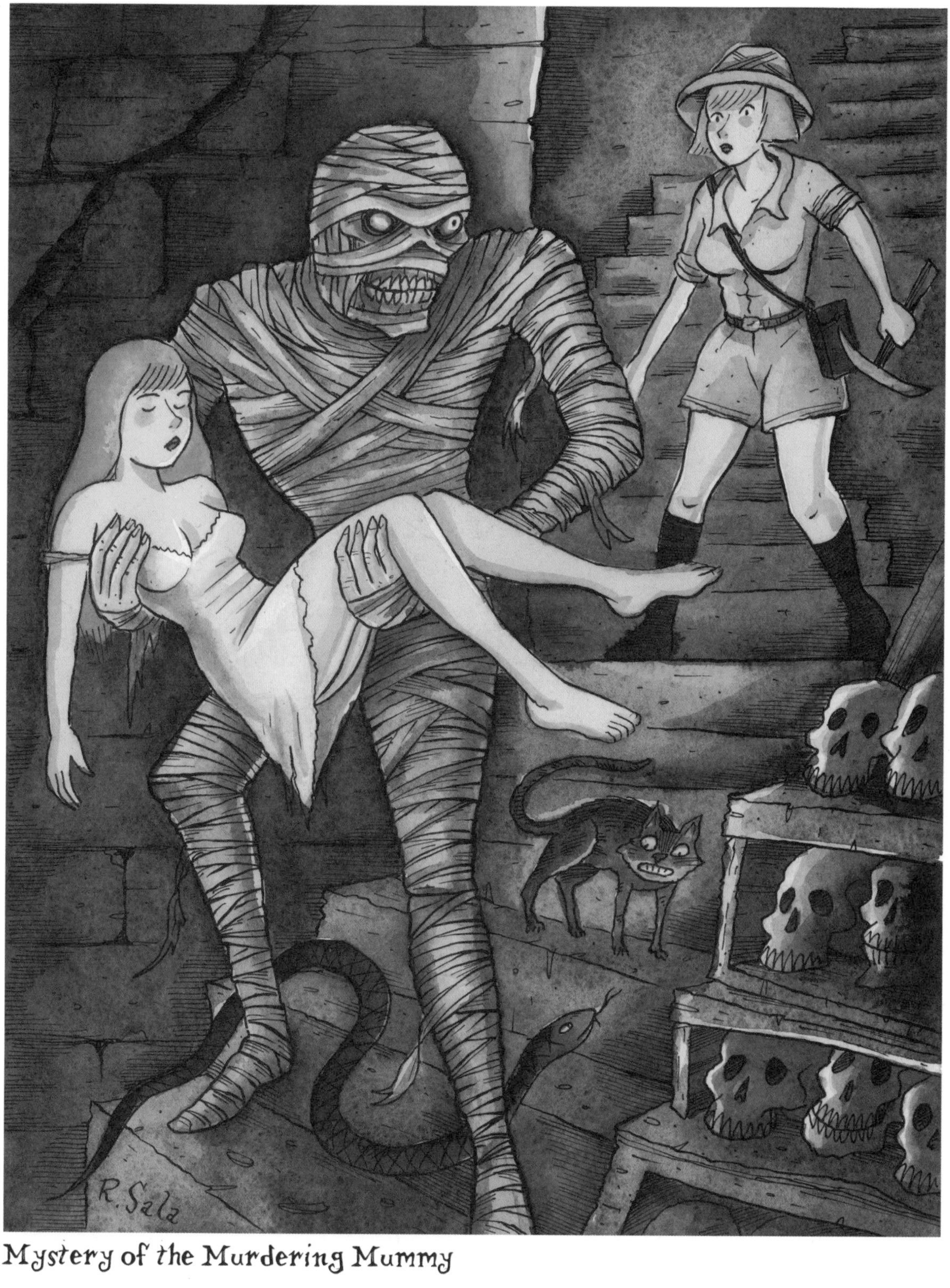
R. Sala
Mystery of the Murdering Mummy

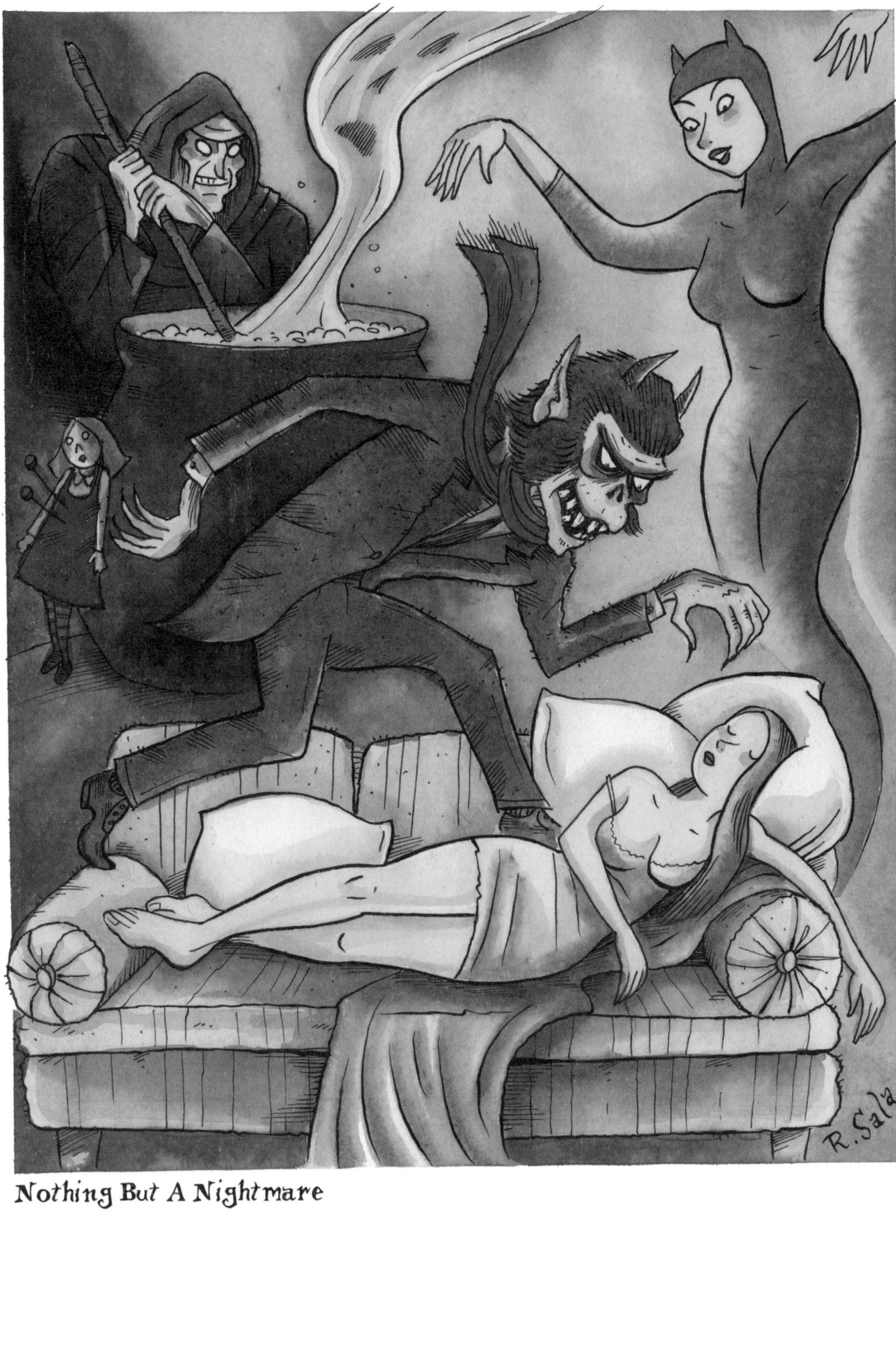
R. Sala

Nothing But A Nightmare

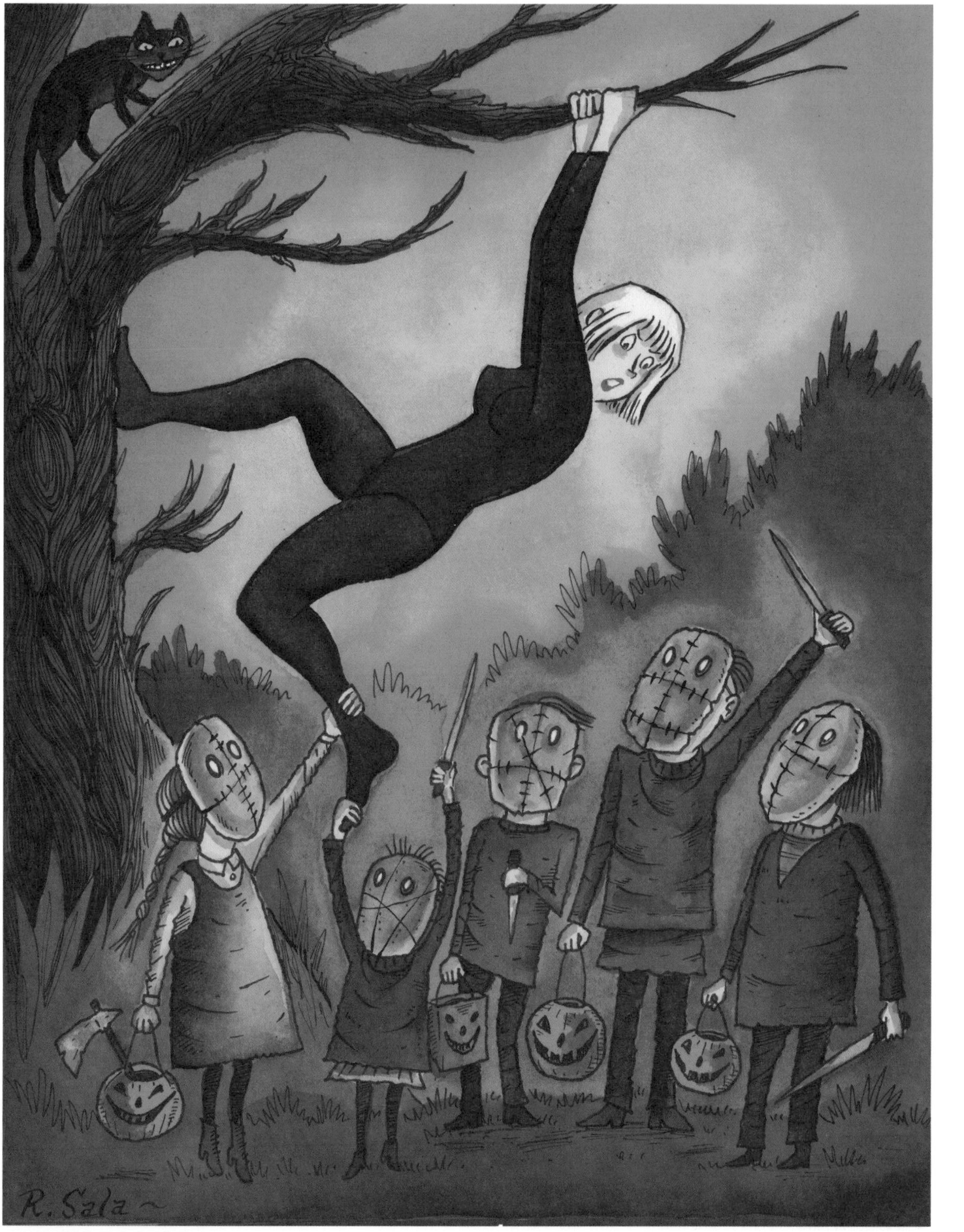
R. Sala

October Orphans

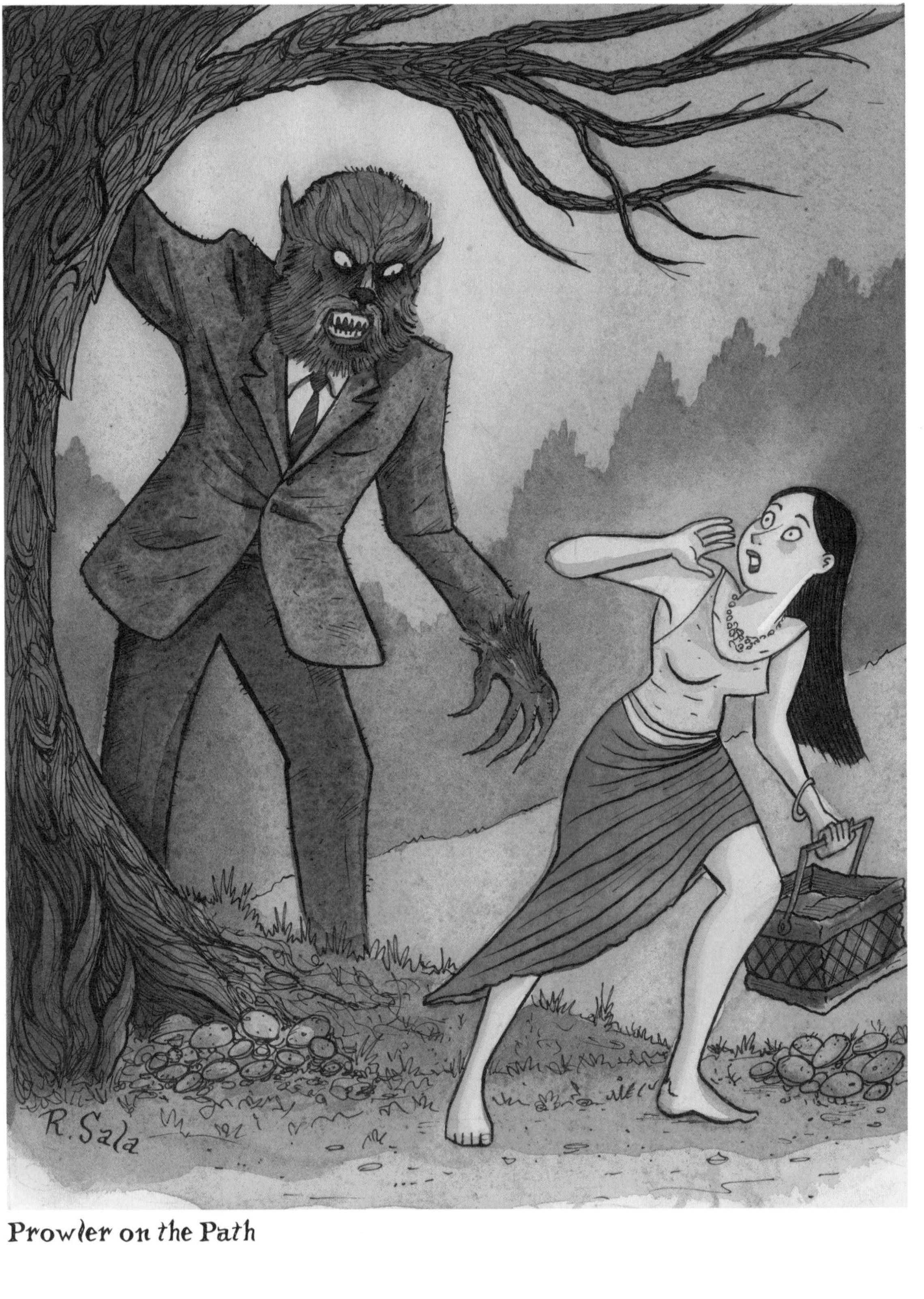
R. Sala

Prowler on the Path

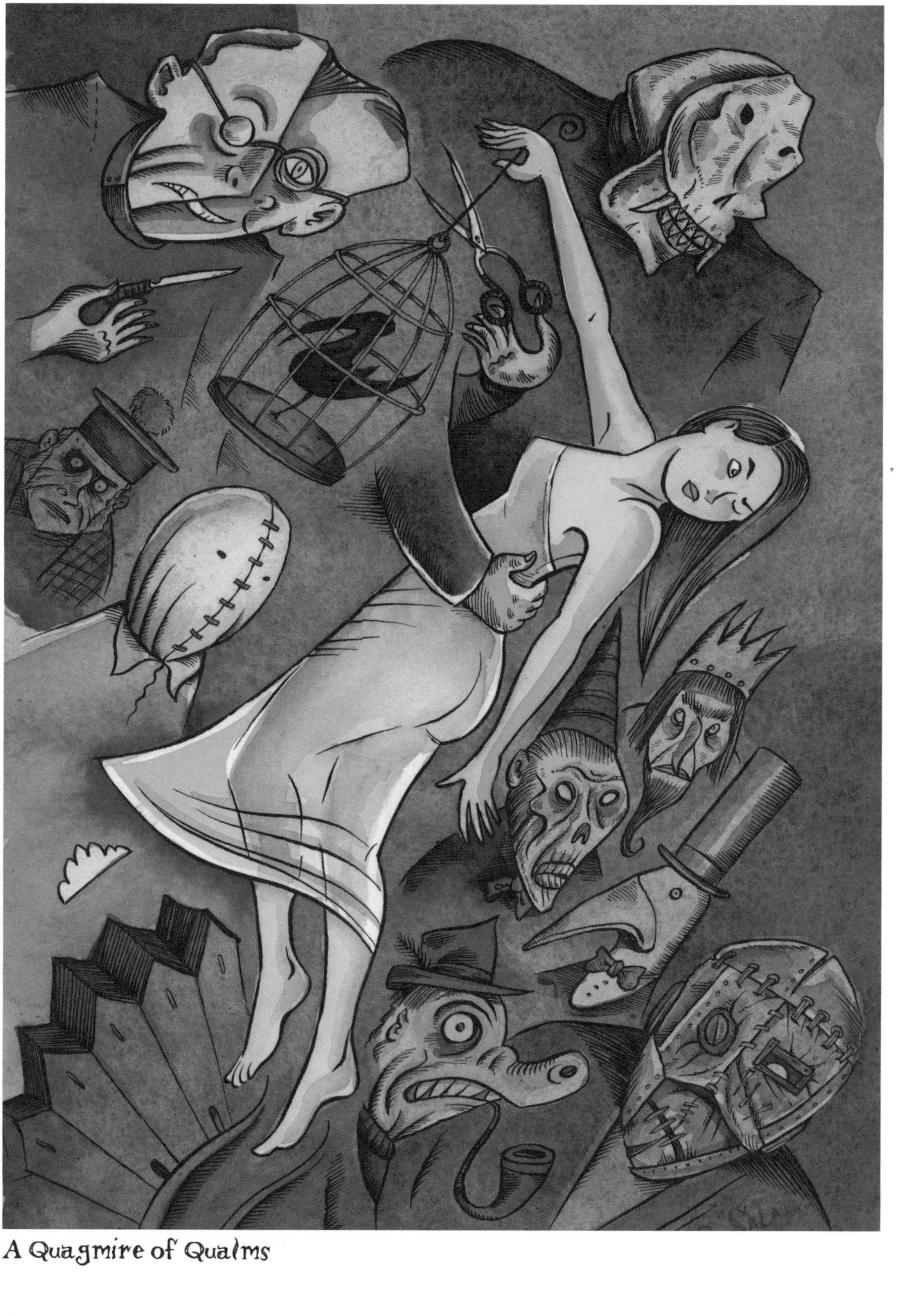

A Quagmire of Qualms

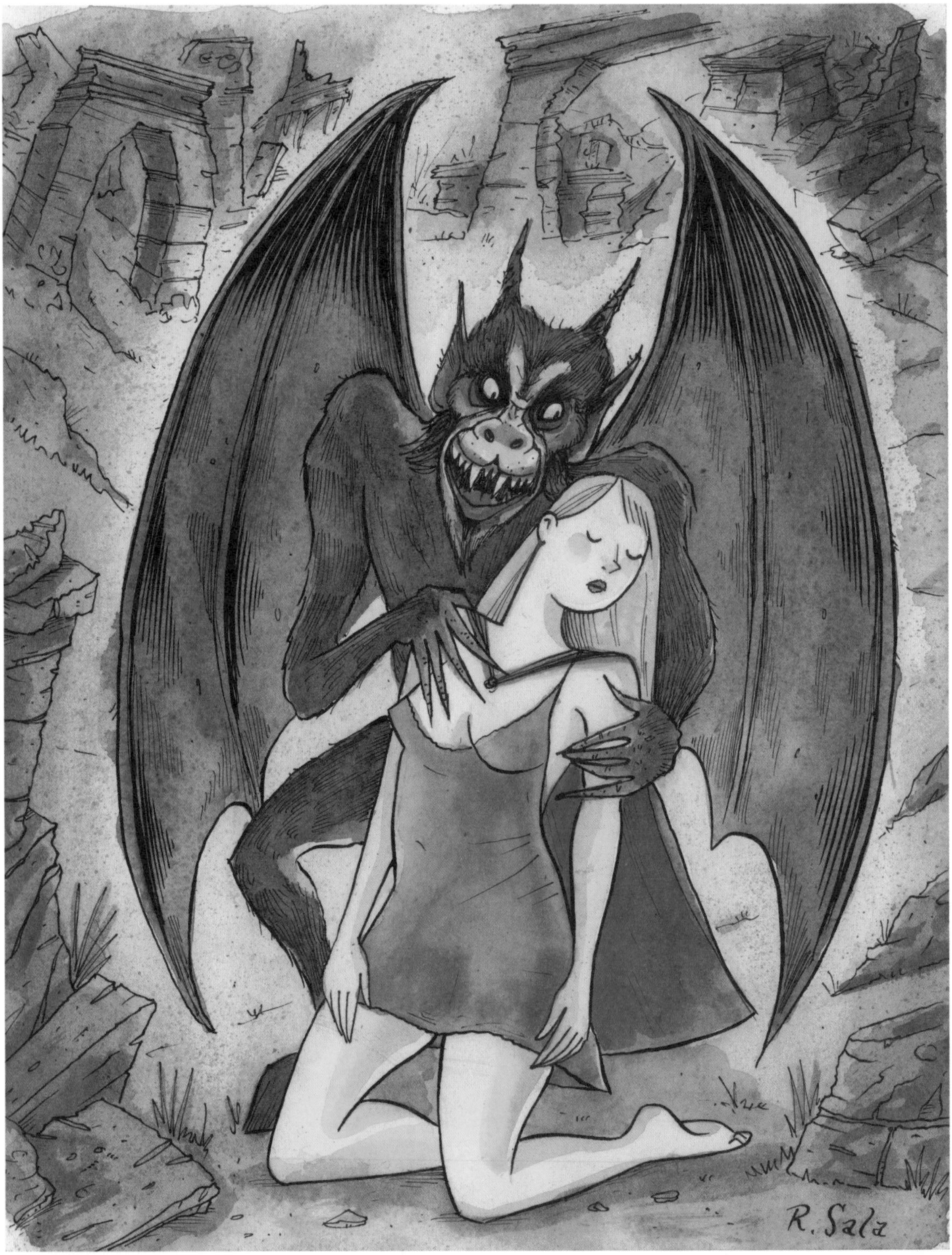
R. Sala

Resident of the Ruins

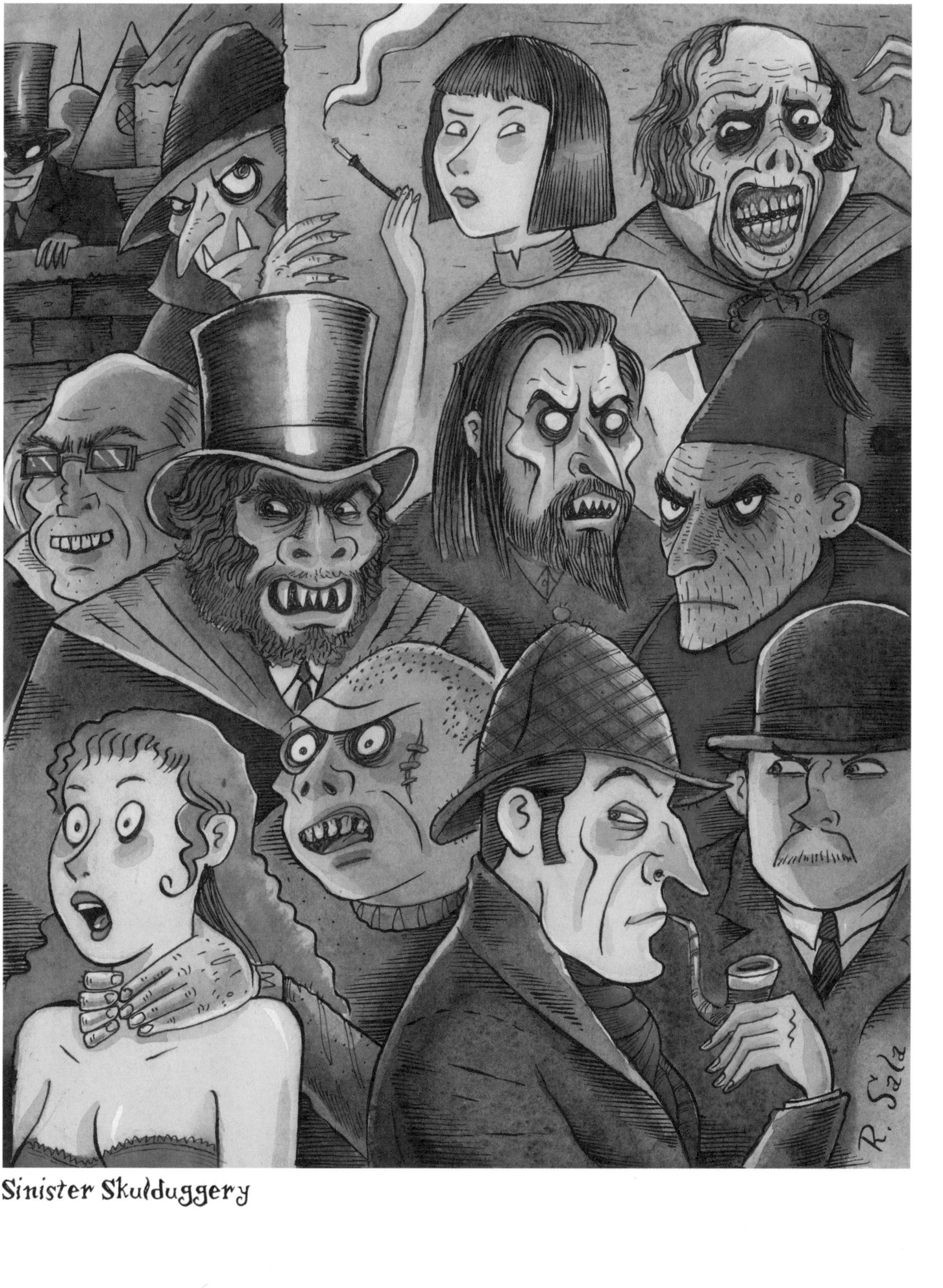
R. Sala

Sinister Skulduggery

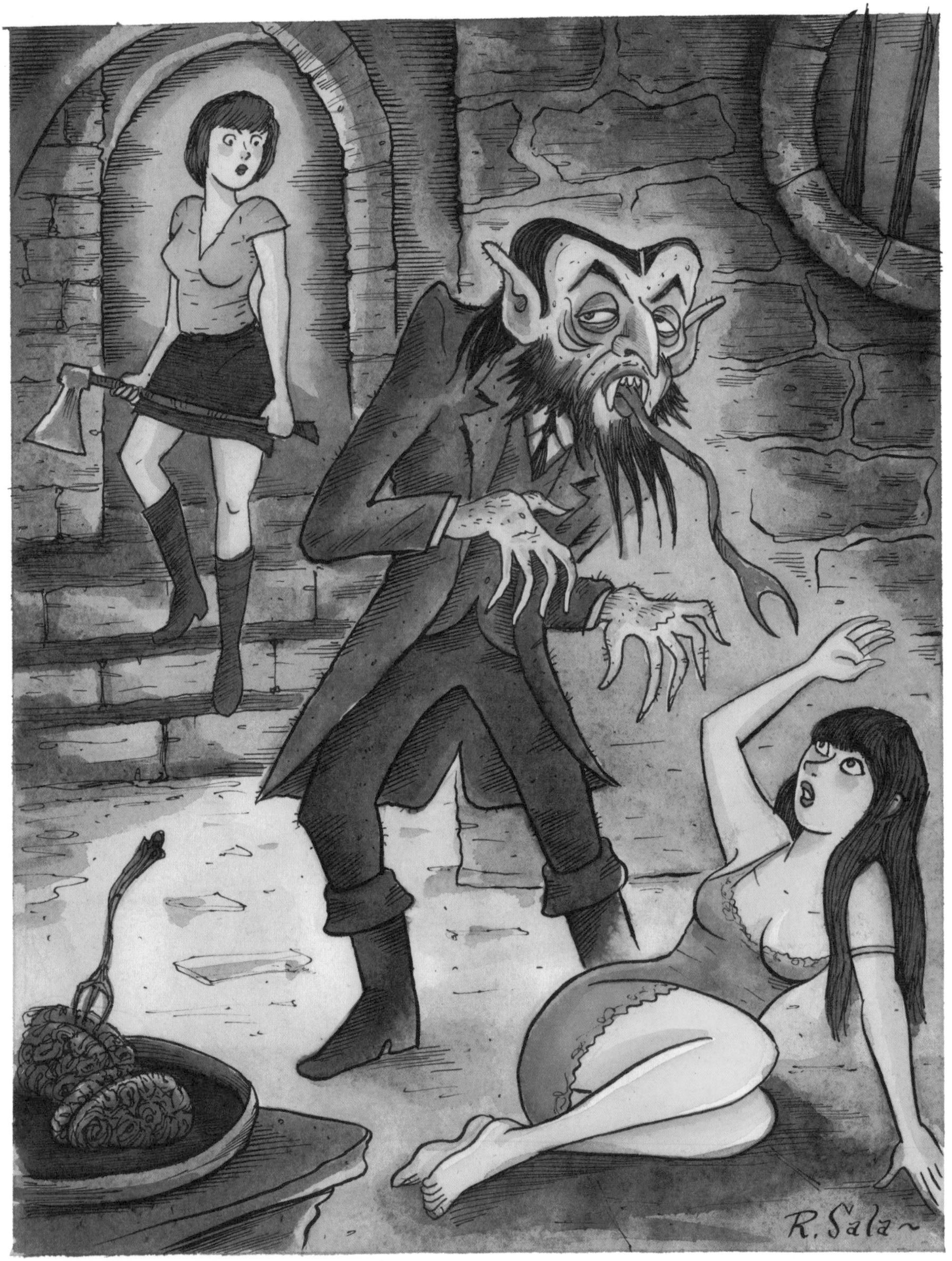
R. Sala
The Terrible Thing in the Tower

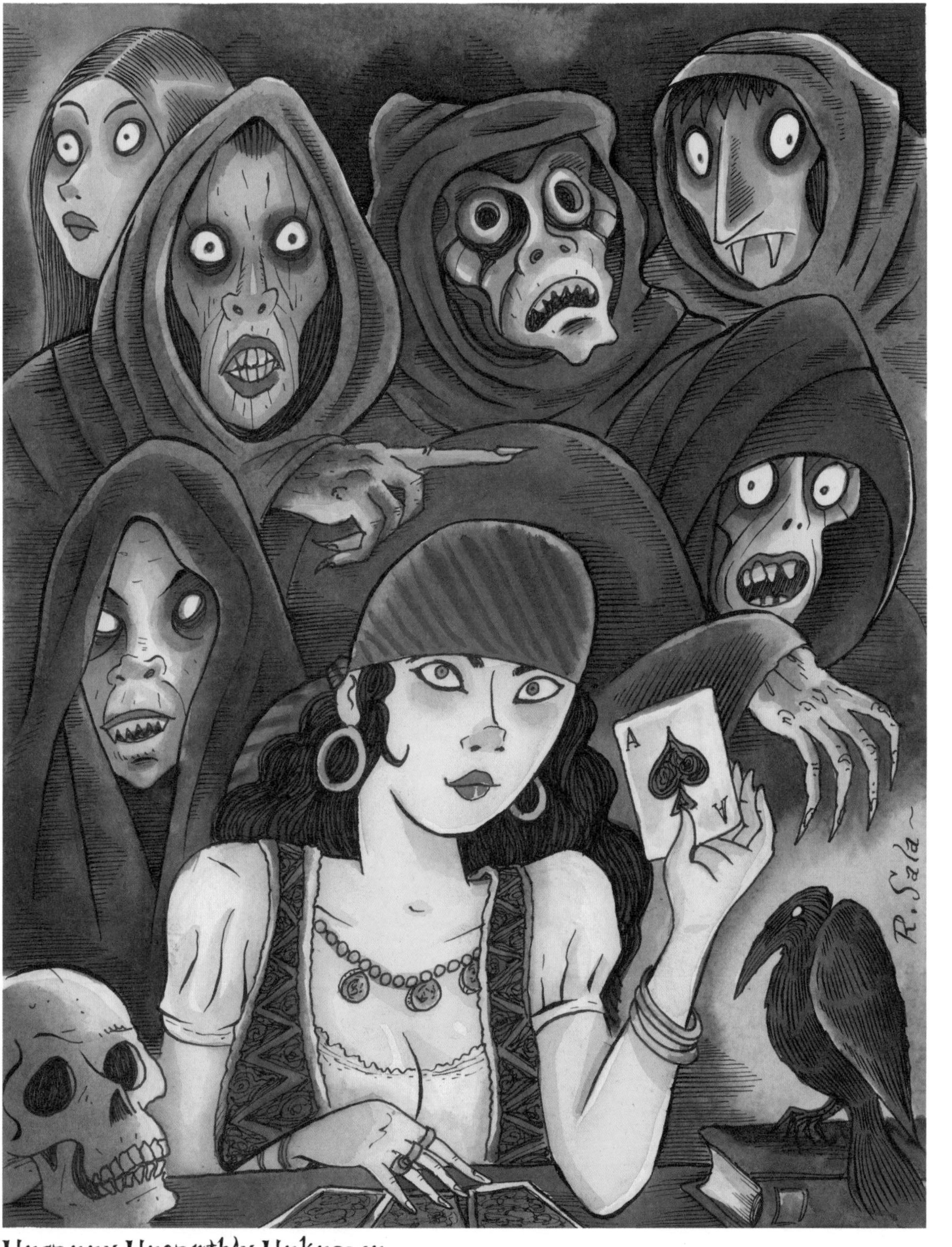
A
A
R. Sala
Uncanny Unearthly Unknown

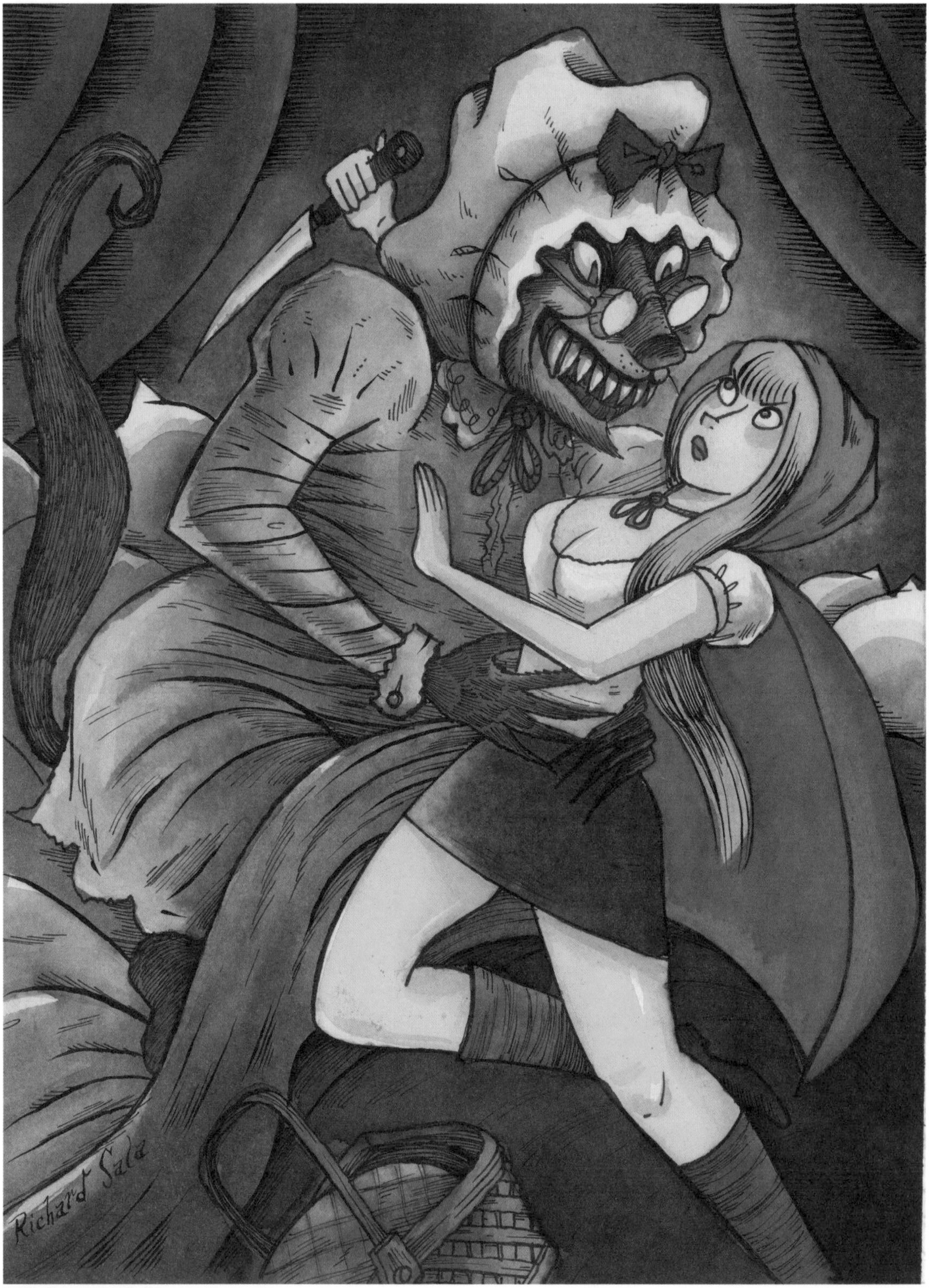
Richard Sala

Violent Visit

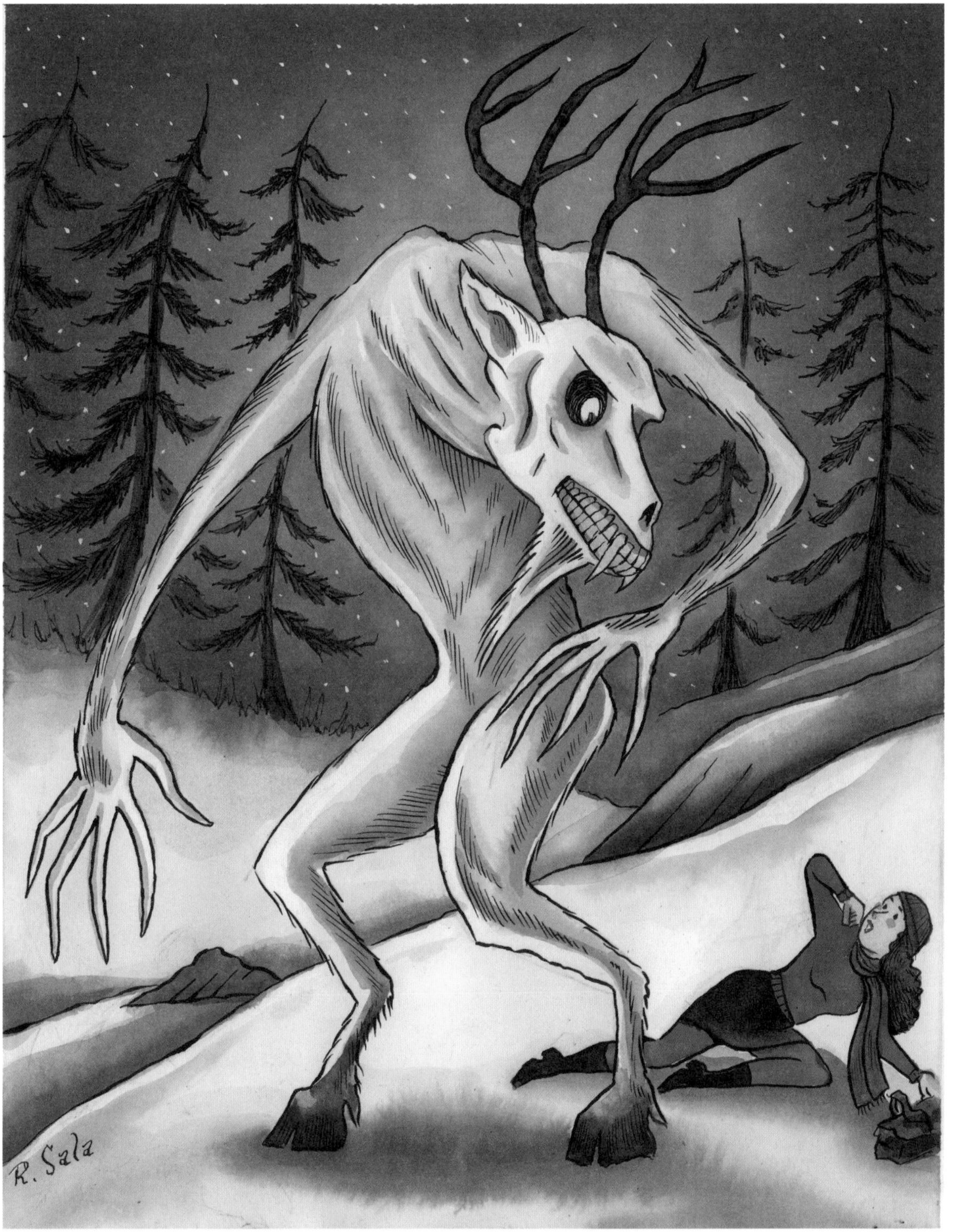
R. Sala

Winter of the Wendigo

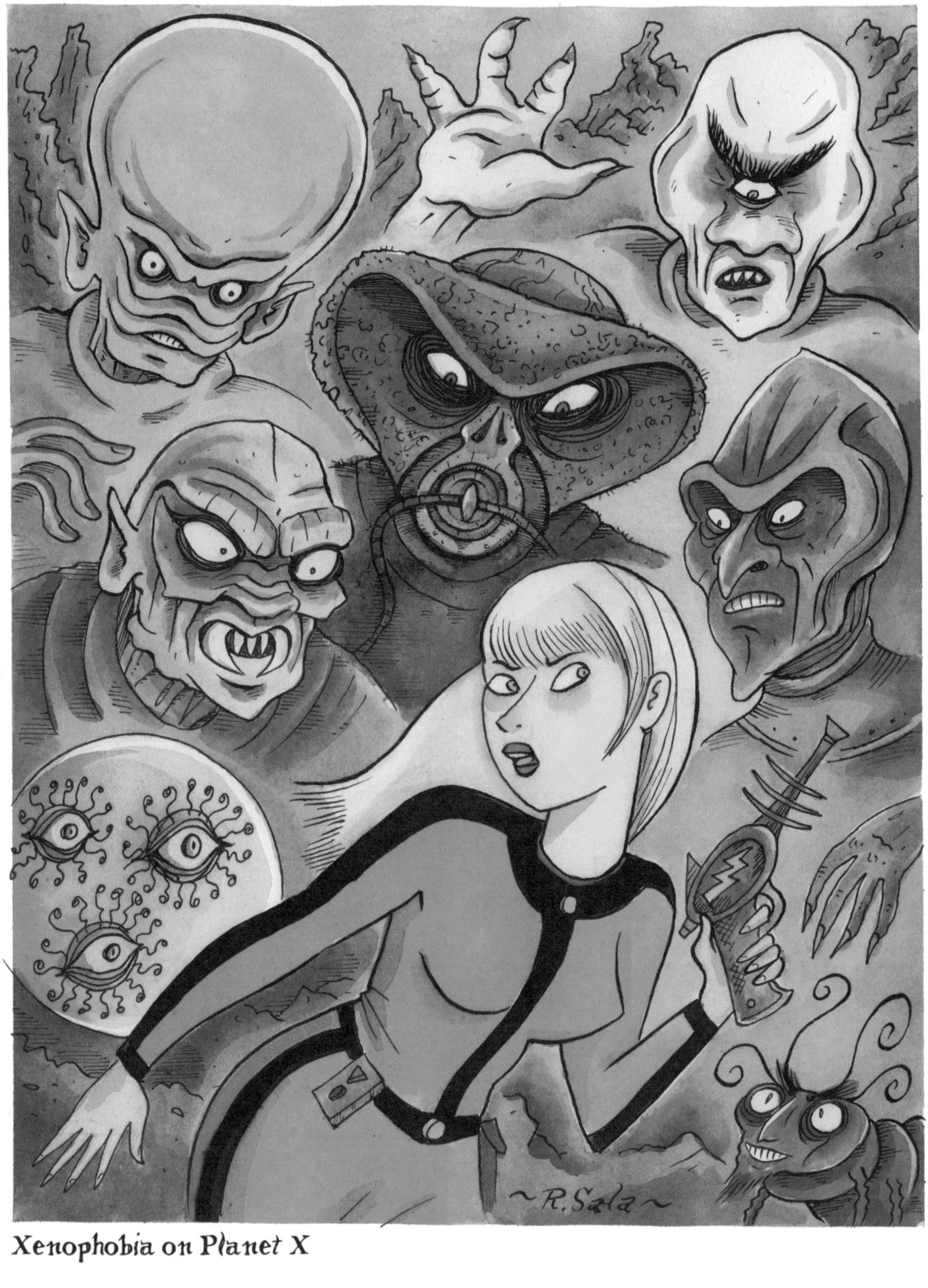
~R.Sala~

Xenophobia on Planet X

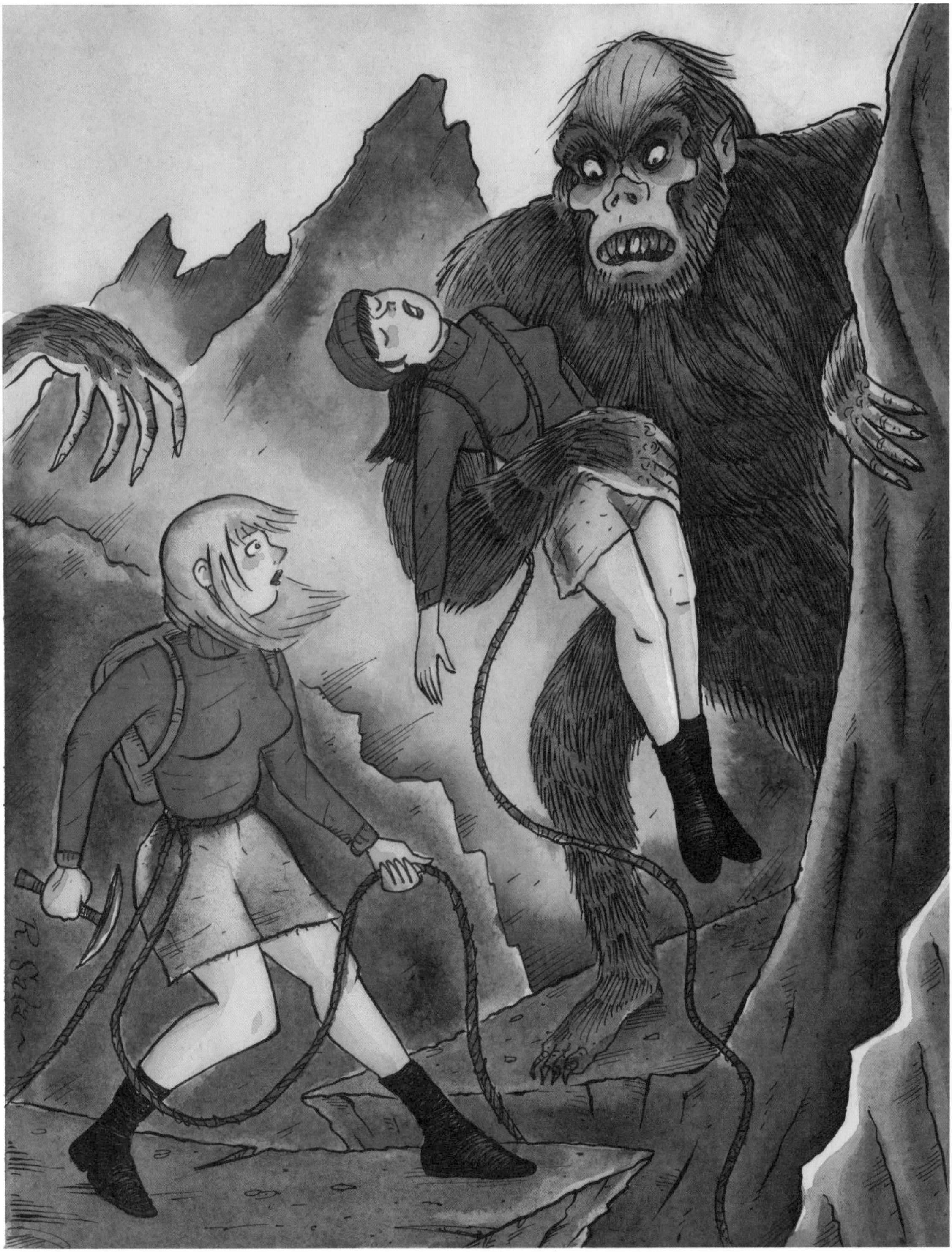

You Found The Yeti

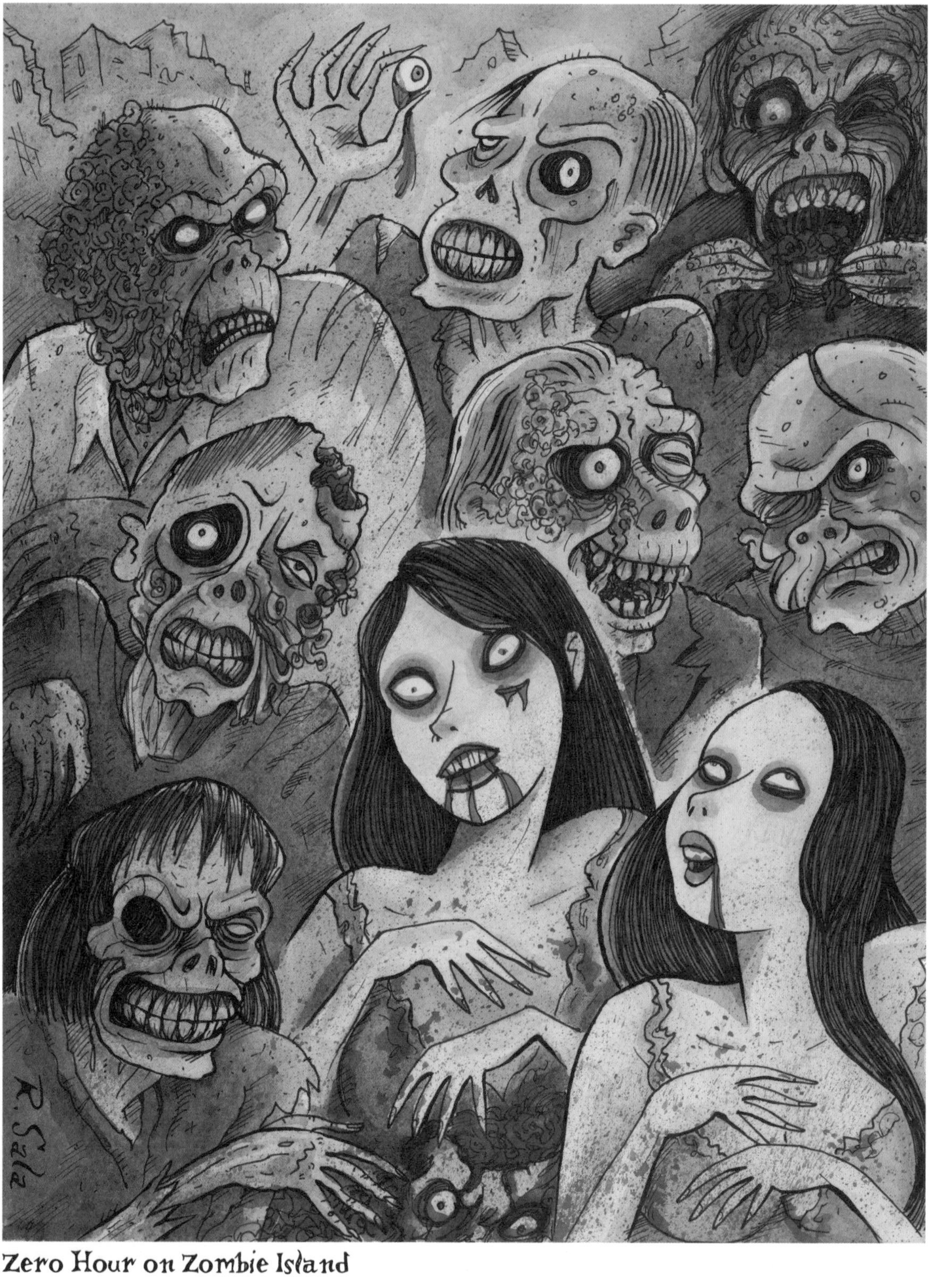
R. Sala

Zero Hour on Zombie Island

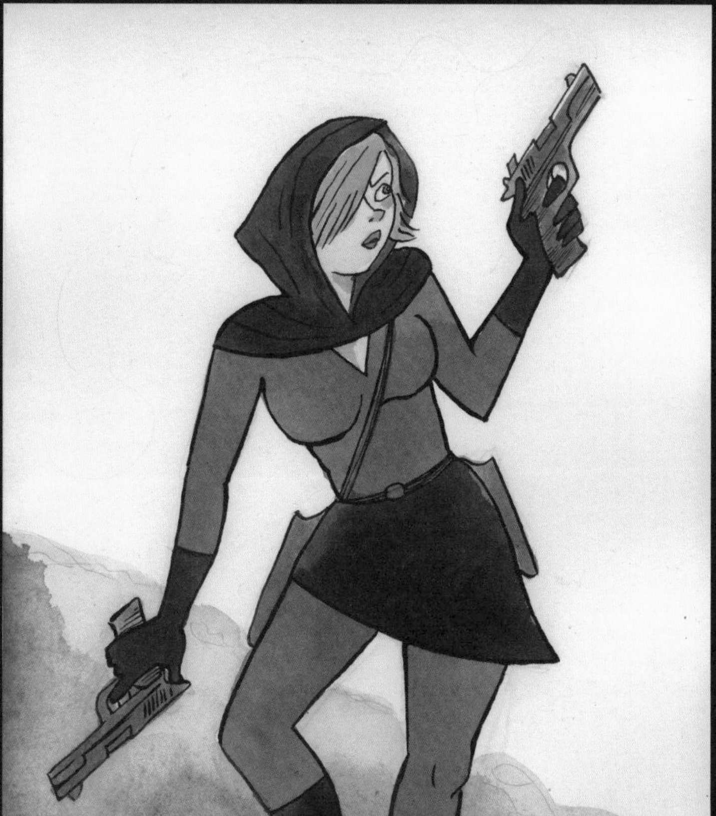
R. Sala

VIOLENZIA RETURNS

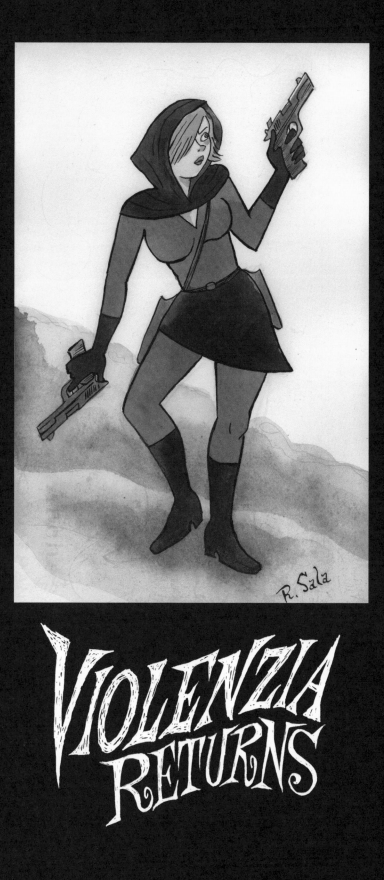

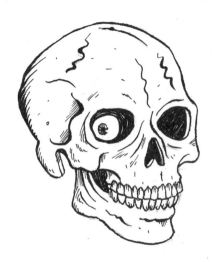

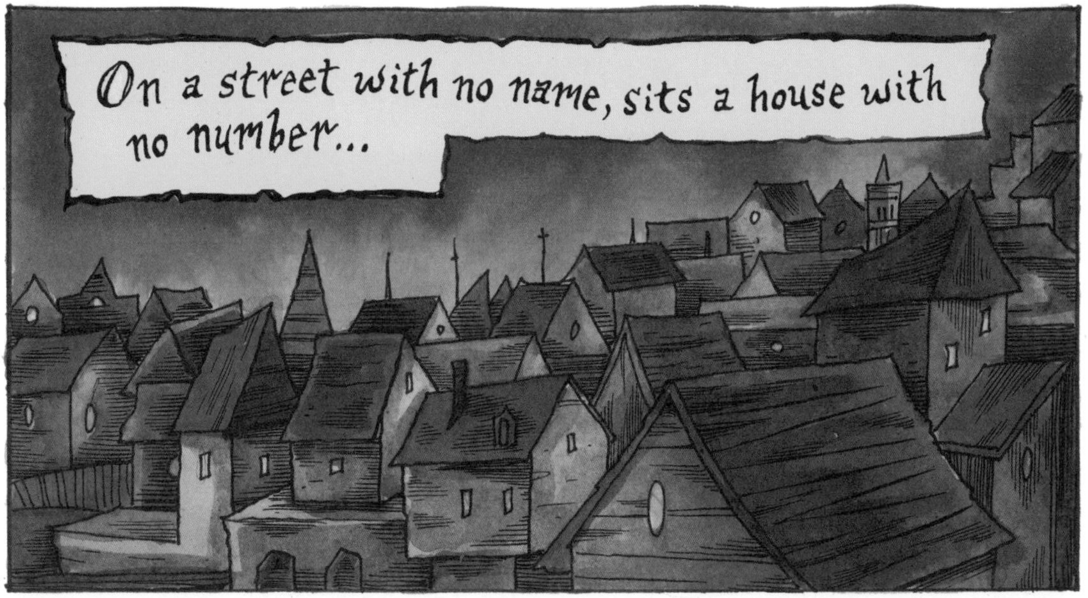
On a street with no name, sits a house with no number...

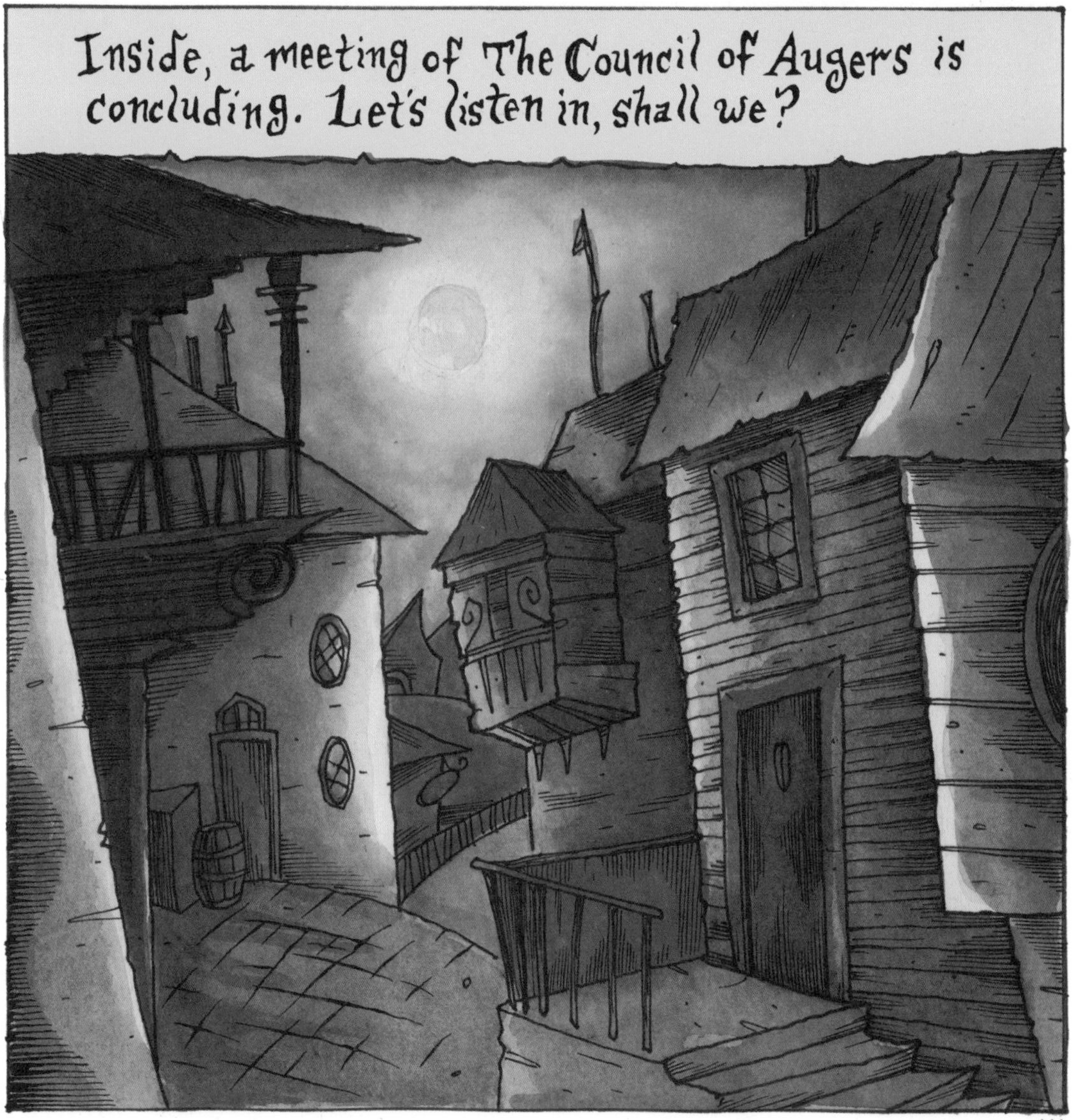
Inside, a meeting of The Council of Augers is concluding. Let's listen in, shall we?

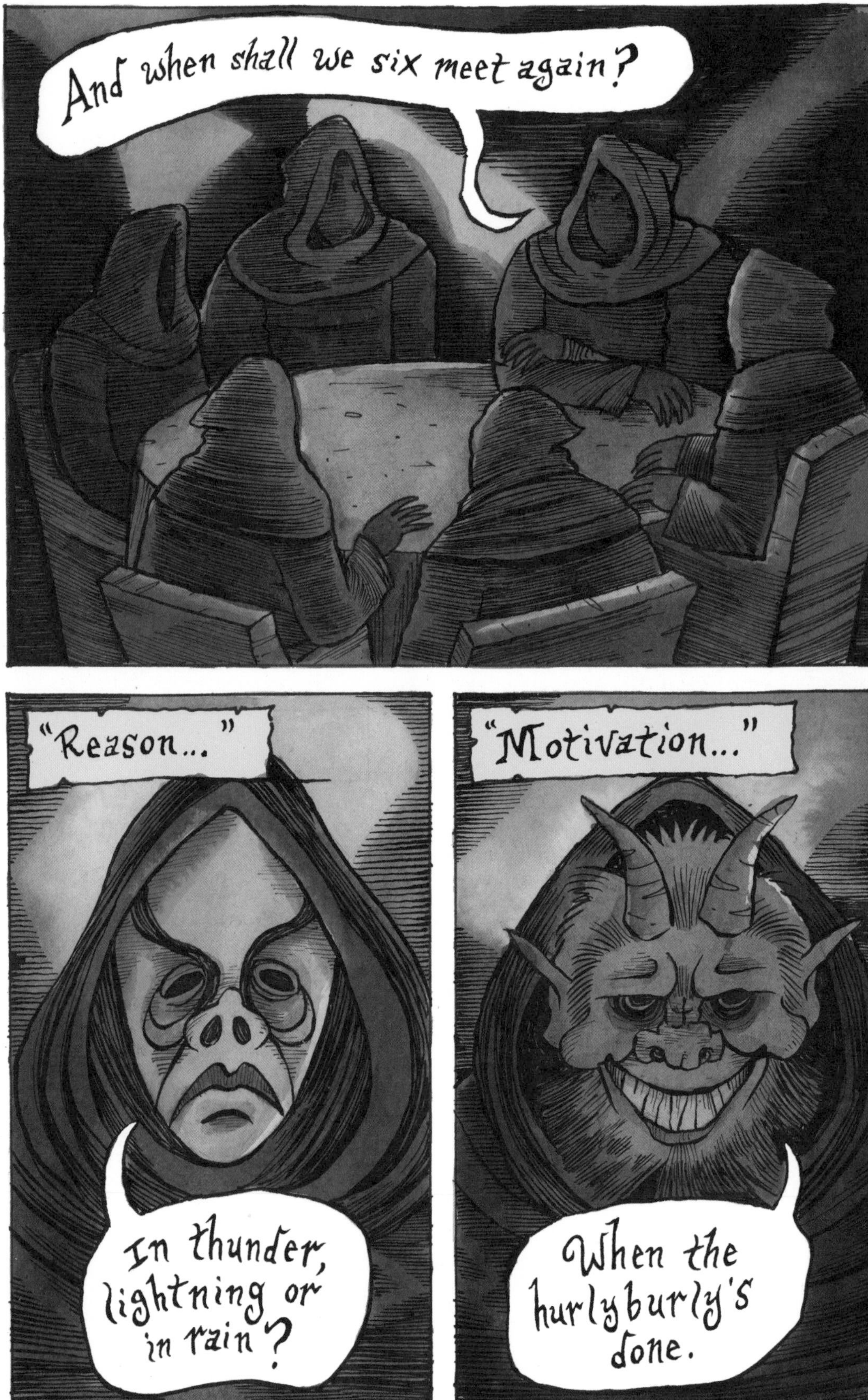
And when shall we six meet again?
"Reason..."
In thunder, lightning or in rain?
"Motivation..."
When the hurlyburly's done.

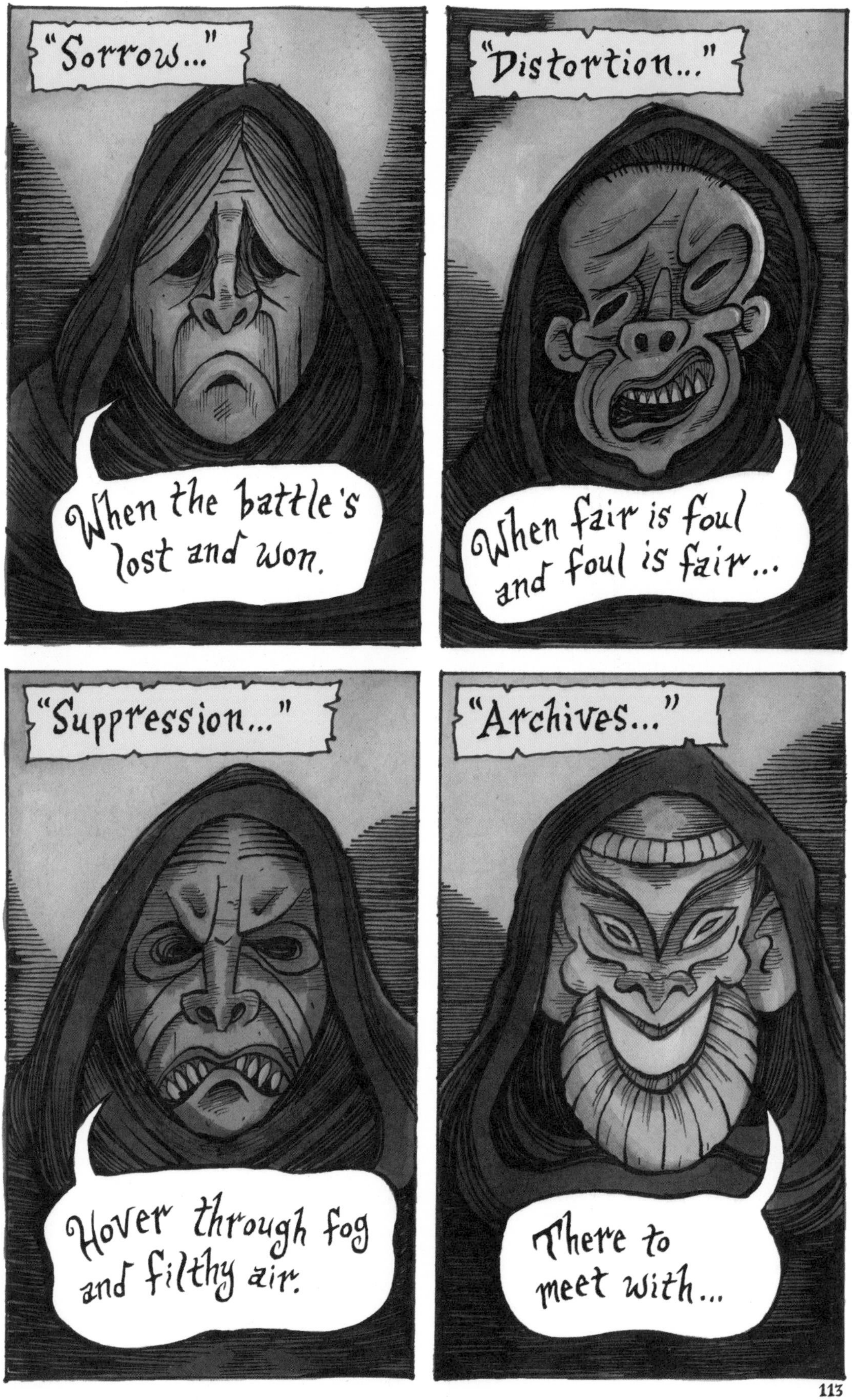
"Sorrow..."
When the battle's lost and won.
"Distortion..."
When fair is foul and foul is fair...
"Suppression..."
Hover through fog and filthy air.
"Archives..."
There to meet with...

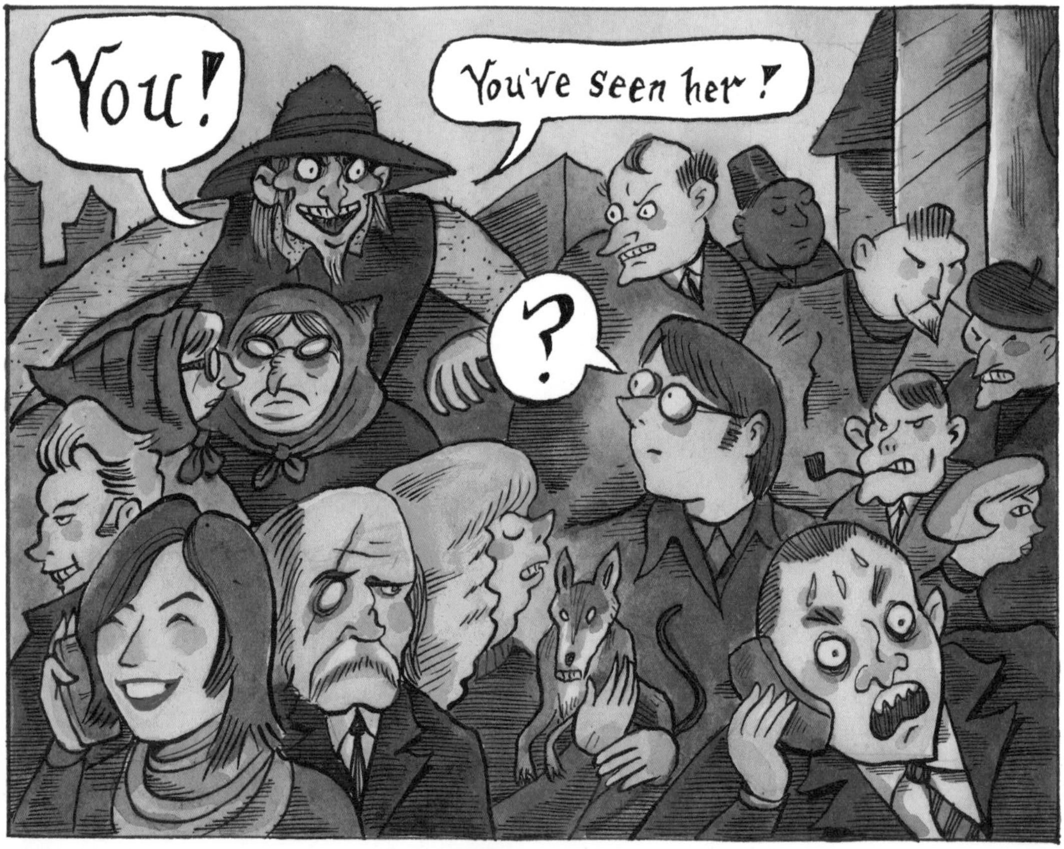
You!
You've seen her!
?
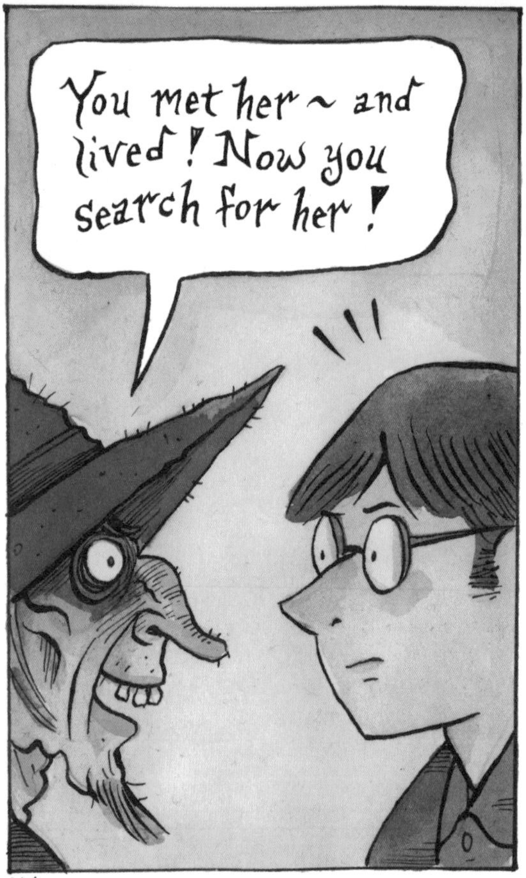
You met her ~ and lived! Now you search for her!
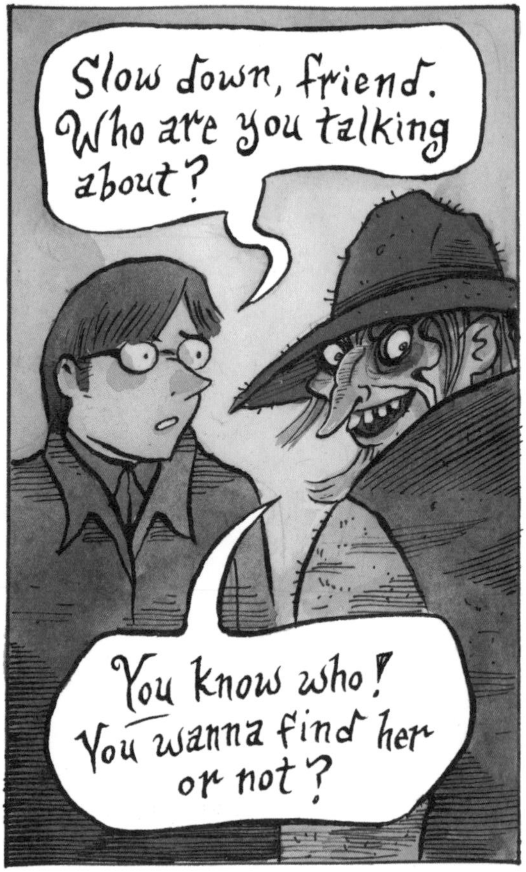
Slow down, friend. Who are you talking about?
You know who! You wanna find her or not?

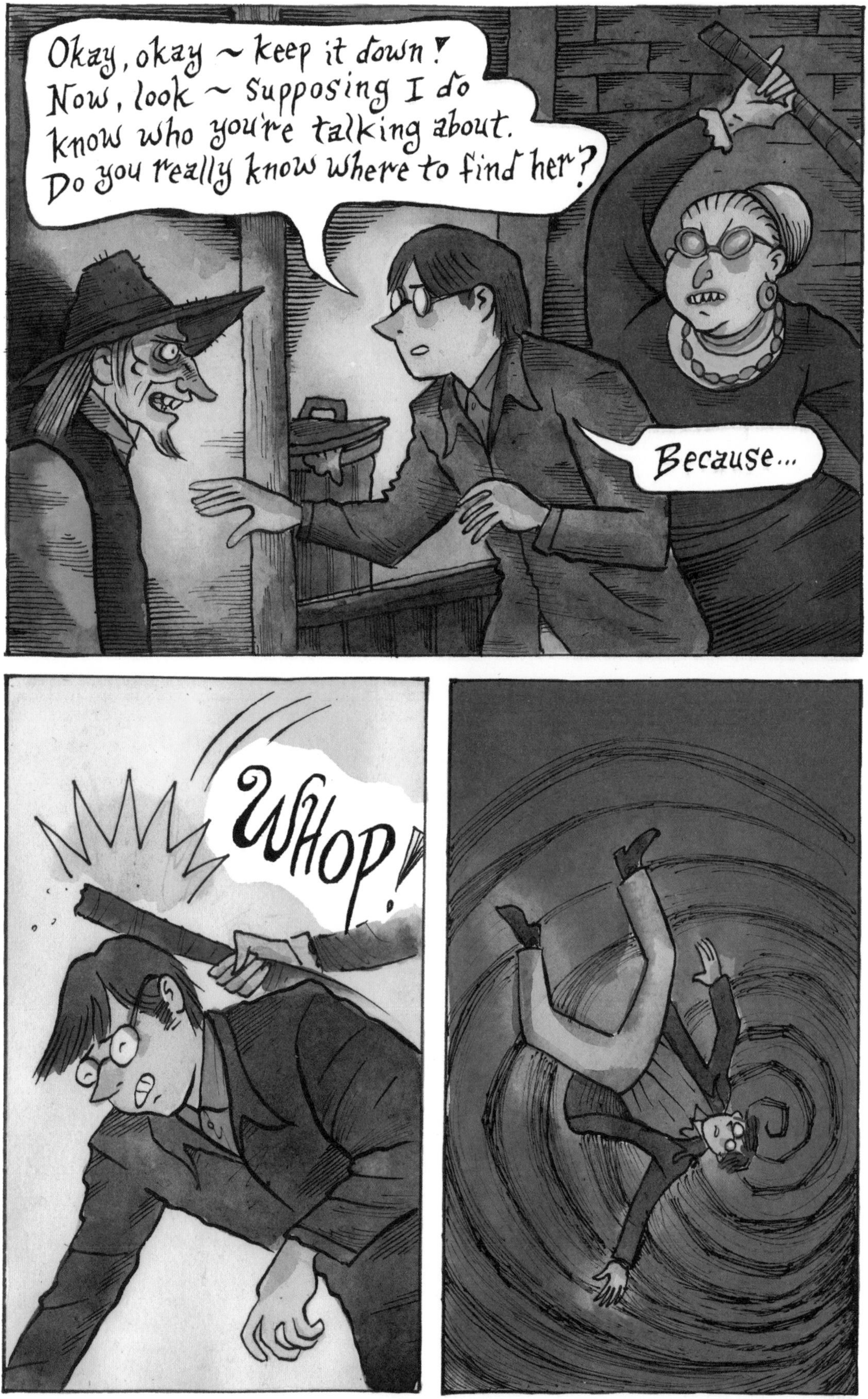
Okay, okay ~ keep it down! Now, look ~ supposing I do know who you're talking about. Do you really know where to find her?
Because...
WHOP!

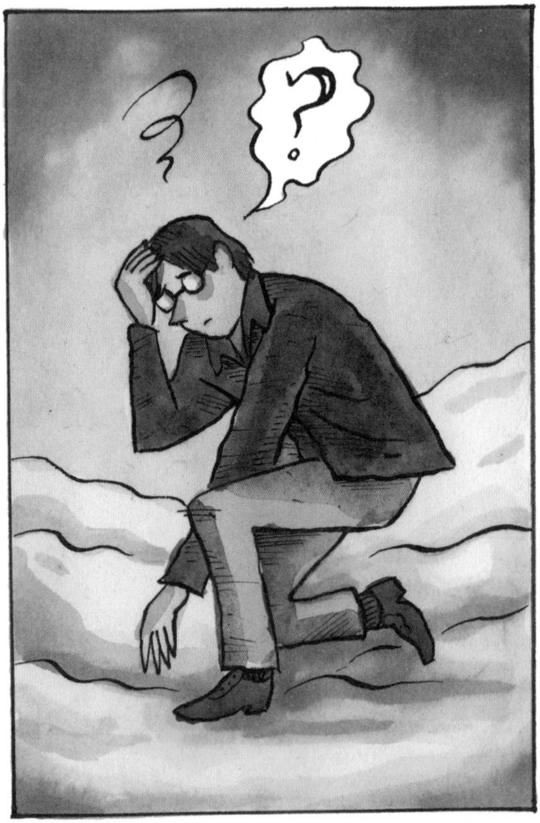
?

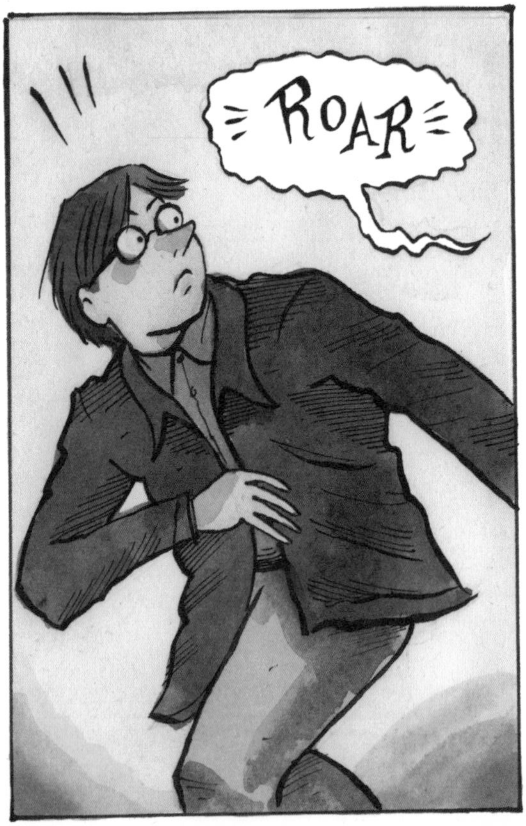
ROAR

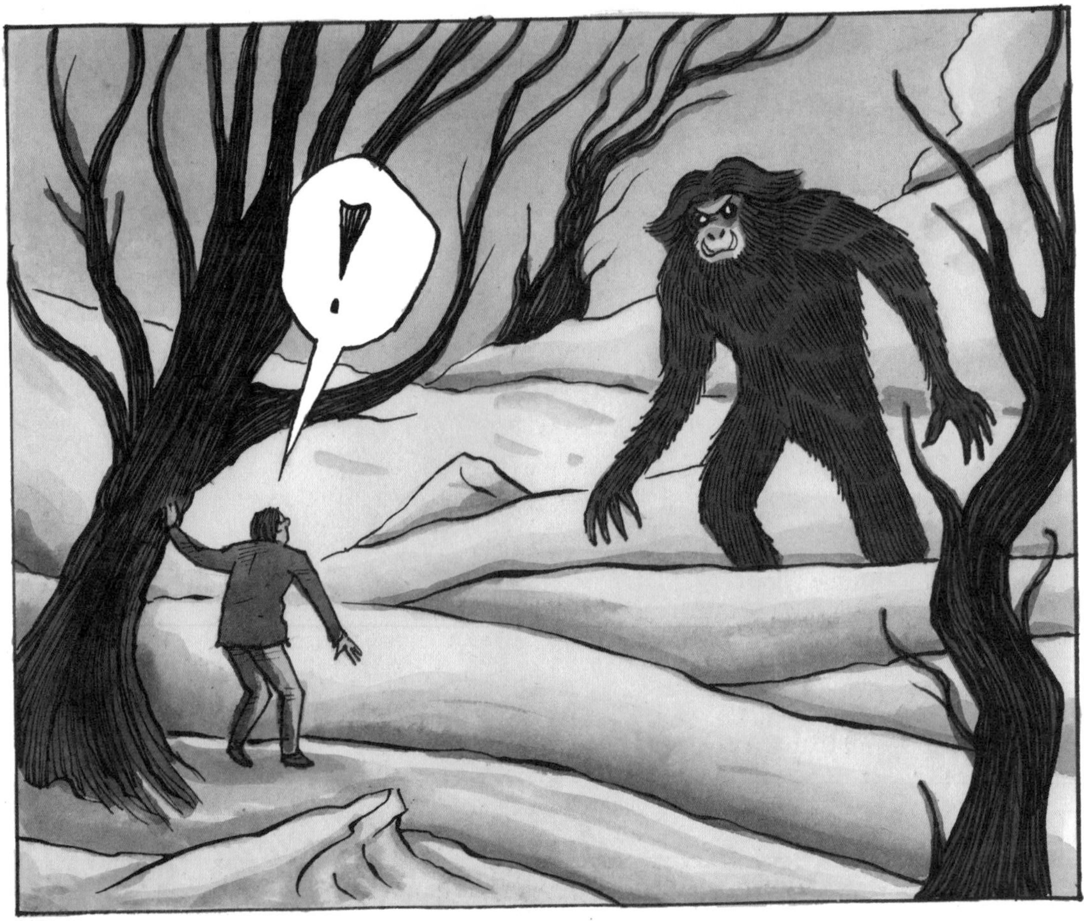
!

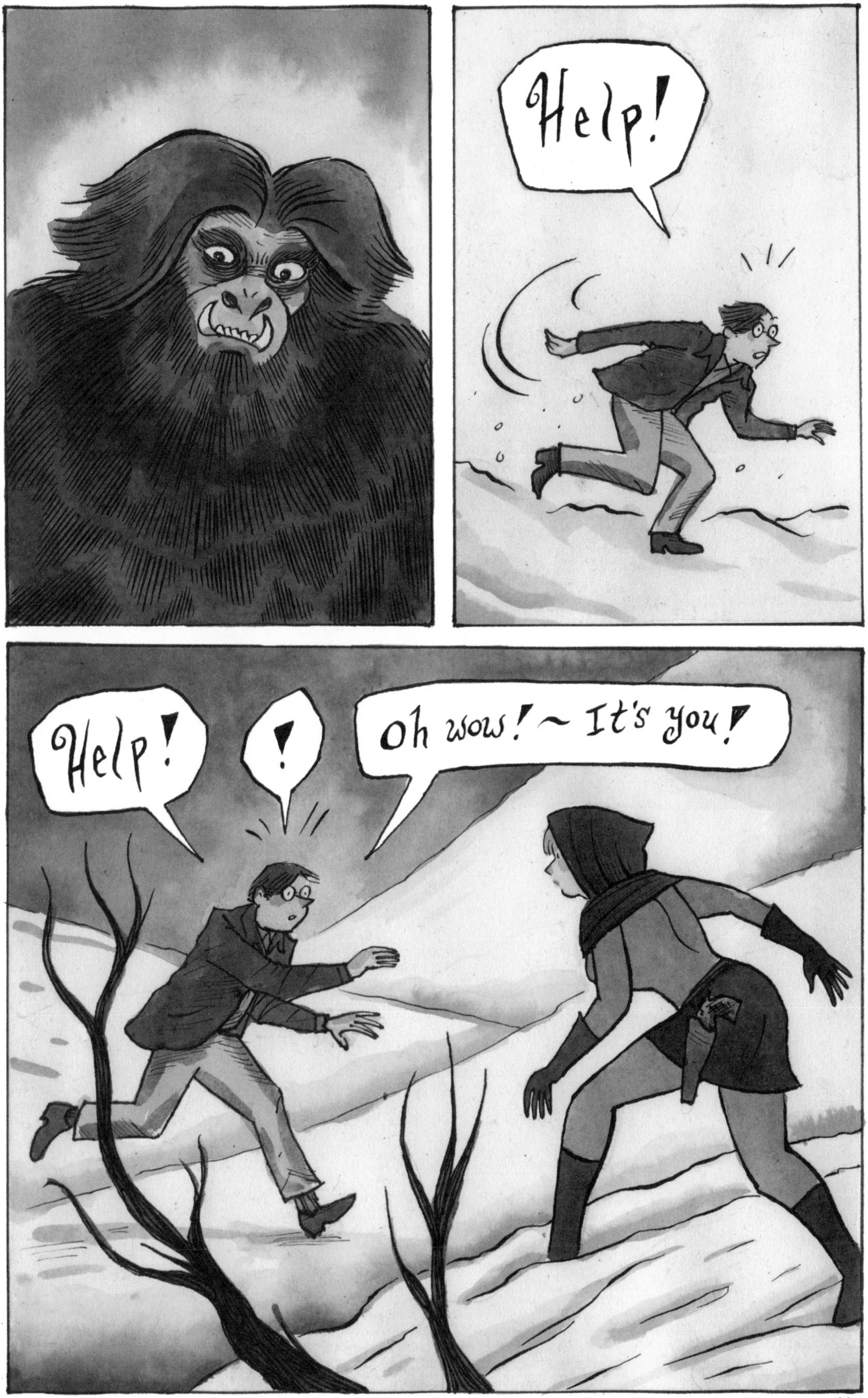
Help!
Help!
!
Oh wow! ~ It's you!

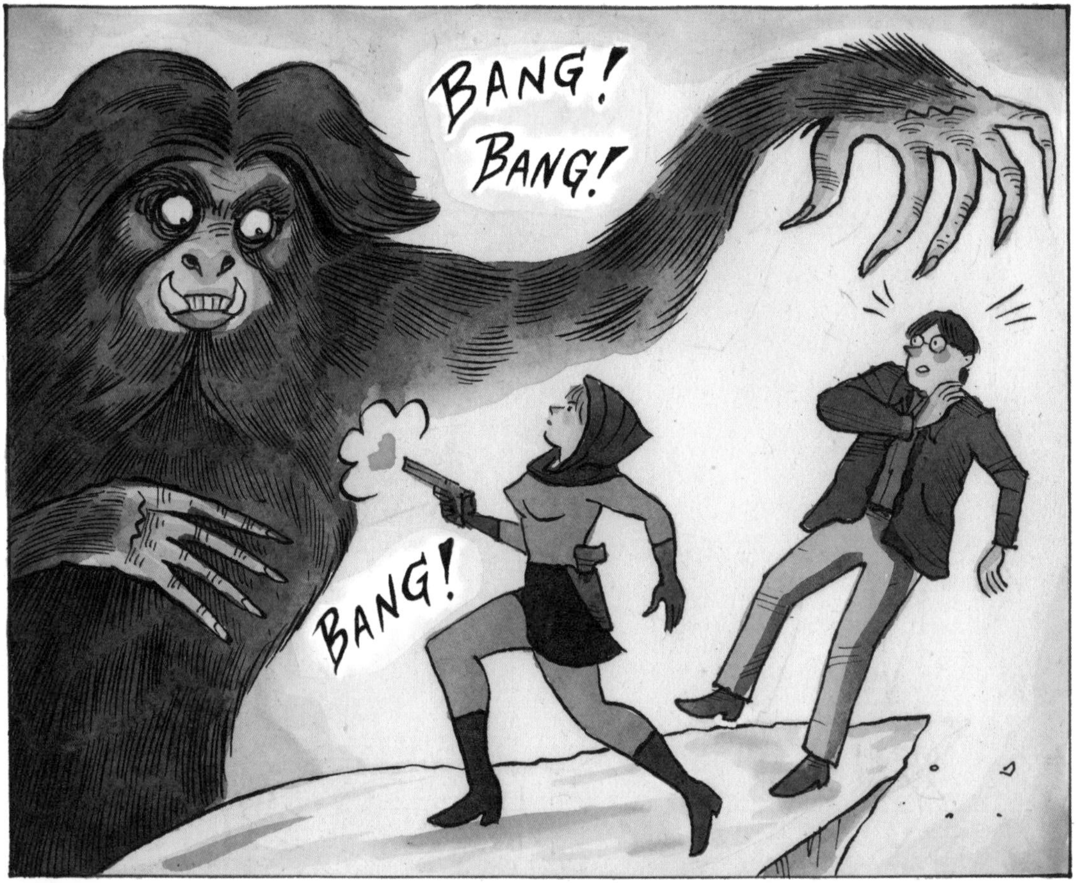
BANG!
BANG!
BANG!

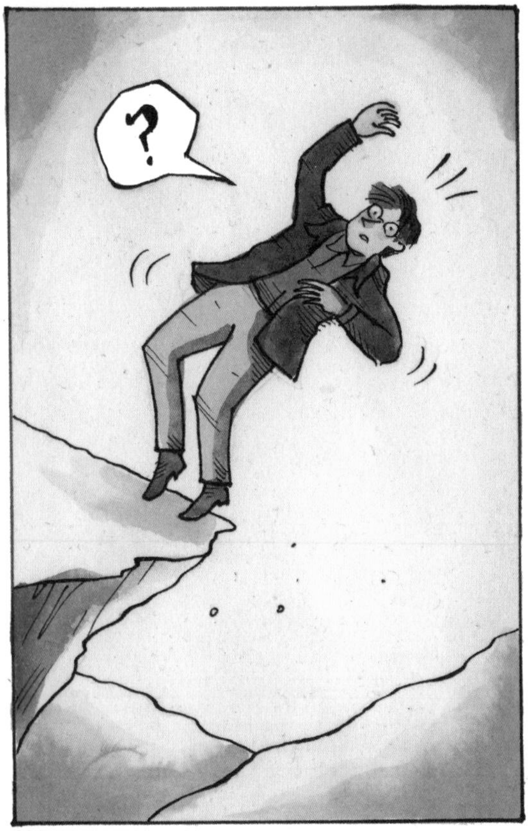
?

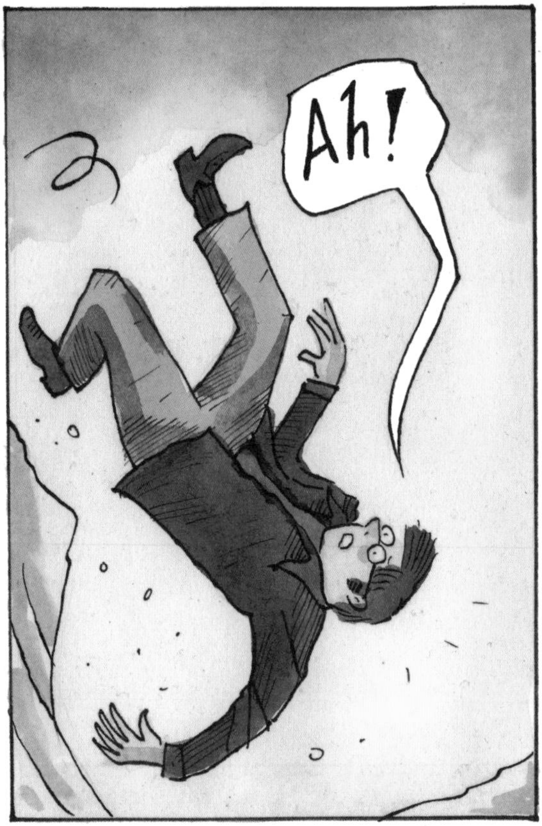
Ah!

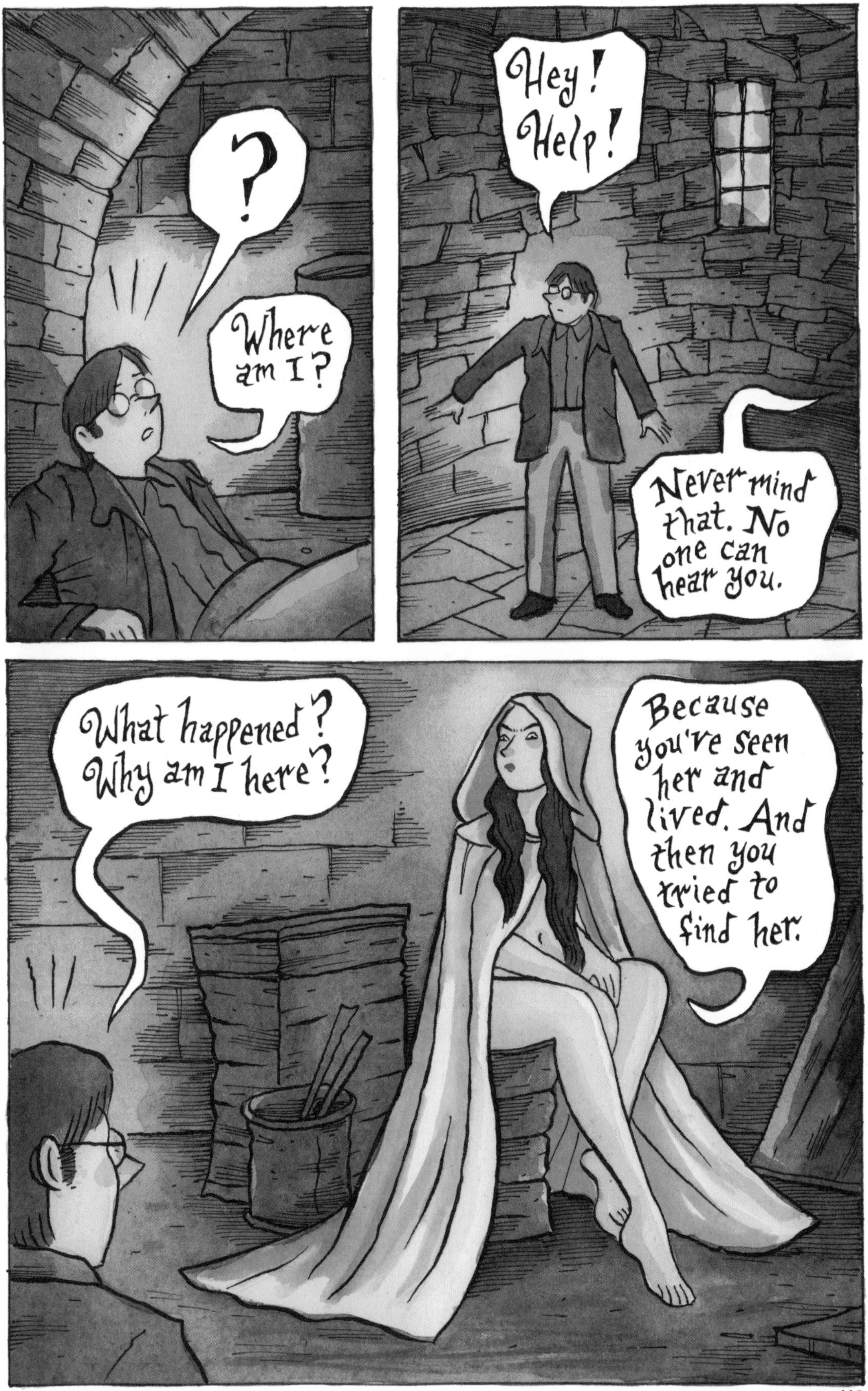
?
Where am I?
Hey! Help!
Never mind that. No one can hear you.
What happened? Why am I here?
Because you've seen her and lived. And then you tried to find her.

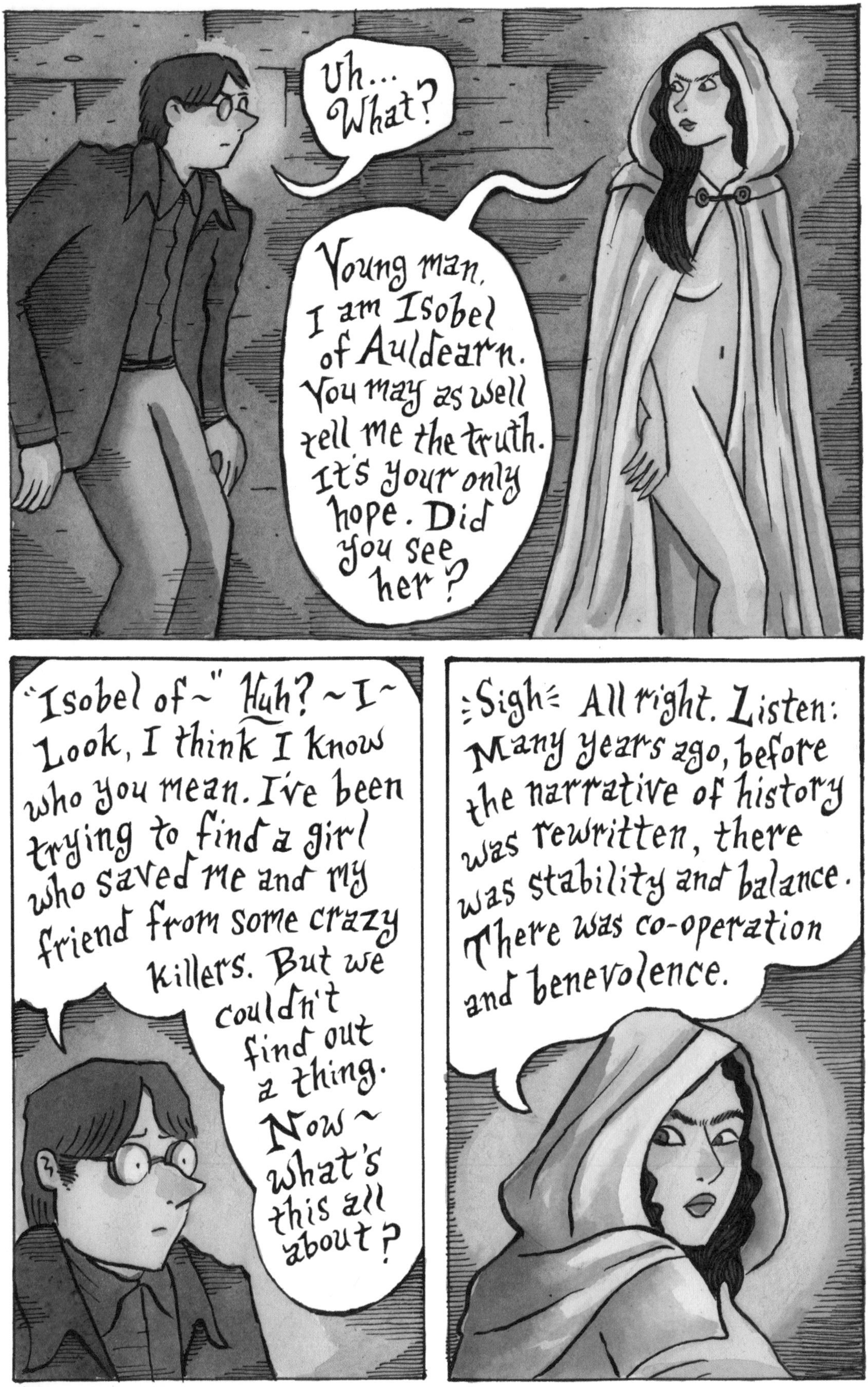
Uh... What?
Young man, I am Isobel of Auldearn. You may as well tell me the truth. It's your only hope. Did you see her?
"Isobel of~" Huh? ~I~ Look, I think I know who you mean. I've been trying to find a girl who saved me and my friend from some crazy killers. But we couldn't find out a thing. Now~ what's this all about?
Sigh All right. Listen: Many years ago, before the narrative of history was rewritten, there was stability and balance. There was co-operation and benevolence.

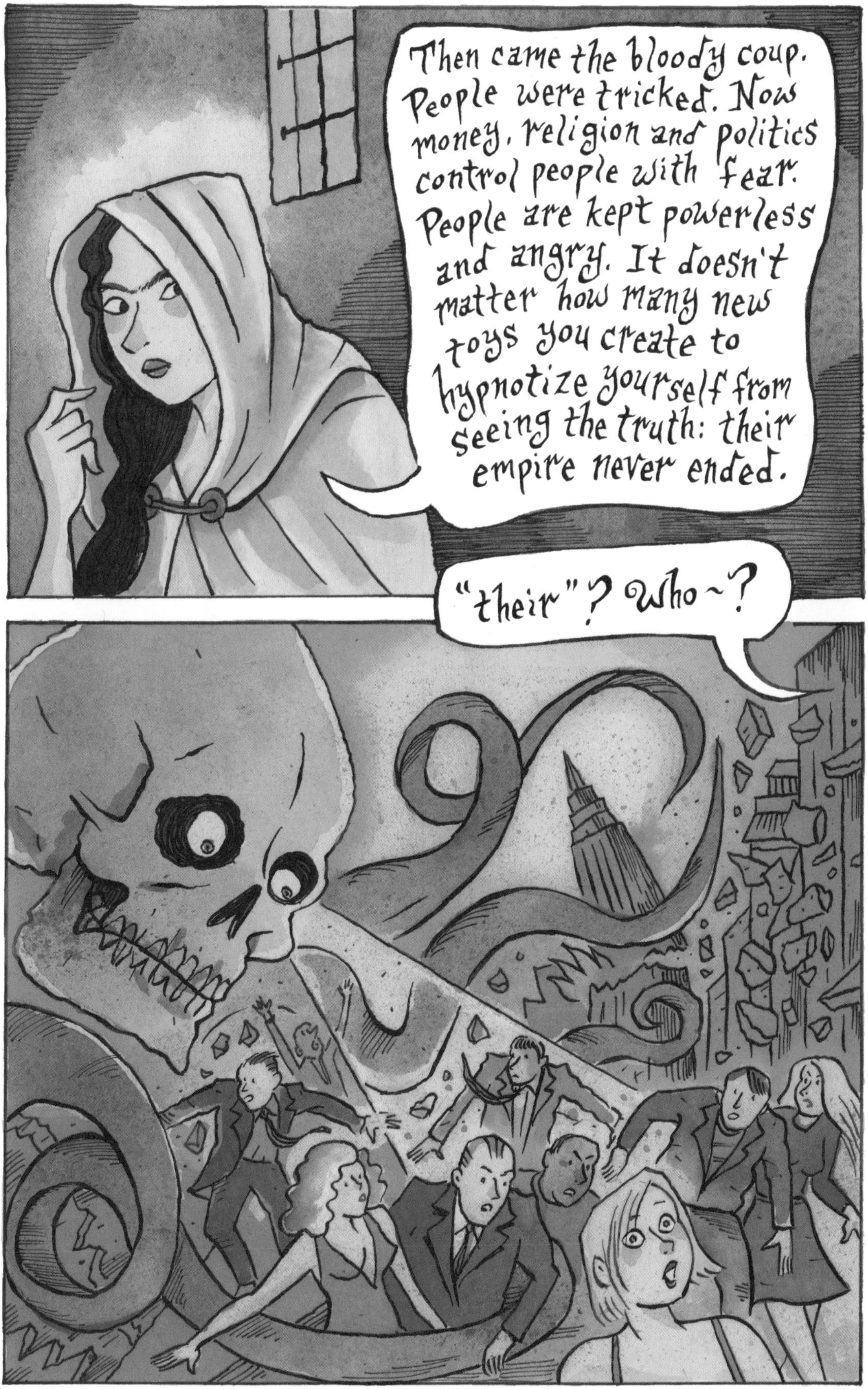
Then came the bloody coup. People were tricked. Now money, religion and politics control people with fear. People are kept powerless and angry. It doesn't matter how many new toys you create to hypnotize yourself from seeing the truth: their empire never ended.
"their"? Who~?

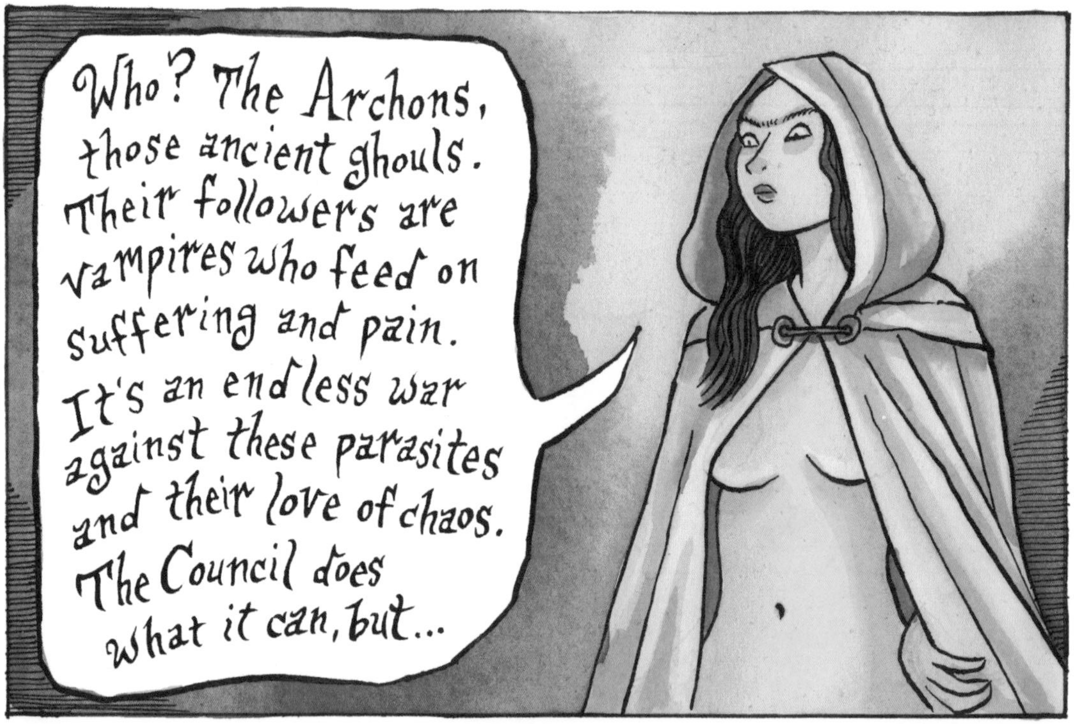
Who? The Archons, those ancient ghouls. Their followers are vampires who feed on suffering and pain. It's an endless war against these parasites and their love of chaos. The Council does what it can, but...

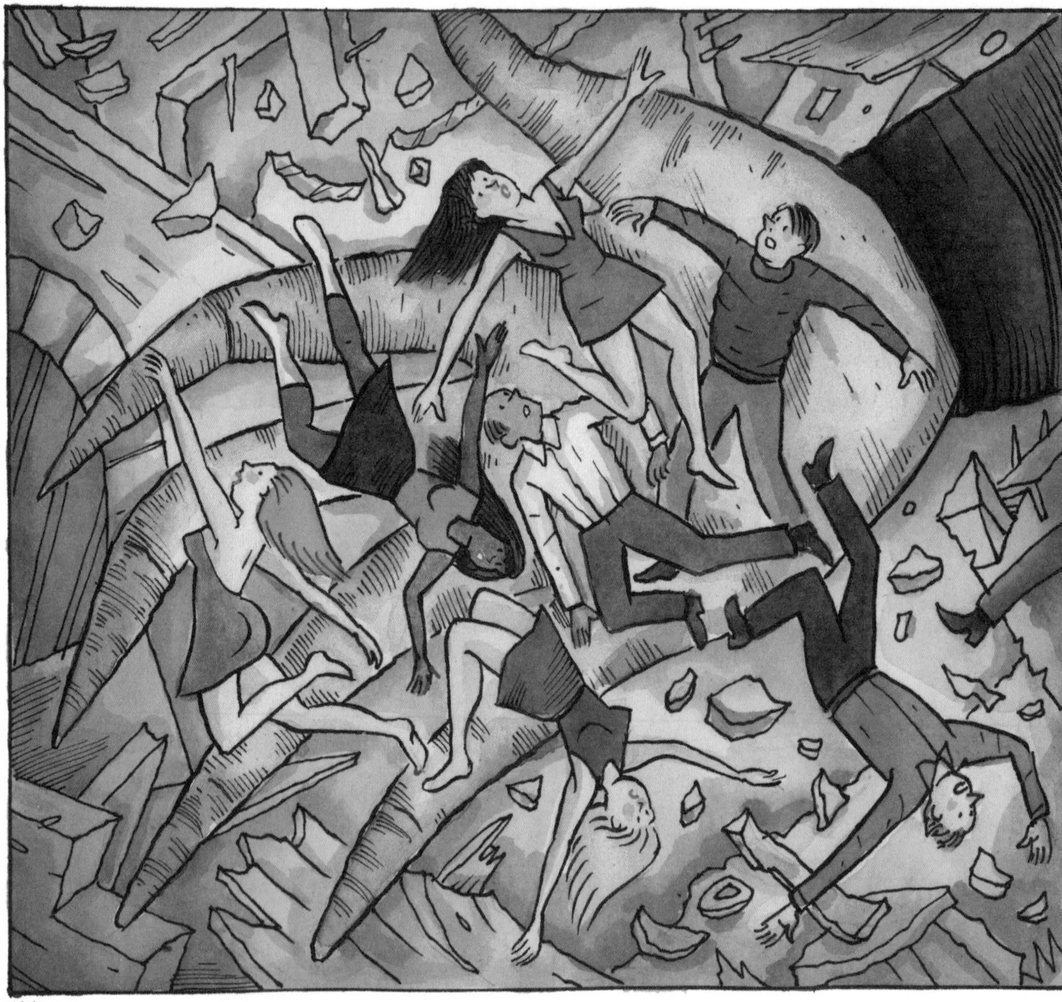

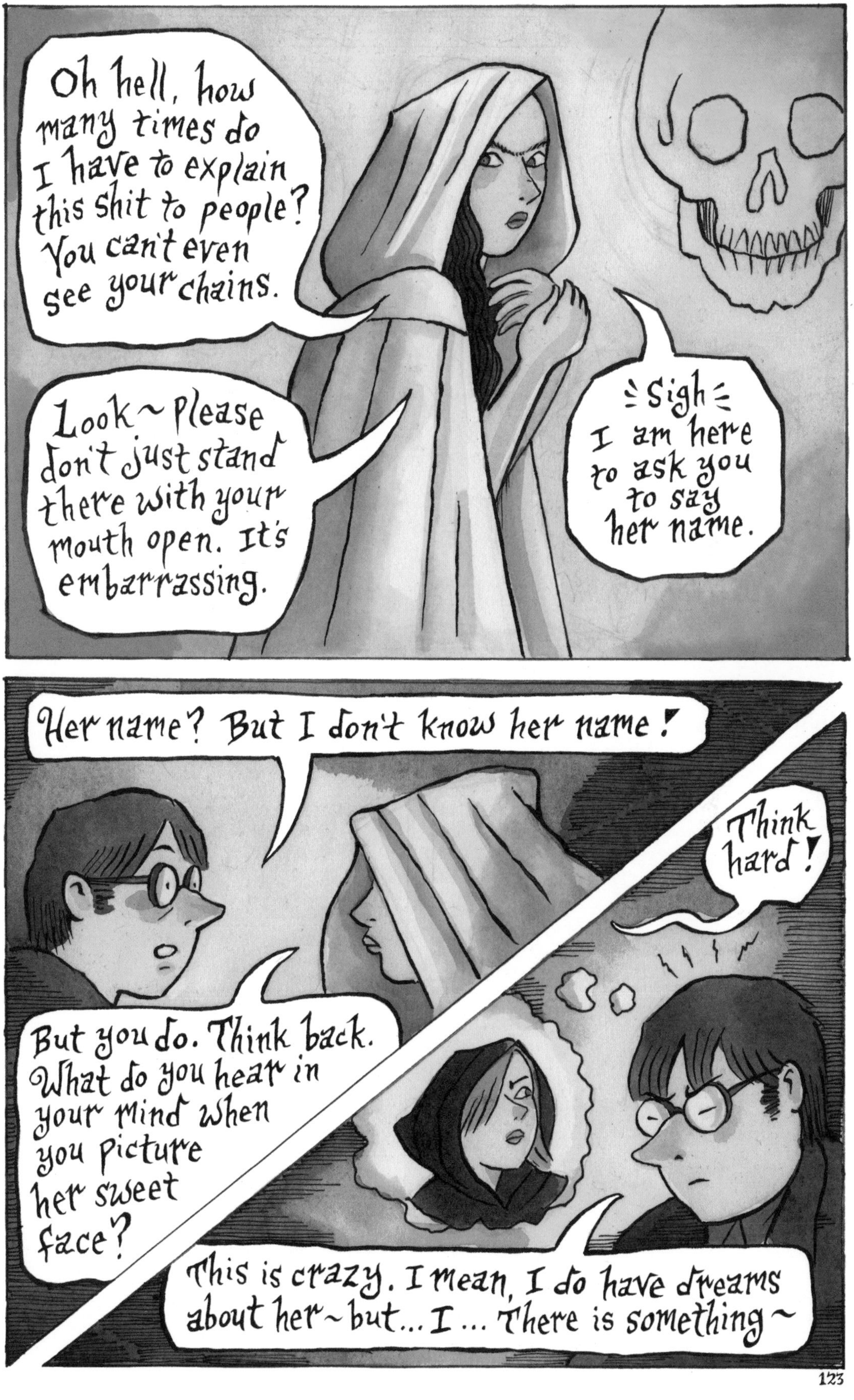
Oh hell, how many times do I have to explain this shit to people? You can't even see your chains.
Look ~ please don't just stand there with your mouth open. It's embarrassing.
Sigh
I am here to ask you to say her name.
Her name? But I don't know her name!
But you do. Think back. What do you hear in your mind when you picture her sweet face?
Think hard!
This is crazy. I mean, I do have dreams about her ~ but... I ... There is something ~

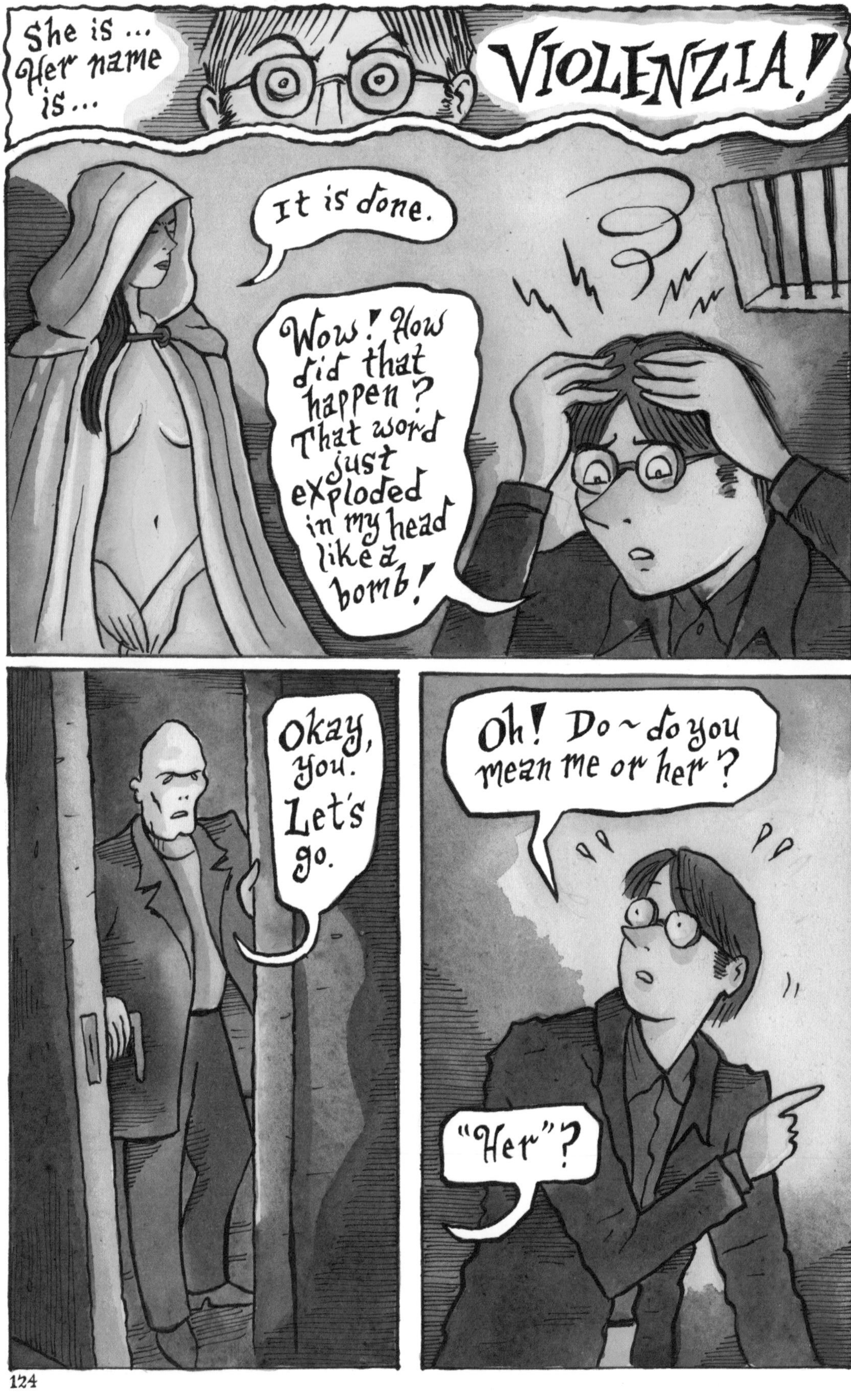
She is ... Her name is ...
VIOLENZIA!
It is done.
Wow! How did that happen? That word just exploded in my head like a bomb!
Okay, You. Let's go.
Oh! Do ~ do you mean me or her?
"Her"?

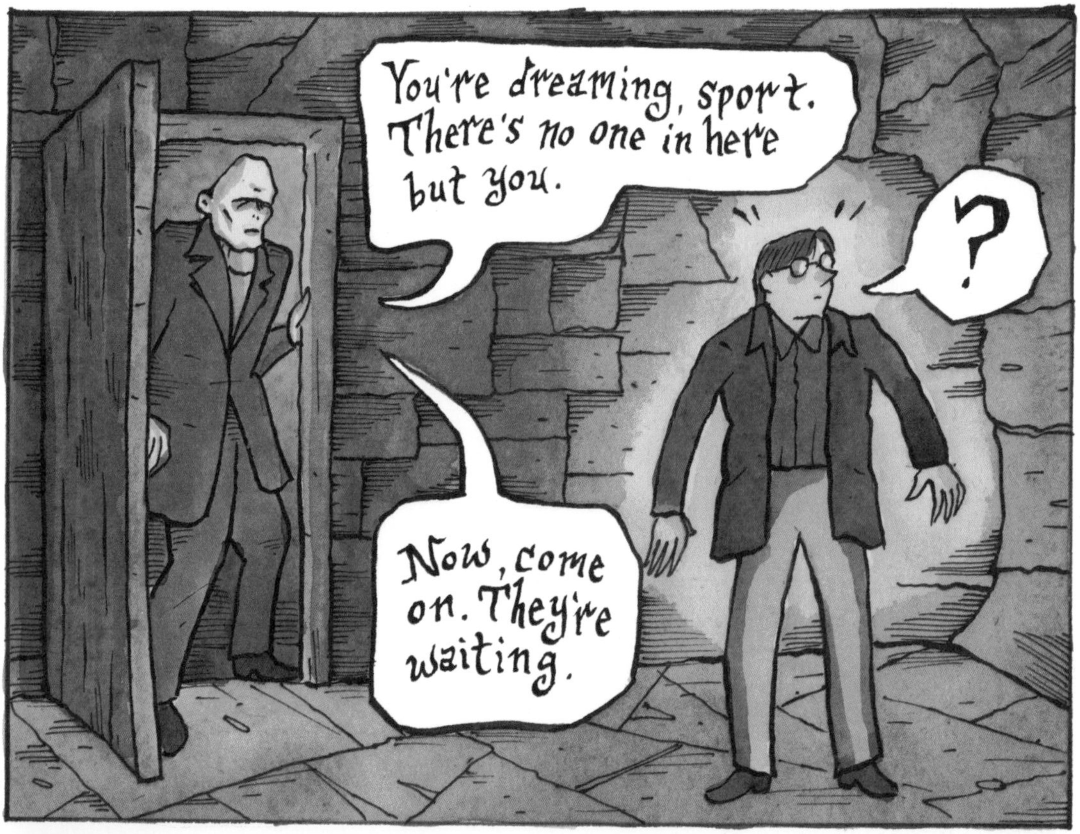
You're dreaming, sport. There's no one in here but you.
?
Now, come on. They're waiting.

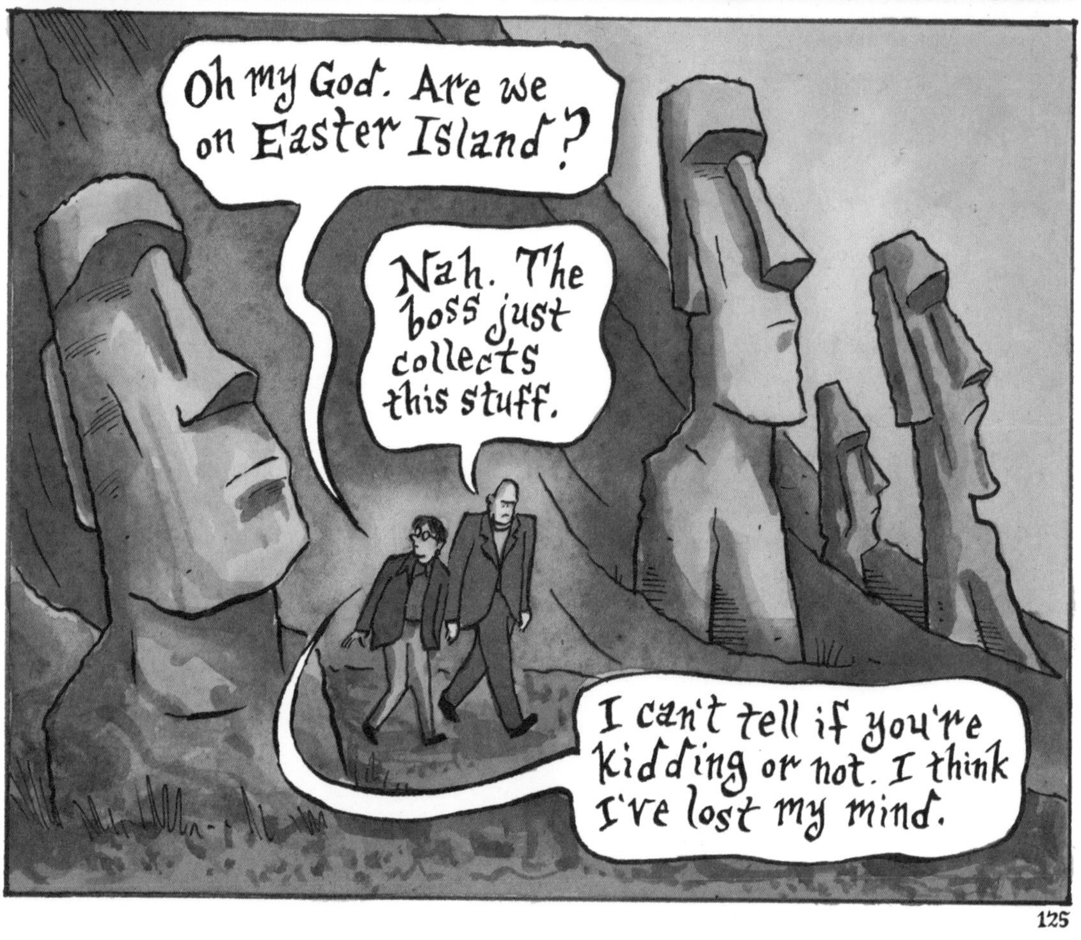
Oh my God. Are we on Easter Island?
Nah. The boss just collects this stuff.
I can't tell if you're kidding or not. I think I've lost my mind.

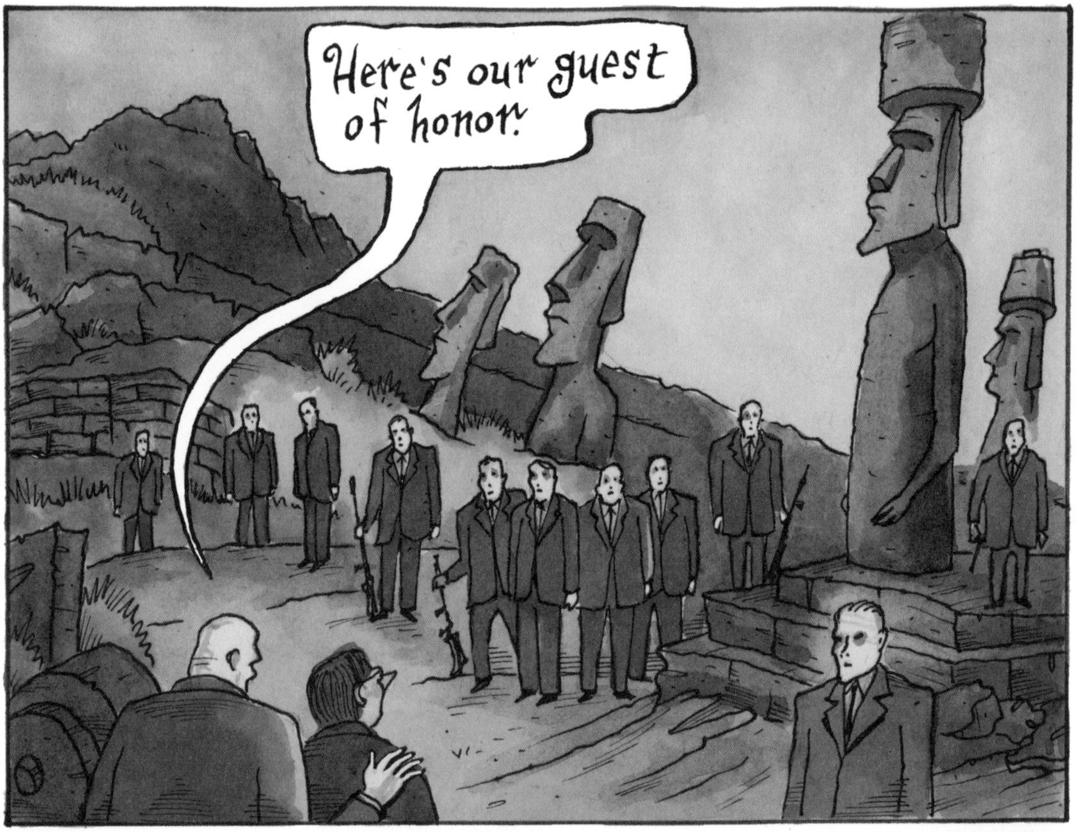
Here's our guest of honor.

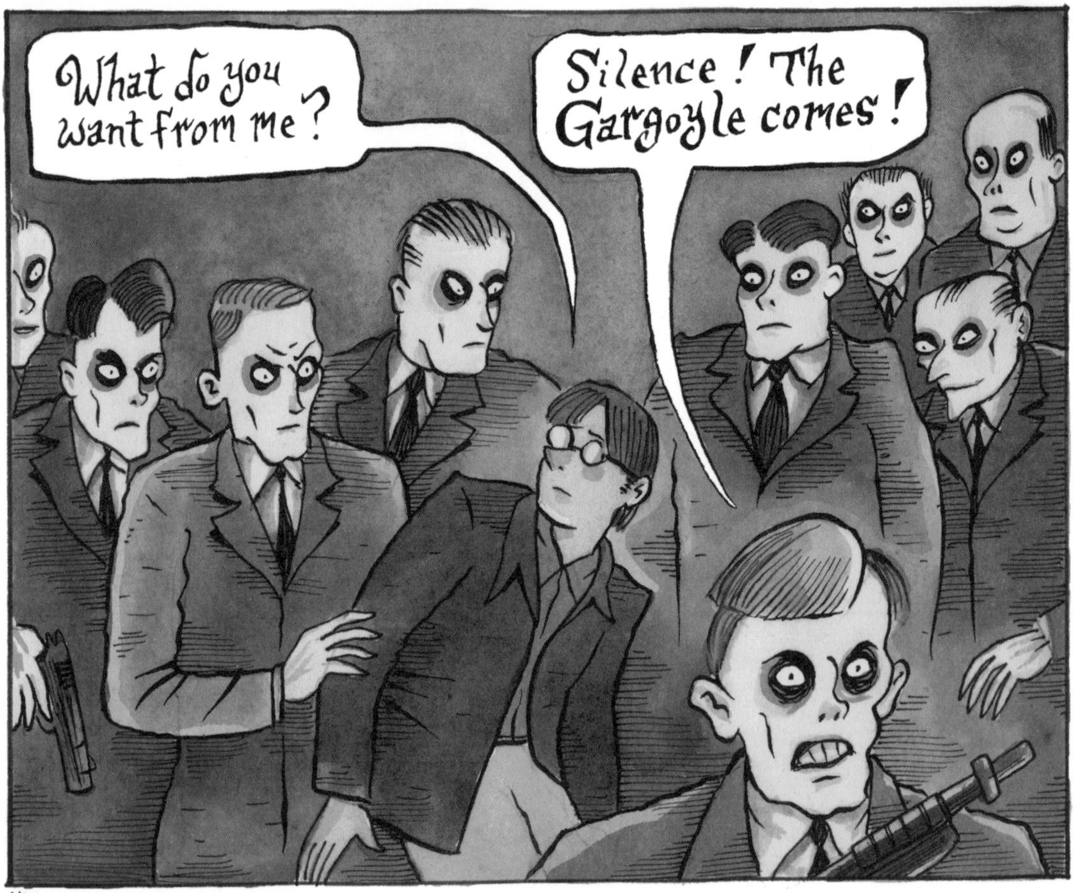
What do you want from me?
Silence! The Gargoyle comes!

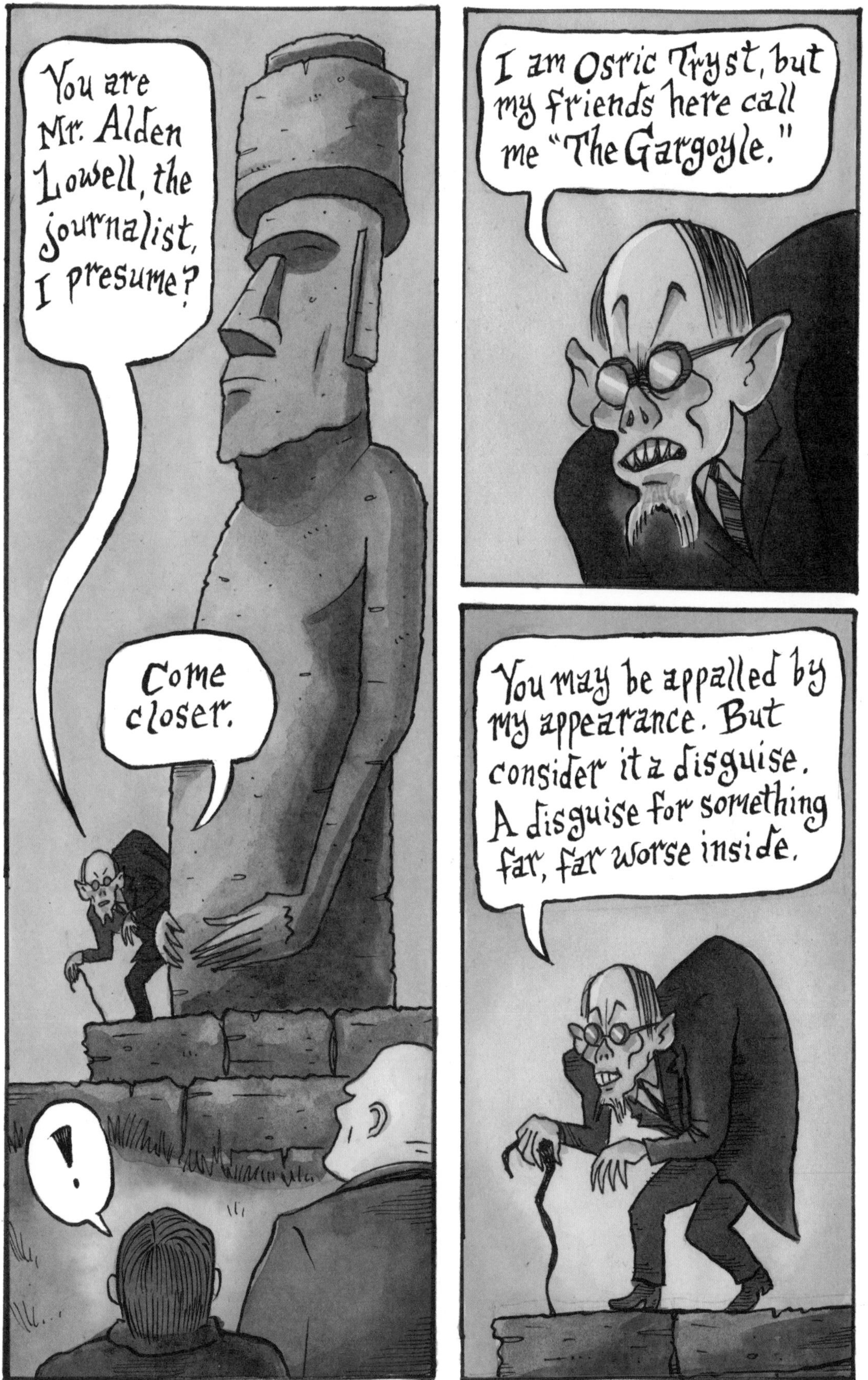
You are Mr. Alden Lowell, the journalist, I presume?
Come closer.
!
I am Osric Tryst, but my friends here call me "The Gargoyle."
You may be appalled by my appearance. But consider it a disguise. A disguise for something far, far worse inside.

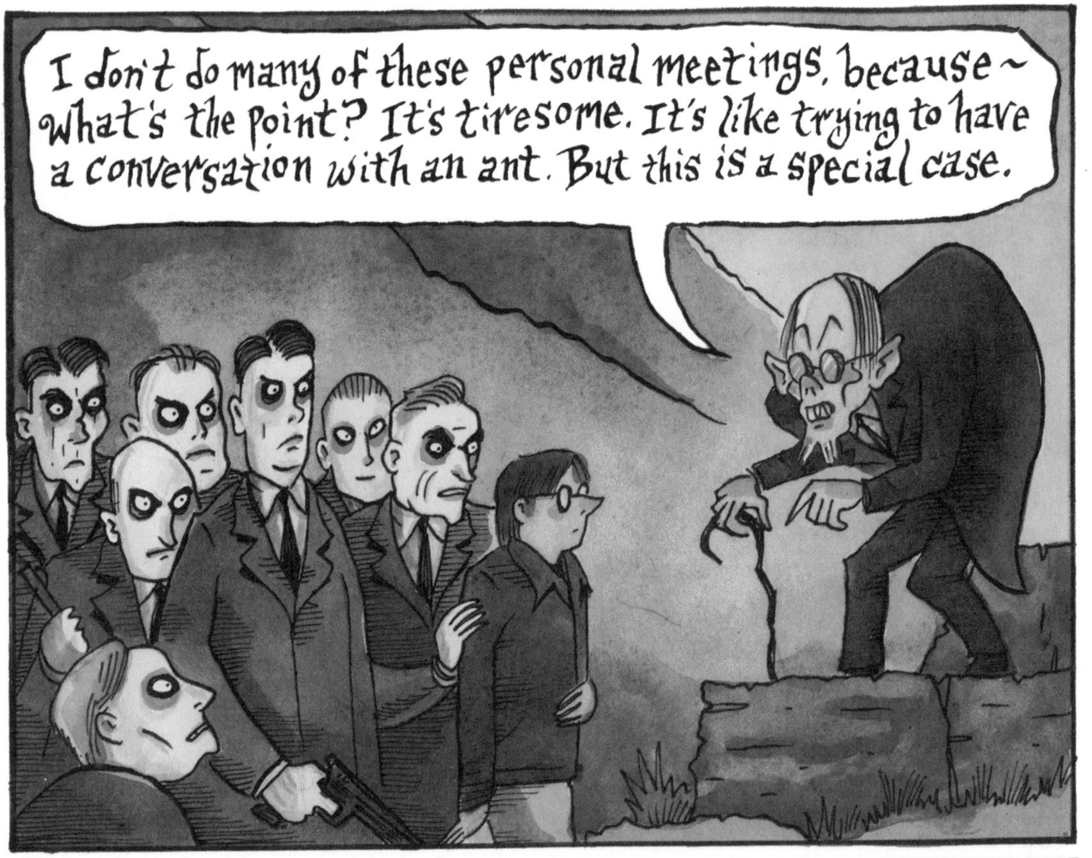
I don't do many of these personal meetings, because ~ what's the point? It's tiresome. It's like trying to have a conversation with an ant. But this is a special case.

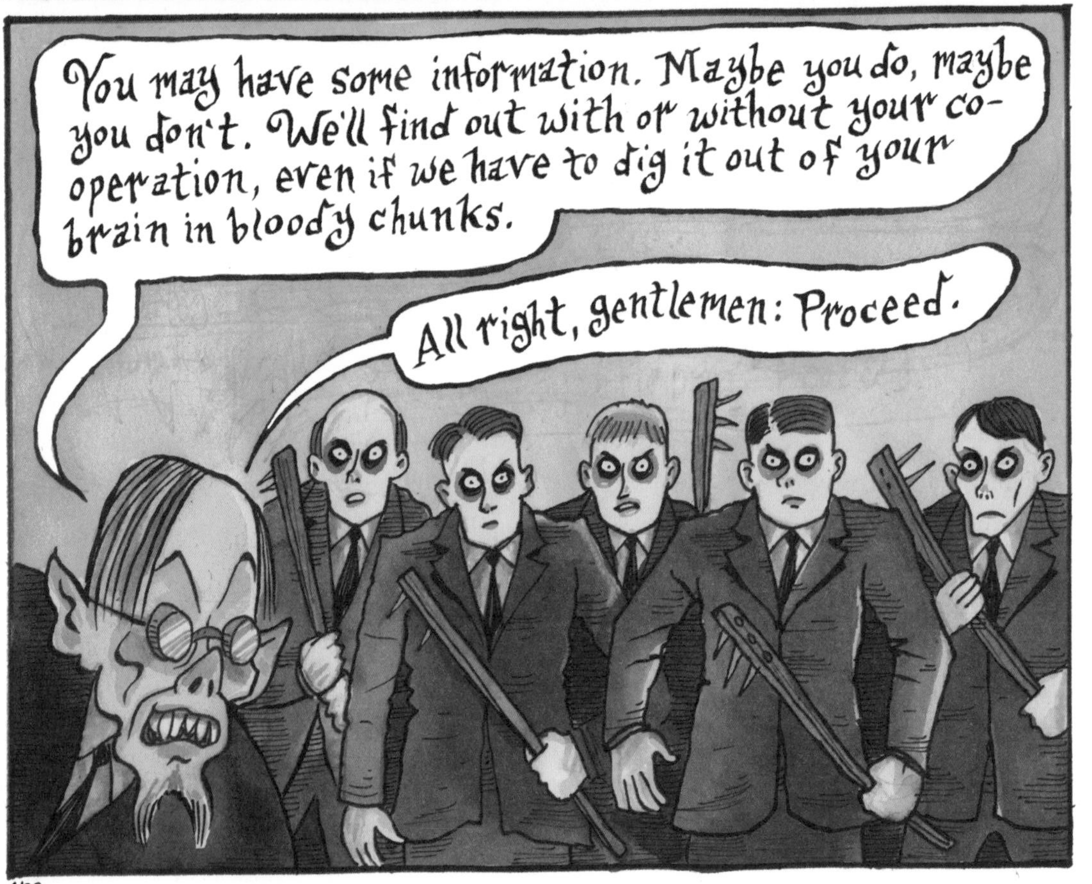
You may have some information. Maybe you do, maybe you don't. We'll find out with or without your co-operation, even if we have to dig it out of your brain in bloody chunks.
All right, gentlemen: Proceed.

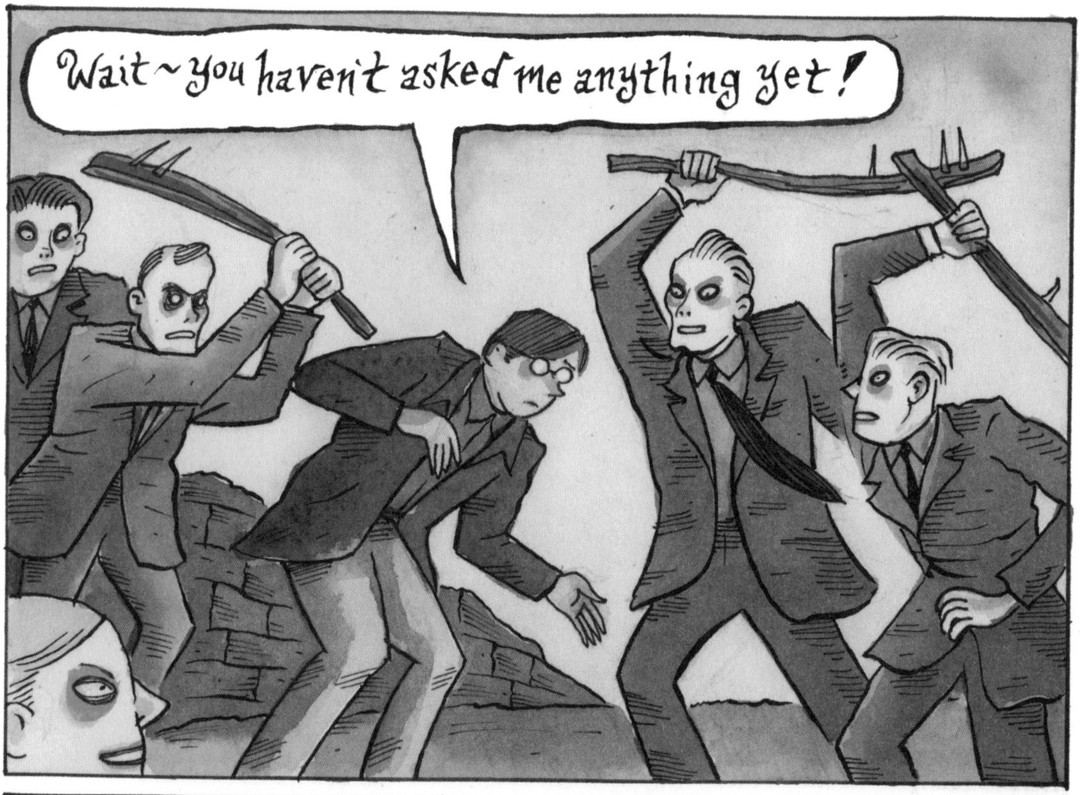
Wait ~ you haven't asked me anything yet!

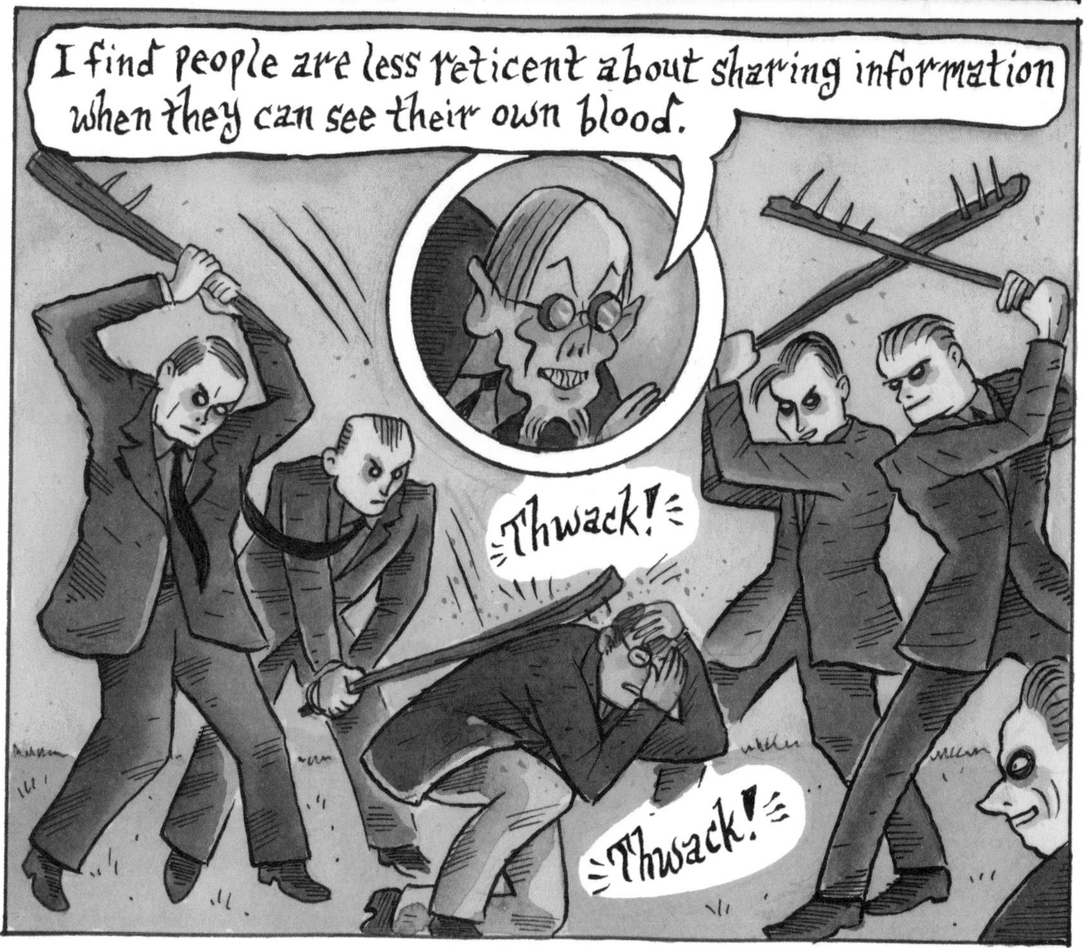
I find people are less reticent about sharing information when they can see their own blood.
Thwack!
Thwack!

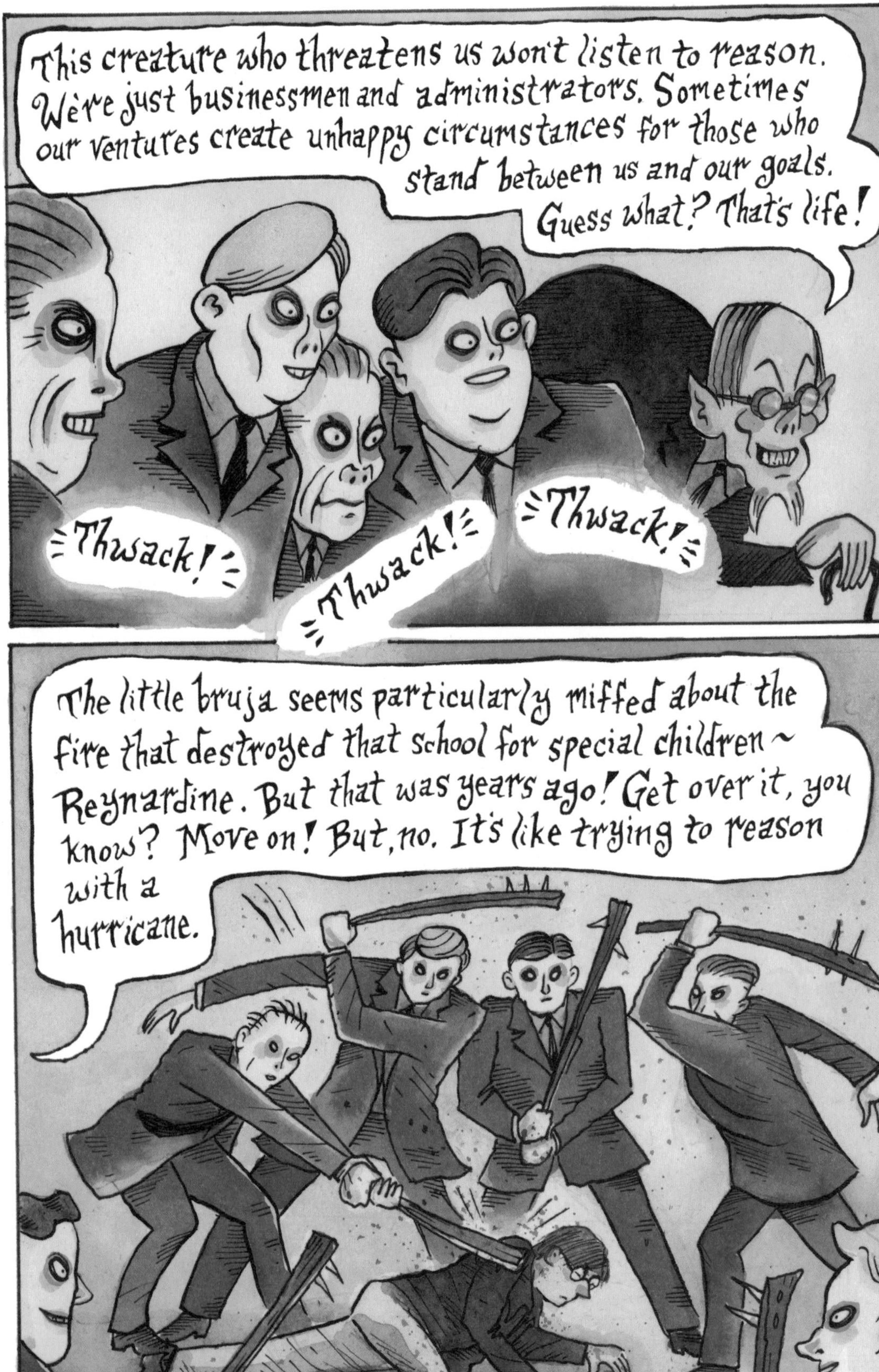
This creature who threatens us won't listen to reason. We're just businessmen and administrators. Sometimes our ventures create unhappy circumstances for those who stand between us and our goals. Guess what? That's life!
Thwack!
Thwack!
Thwack!
The little bruja seems particularly miffed about the fire that destroyed that school for special children ~ Reynardine. But that was years ago! Get over it, you know? Move on! But, no. It's like trying to reason with a hurricane.

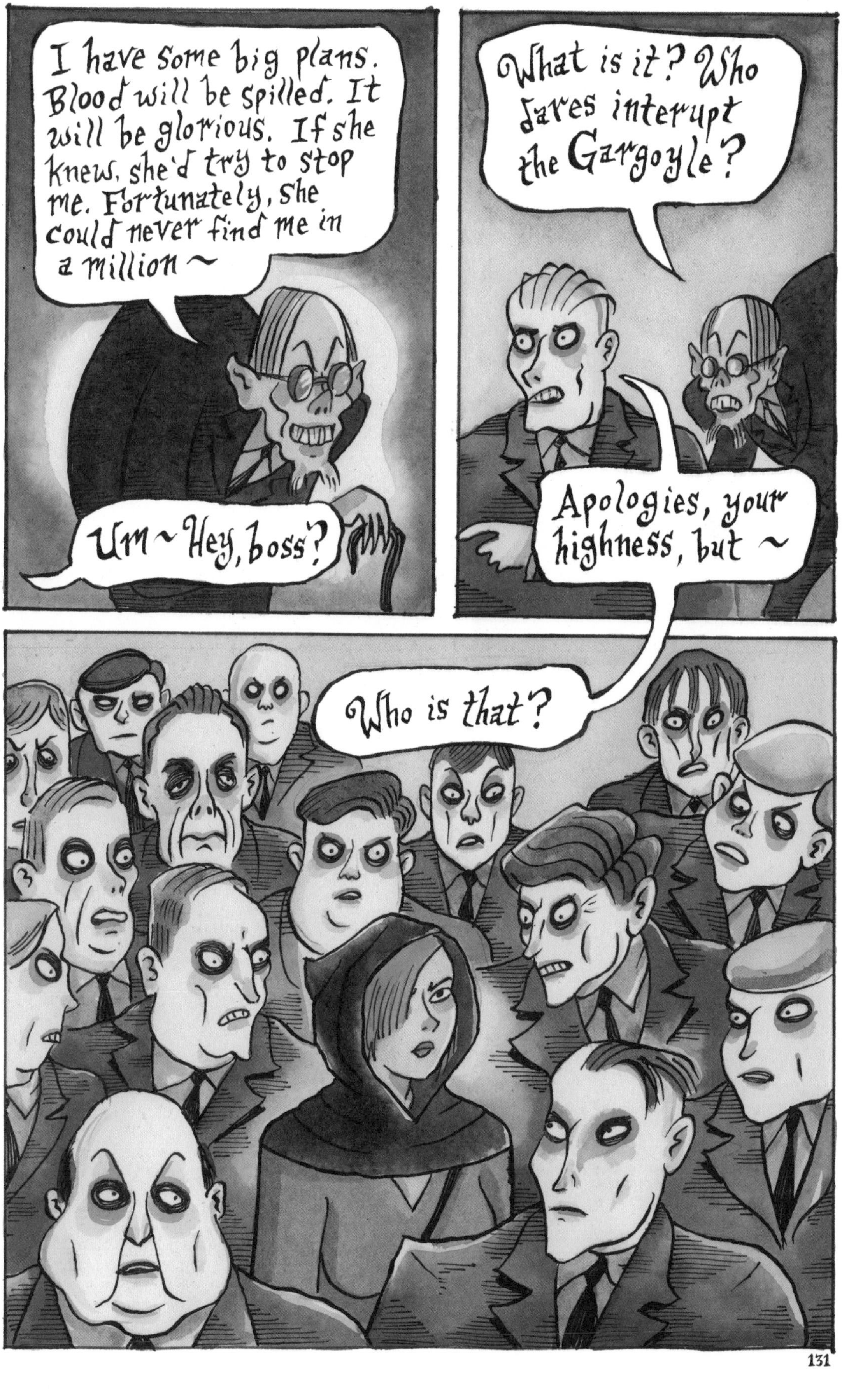
I have some big plans. Blood will be spilled. It will be glorious. If she knew, she'd try to stop me. Fortunately, she could never find me in a million ~
Um ~ Hey, boss?
What is it? Who dares interupt the Gargoyle?
Apologies, your highness, but ~
Who is that?

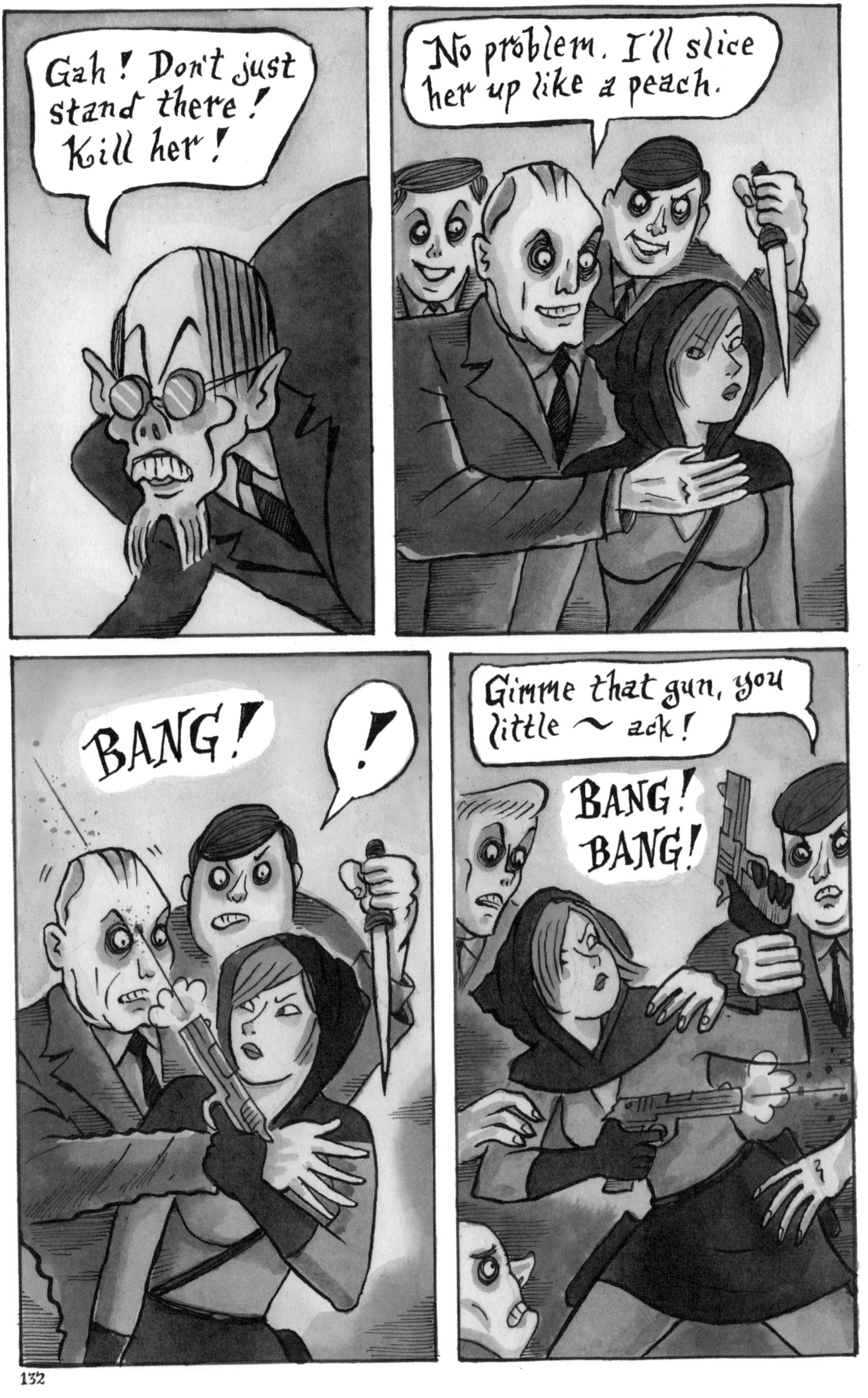
Gah! Don't just stand there! Kill her!
No problem. I'll slice her up like a peach.
BANG!
!
Gimme that gun, you little ~ ack!
BANG! BANG!

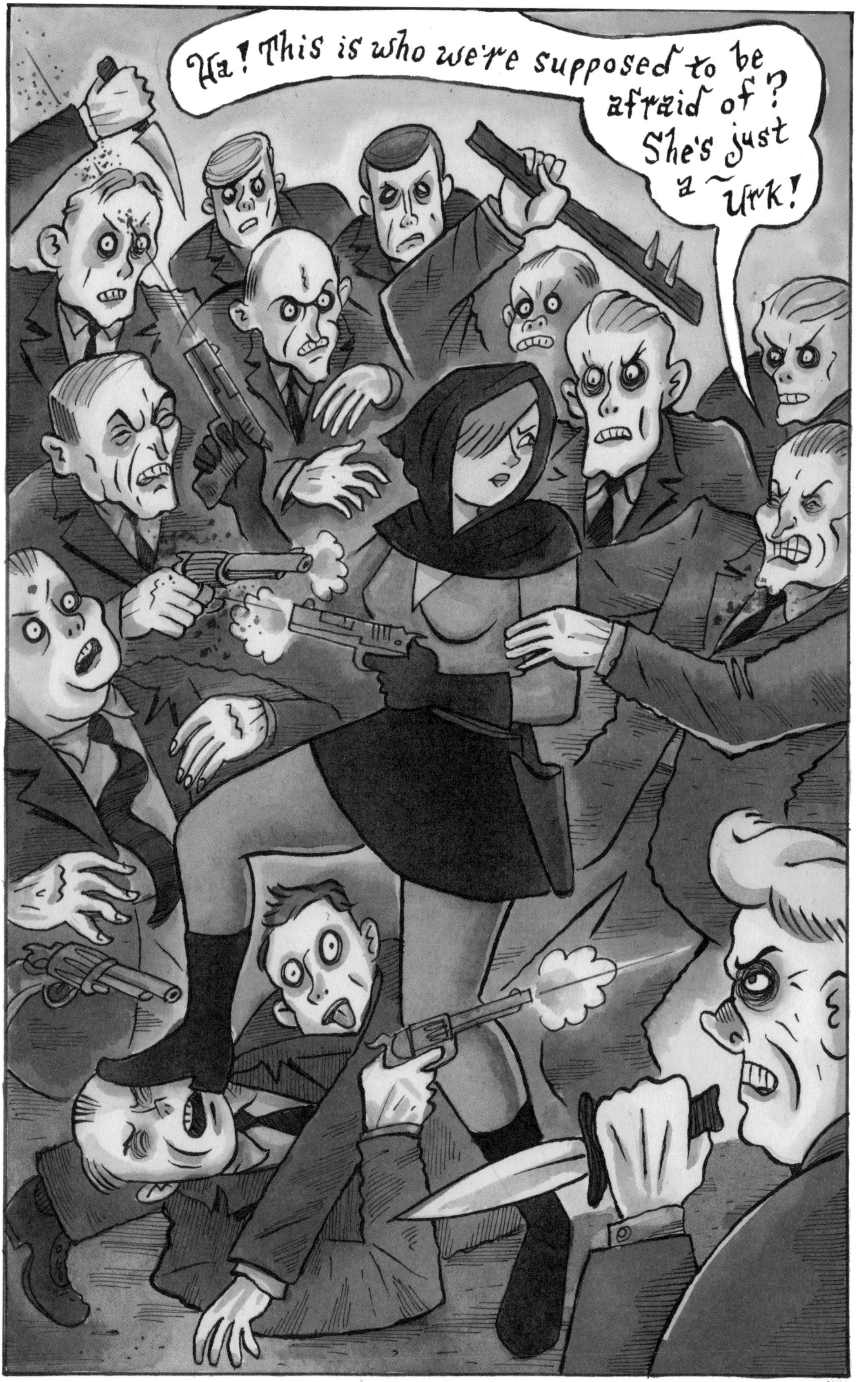
Ha! This is who we're supposed to be afraid of? She's just a ~Urk!

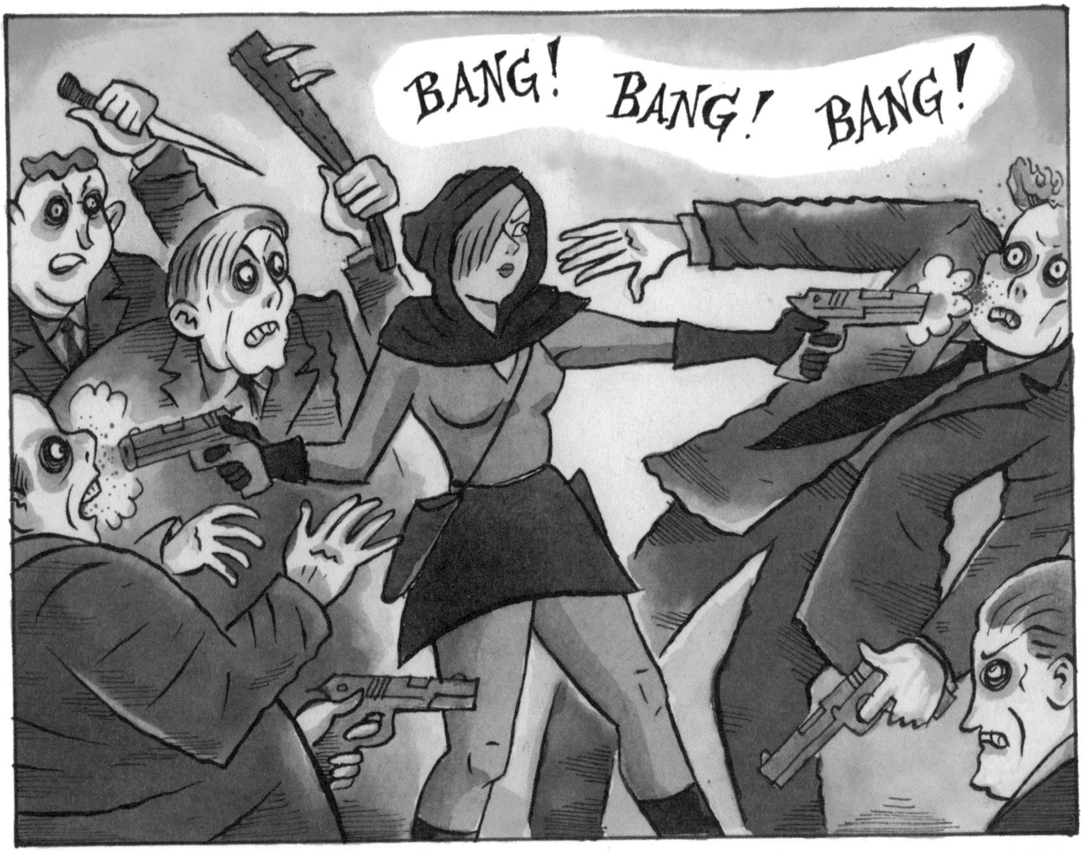
BANG! BANG! BANG!

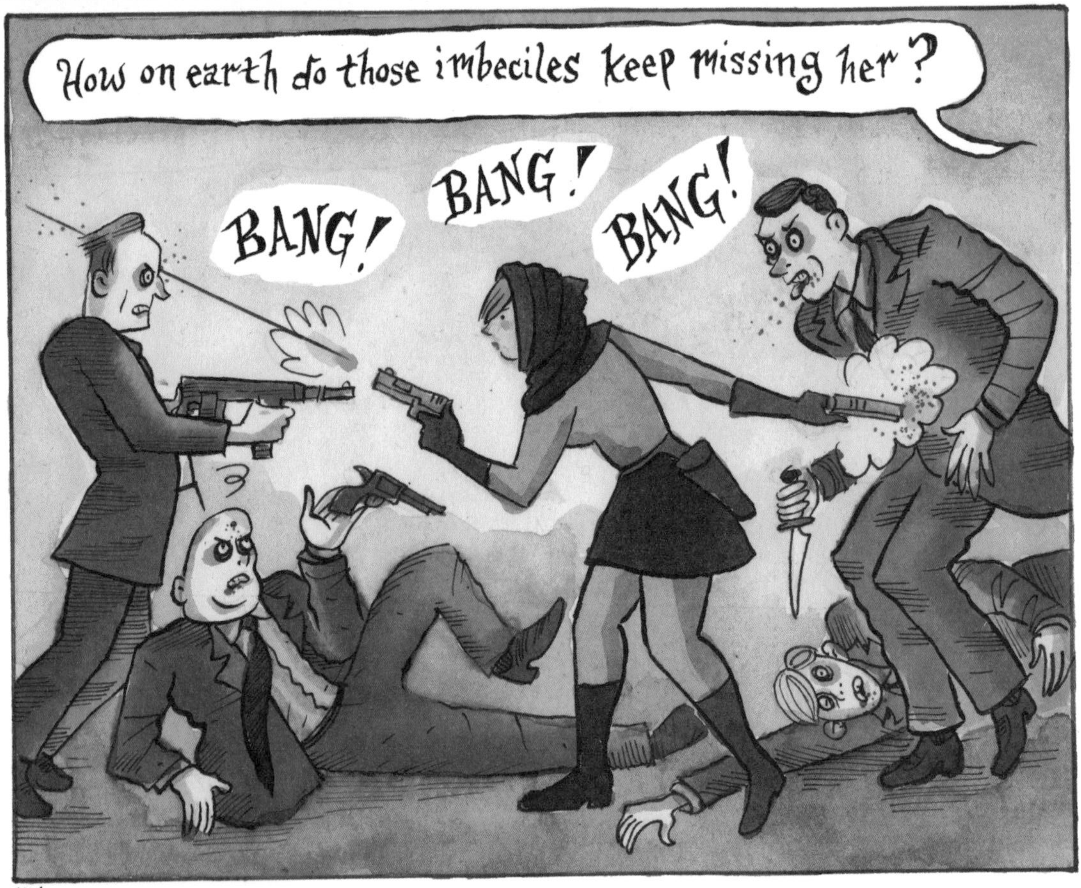
How on earth do those imbeciles keep missing her?
BANG!
BANG!
BANG!

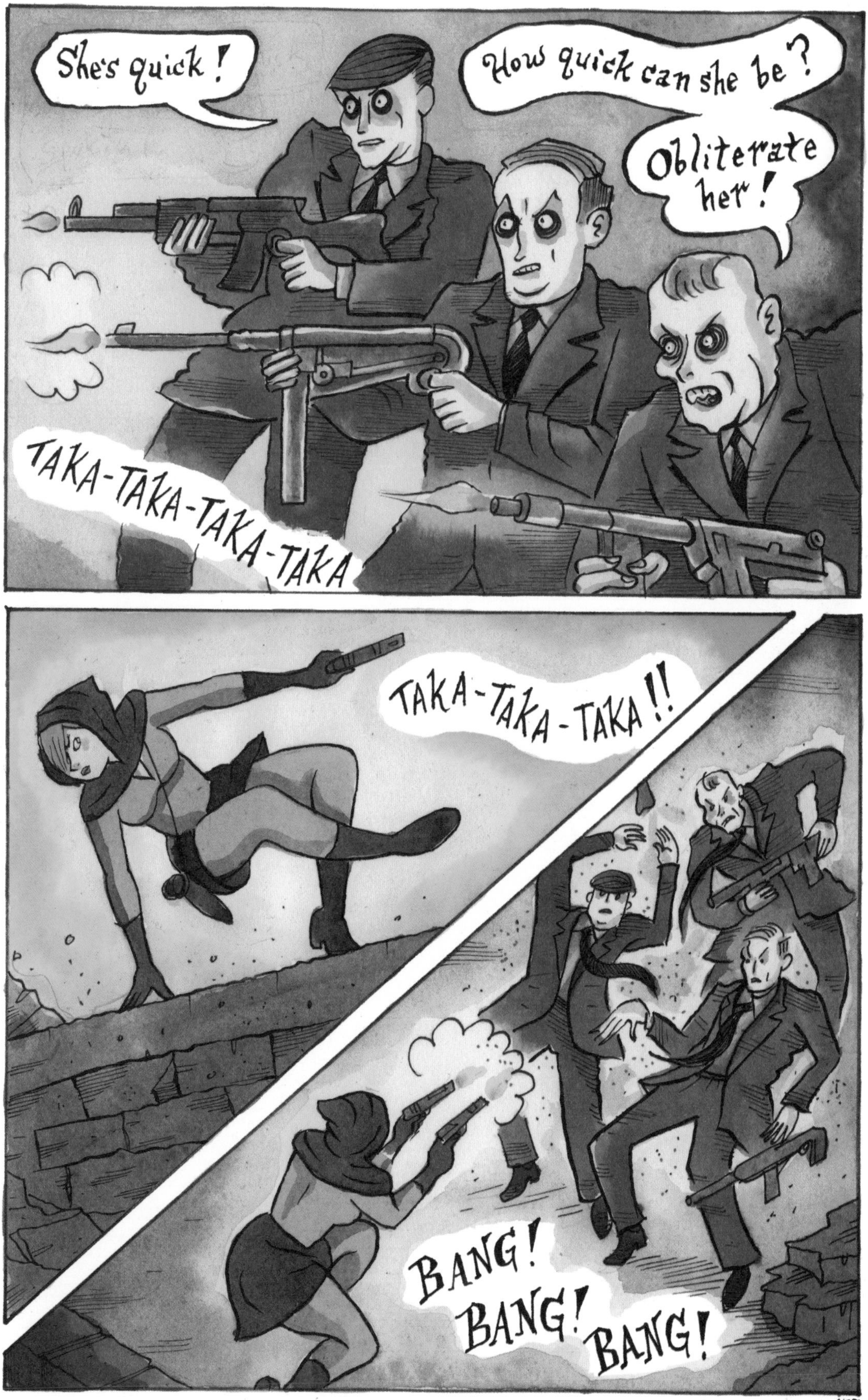
She's quick!
How quick can she be?
Obliterate her!
TAKA-TAKA-TAKA-TAKA
TAKA-TAKA-TAKA!!
BANG! BANG! BANG!

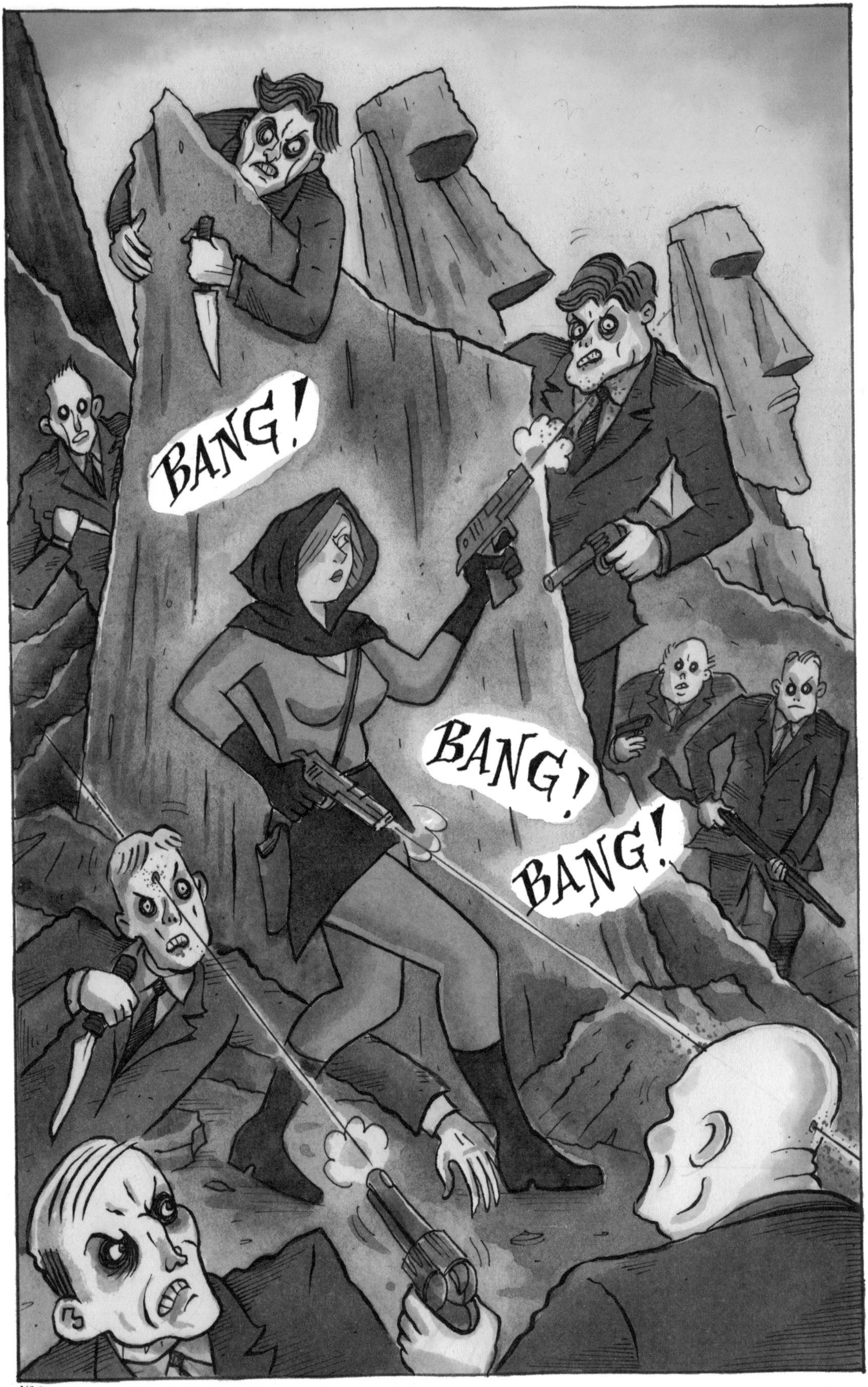
BANG!
BANG!
BANG!

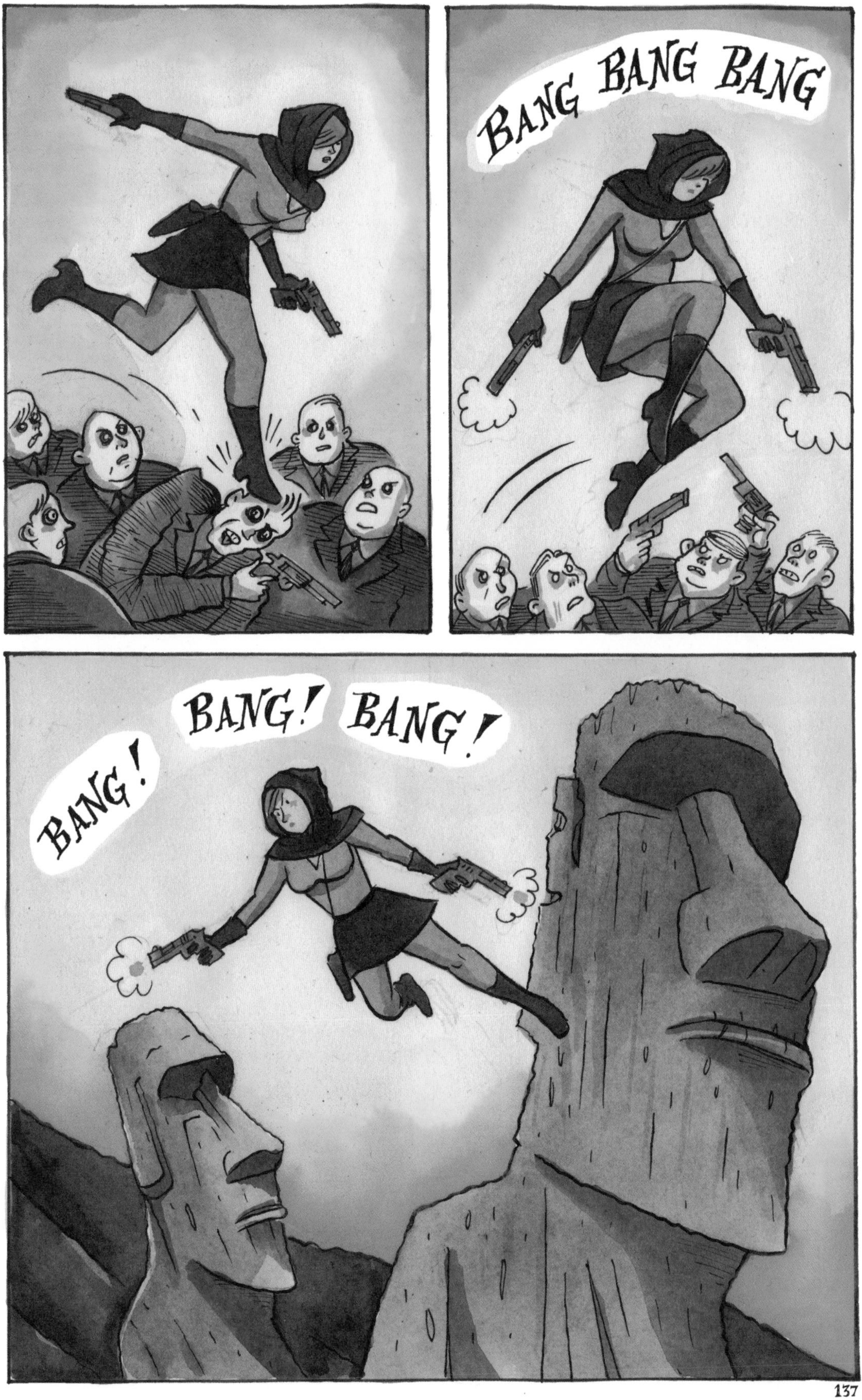
BANG BANG BANG
BANG!
BANG!
BANG!

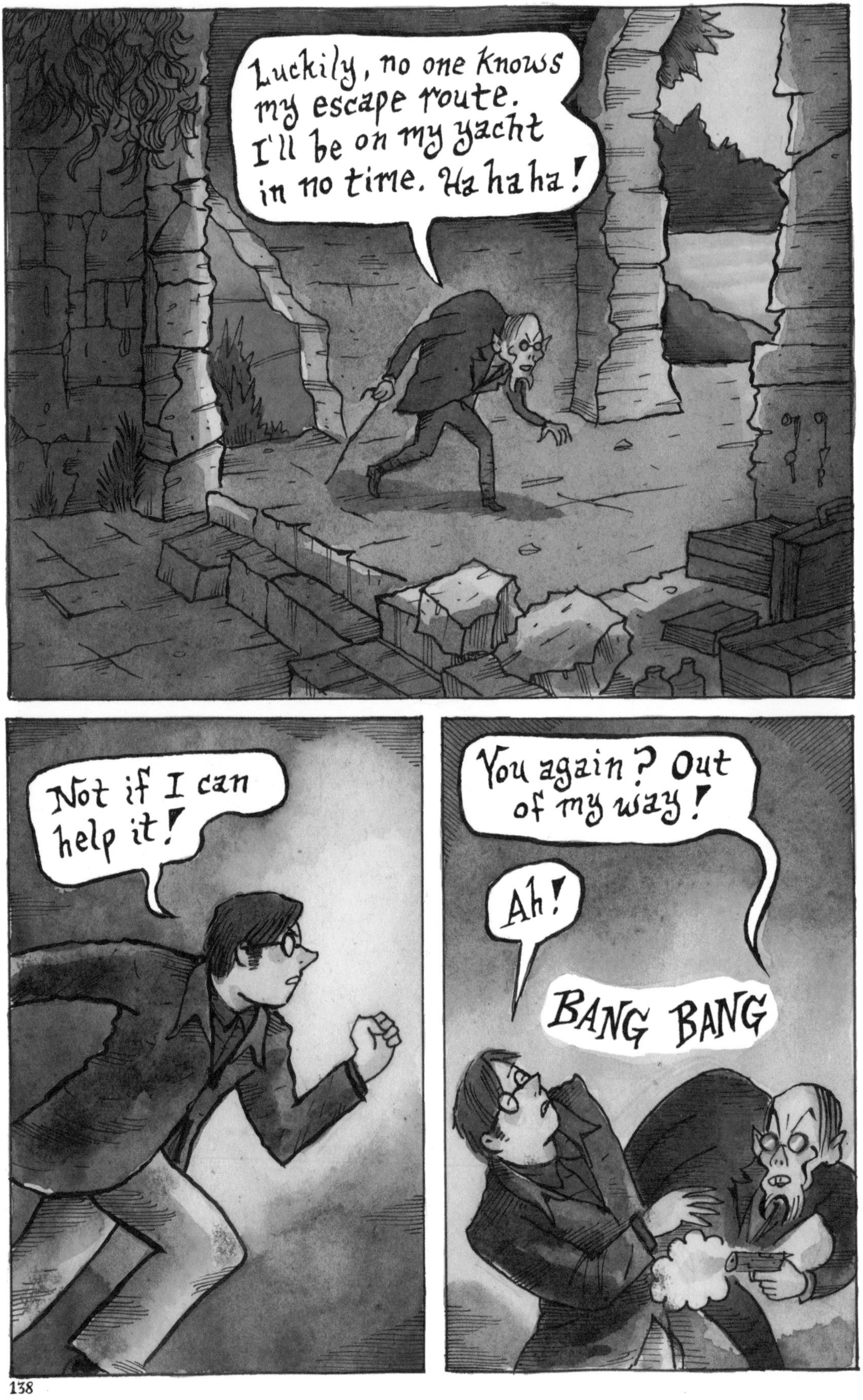
Luckily, no one knows my escape route. I'll be on my yacht in no time. Ha ha ha!
Not if I can help it!
You again? Out of my way!
Ah!
BANG BANG

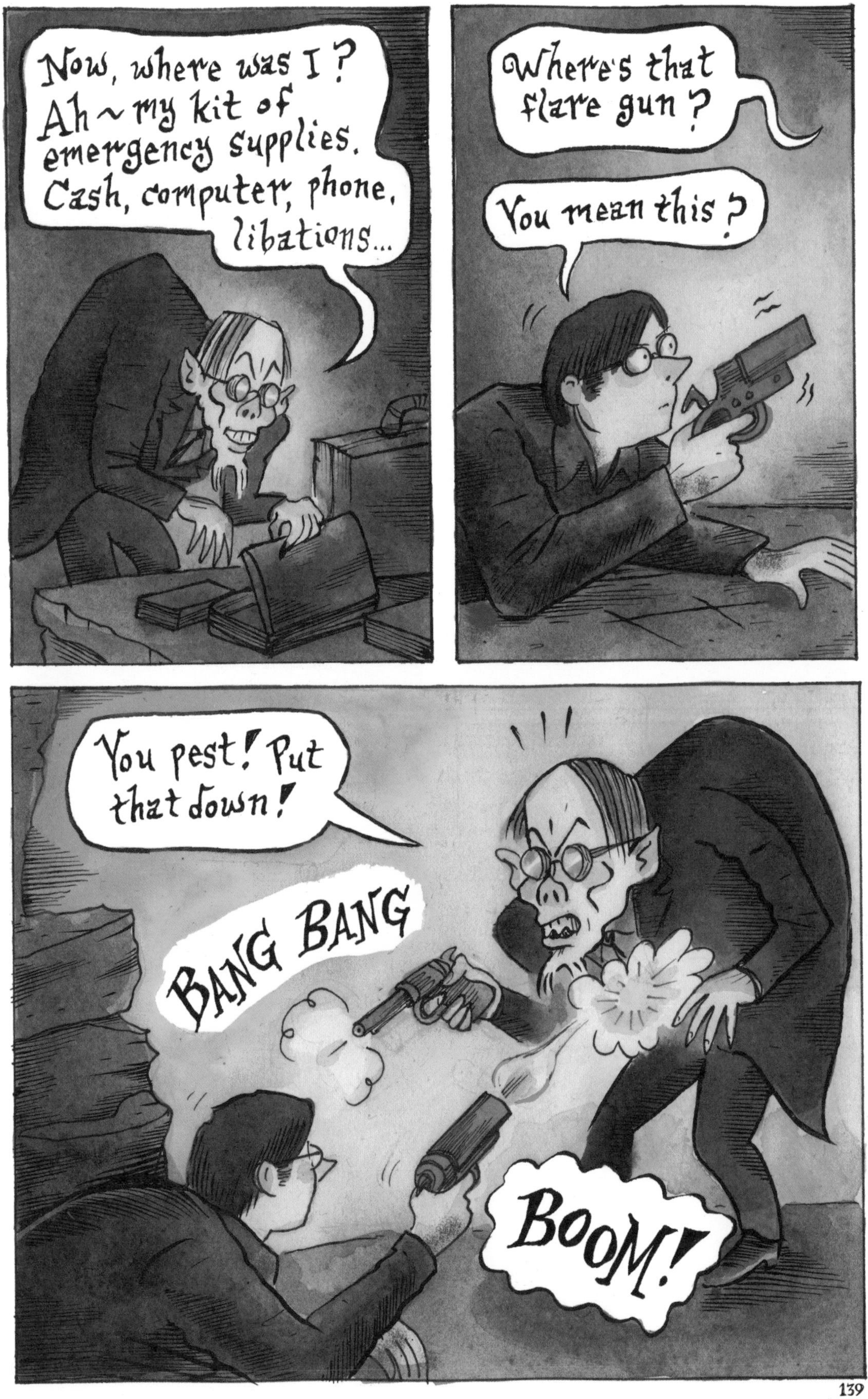
Now, where was I? Ah ~ my kit of emergency supplies. Cash, computer, phone, libations...
Where's that flare gun?
You mean this?
You pest! Put that down!
BANG BANG
BOOM!

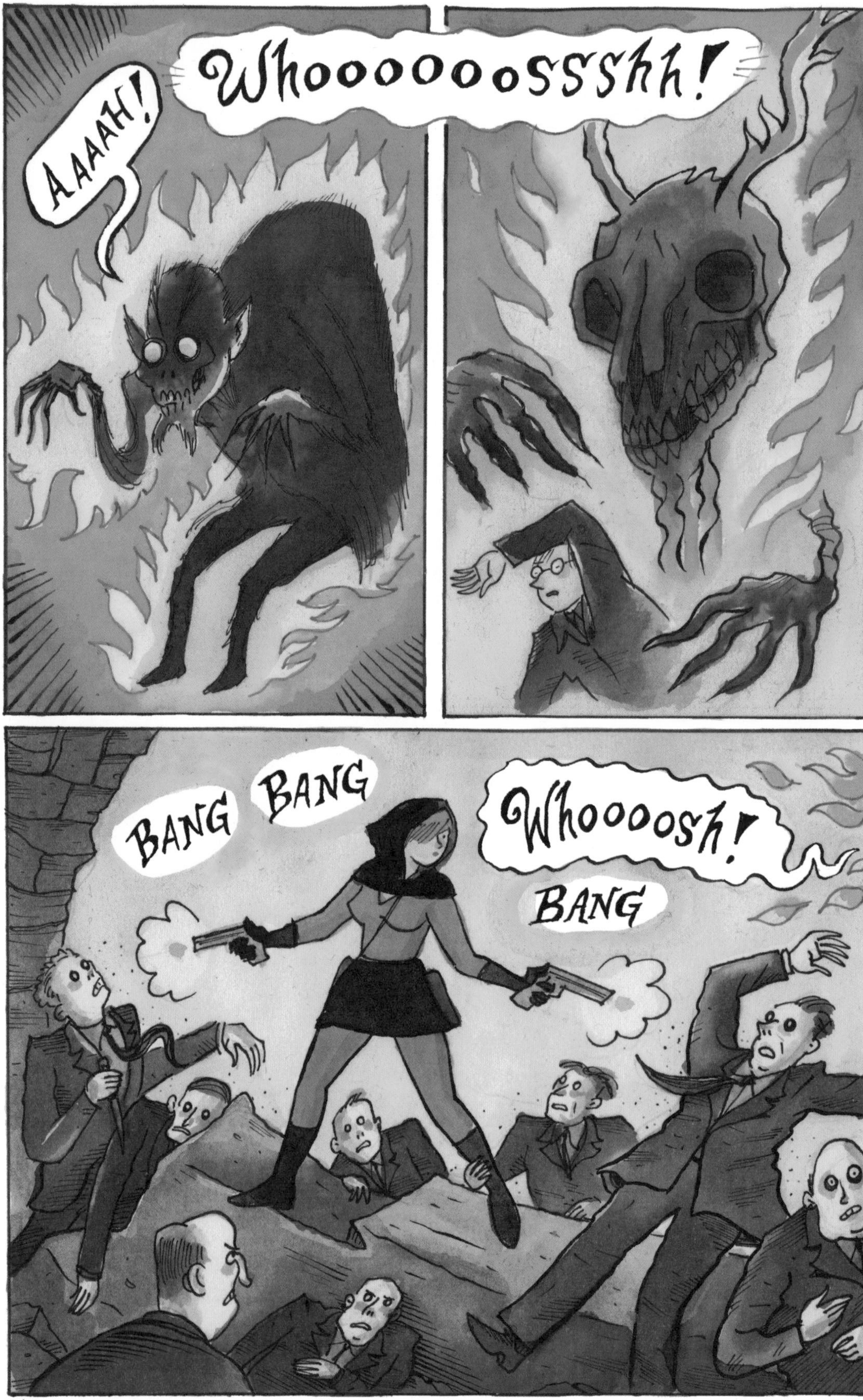
AAAAH!
WhooooooSSShh!
BANG
BANG
Whoooosh!
BANG

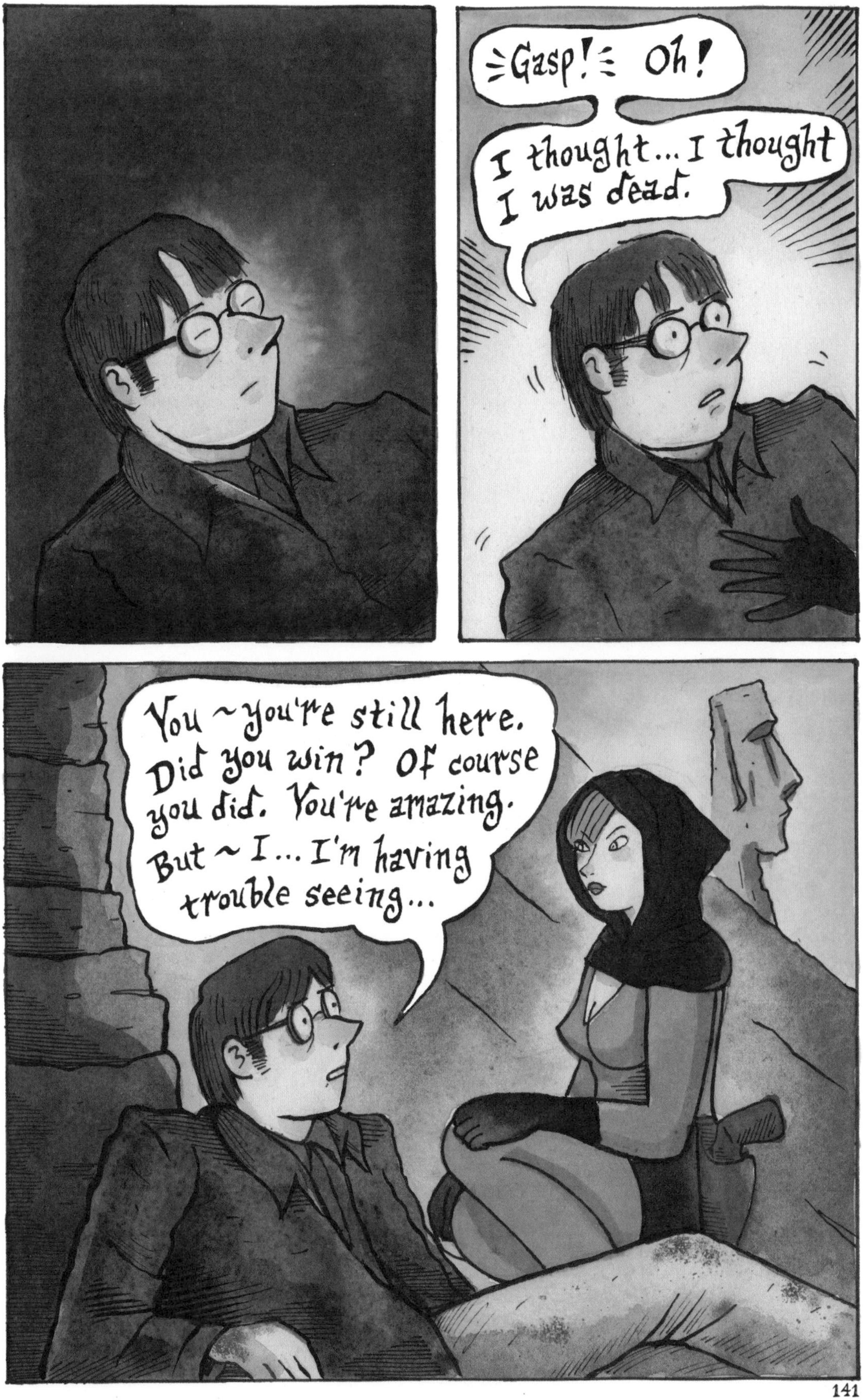
Gasp! Oh!
I thought... I thought I was dead.
You ~ you're still here. Did you win? Of course you did. You're amazing. But ~ I... I'm having trouble seeing...

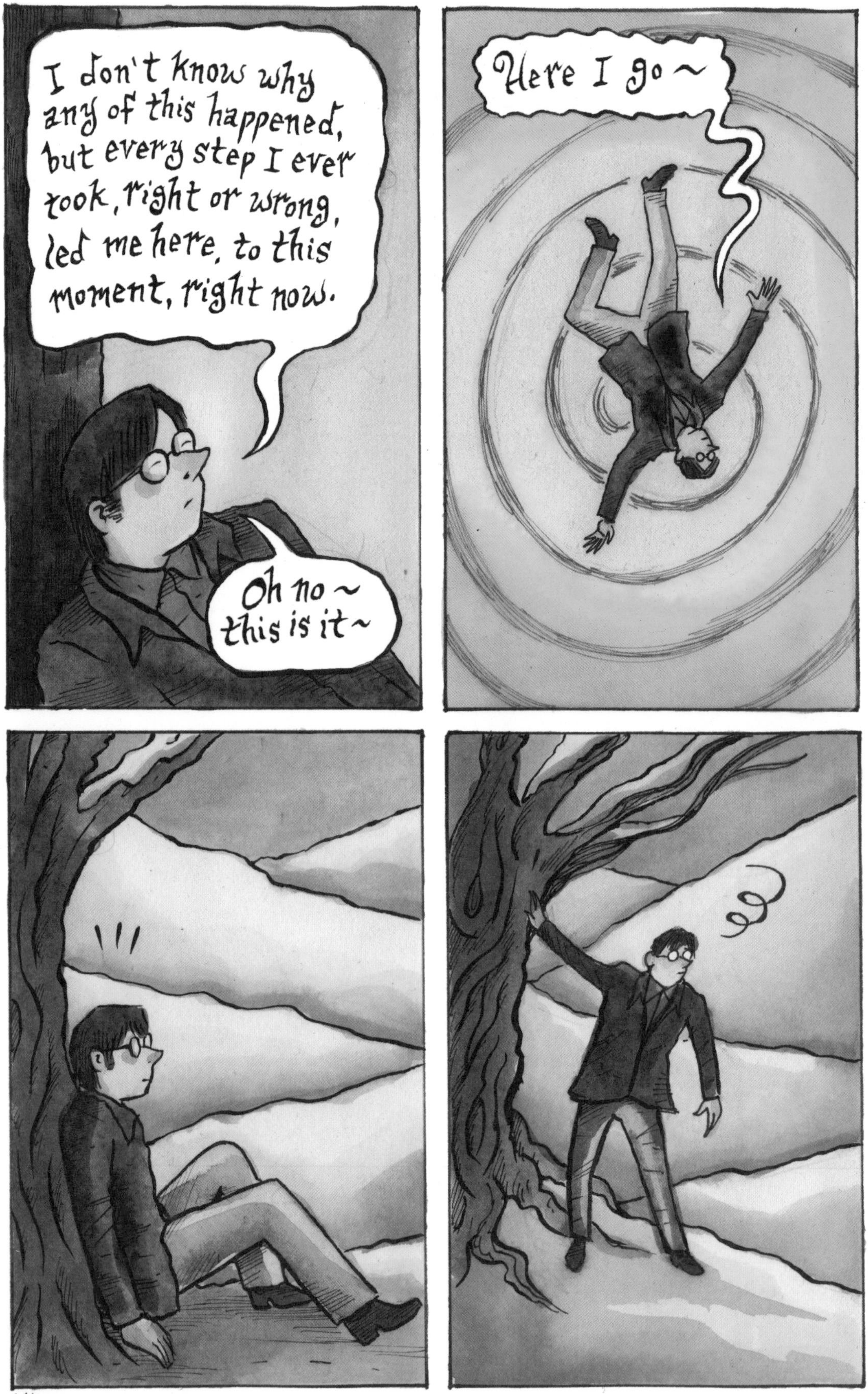
I don't know why any of this happened, but every step I ever took, right or wrong, led me here, to this moment, right now.
Oh no ~ this is it ~
Here I go ~

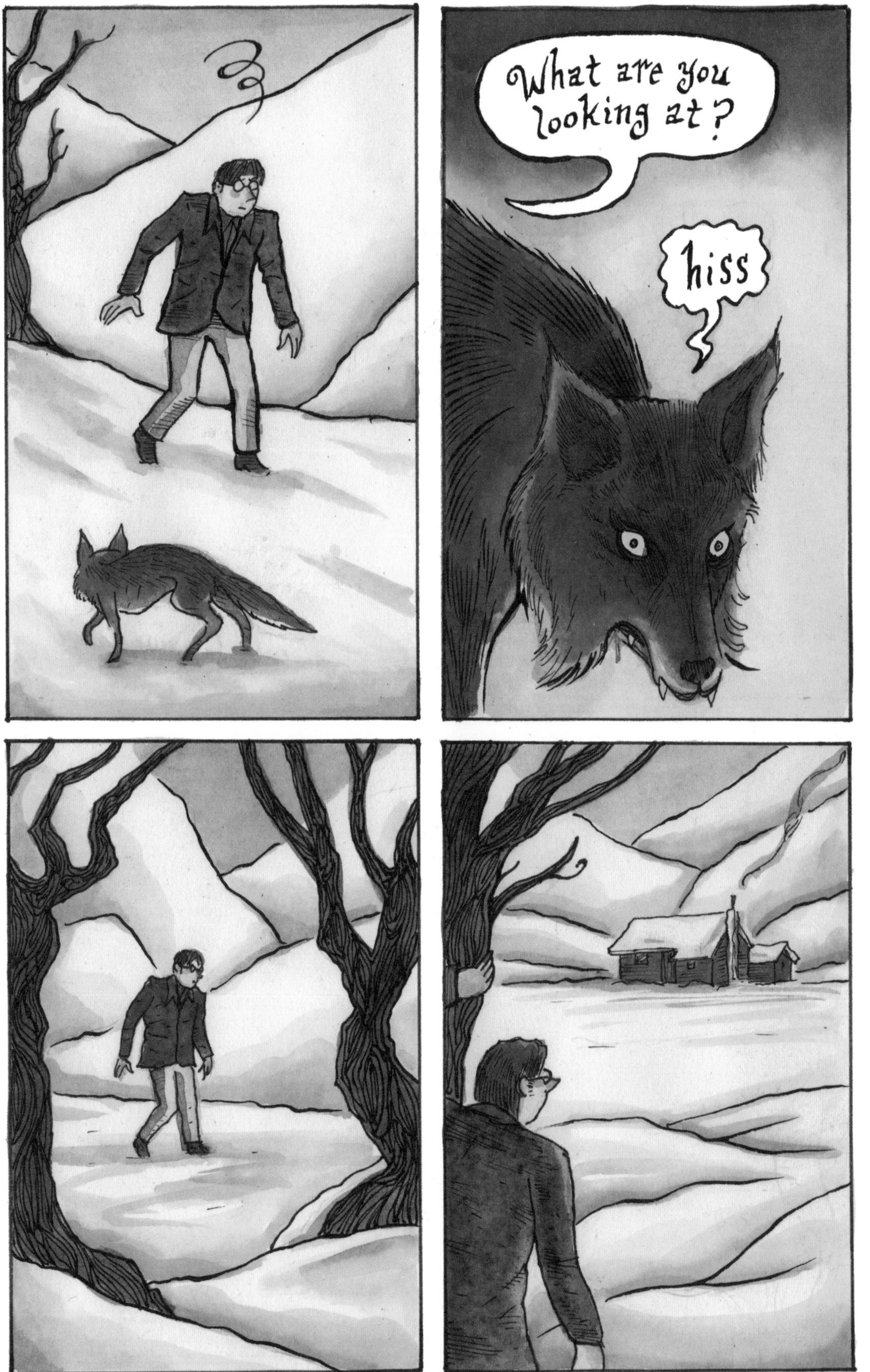
What are you looking at?
hiss

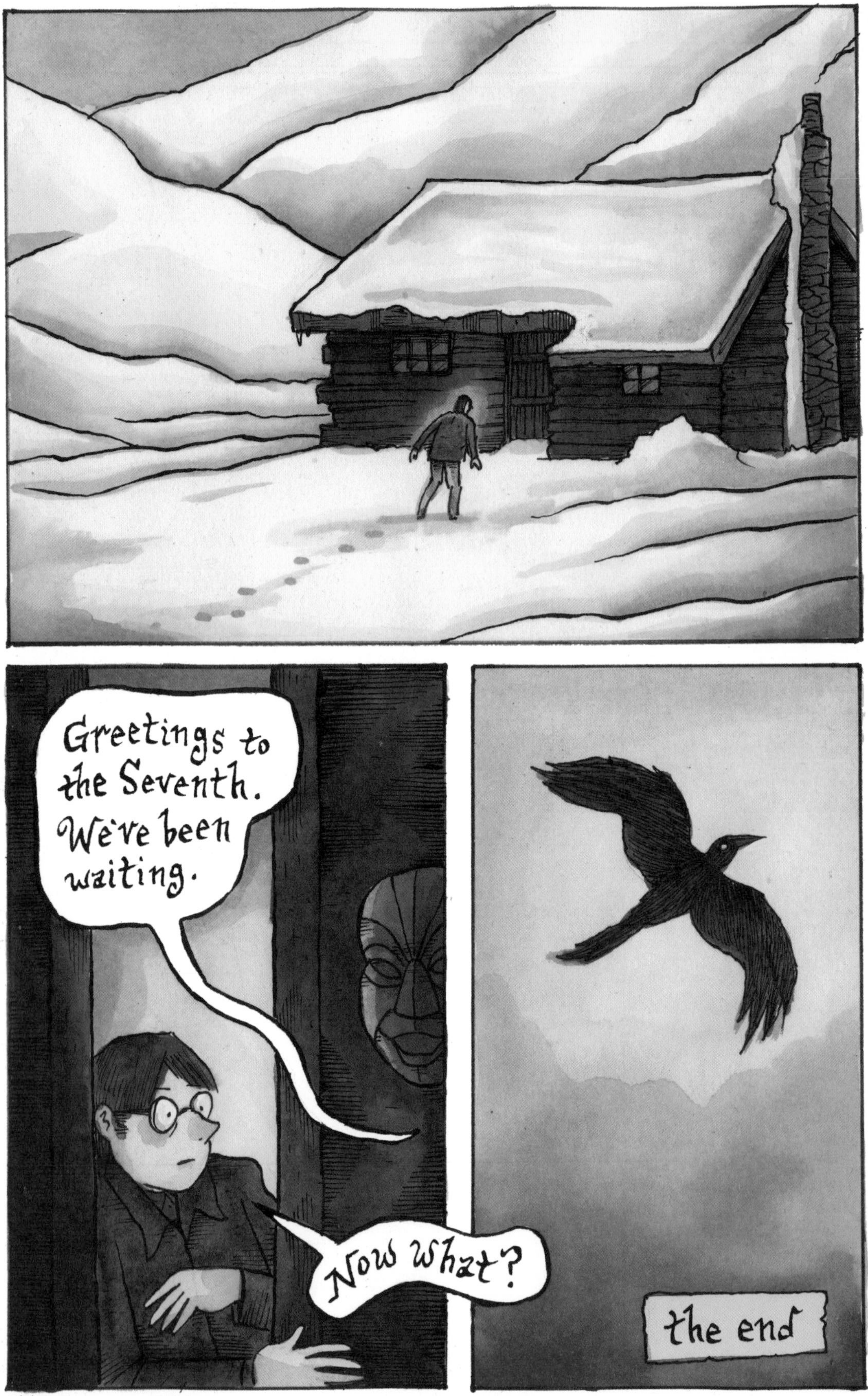
Greetings to the Seventh. We've been waiting.
Now What?
the end